pleasure
packing

FOR THE '80s

ACKNOWLEDGEMENTS
First Edition

I want to express my thanks for invaluable help to Shelby Chapel, Kathleen Cox, Warren Dayton, Jim Edmondson, Mark Erickson, Don Evers, Jack Gilbert, Mike Harding, Dr. Andrew Mirov and Holly Schenck.

Second Edition

For help on the revision I am grateful to Bill Arrigi, Dave Beck, Dave Curtis, Bob DeWolf, Mark Erickson, Dean Holland, Paul Kramer, Roger Neale, Peter Noone, George Rudolph, John Schelling, Dean Schubert, Daniel Shurman, Jack Stephenson and Fred Williams.

— Bob Wood

FUTURE EDITIONS

To keep this book current and up-to-date, revised editions will be issued from time to time. Readers are invited to contribute, comment and correct.

pleasure packing

FOR THE '80s

by Robert S. Wood

Illustrations
by Warren Dayton
and the author
Cover photos
by Ted Streshinsky

Ten Speed Press

STARTING OFF

Awakened in the dark
by the purling of Robins
I set myself deeper
in the frost stiff bag
and sink into sleep
as the day takes hold.

With new melted ice
from a rock bound pool
we wash back the night
from our cobwebbed faces
and breakfast on apples
from my father's farm.

As the sun breaks free
from the shadowed trees
and the stillness gives way
to the clamor of day
we gather our gear
and make ready to go.

Then with tentative steps
under unaccustomed loads
we set forth out the trail
in the growing light
through the warming air
on the first long trip
of the new found summer.

TABLE OF CONTENTS

PLEASURE PACKING??

Anyone can backpack in comparative misery—and many people regularly do. Every summer I shudder at the number of people struggling through the wilds, plagued by poor equipment and a lack of experience, unable to enjoy the country around them. Backpacking becomes ridiculous when the misery clearly outweighs the pleasure. But when a trip can be made in relative comfort, all the joys of living and traveling in the wilds will unfold. My hope is to help the reader achieve the level of comfort that turns backpacking into PLEASURE PACKING.

PLEASURE PACKING is anything but simple, especially for the highly civilized, city-oriented individual. The first probelm is weight. Comfort means equipment and equipment means weight. Comfort in camp (ample equipment) often means sacrificing comfort and mobility on the trail. And comfort on the trail (a light pack) often comes at the expense of comfort in camp. The backpacker seemingly must choose between the freedom and mobility of a small pack and the shelter and comfort of a happy camp.

But weight is not the only problem. All the gear in the world will not ensure comfort for the hiker who knows nothing about conditioning, trip planning, efficient walking, choosing a campsite, wilderness cookery—in short, technique.

So comfort in the wilds comes from carrying just the right gear and knowing precisely how to use it. And that is exactly what PLEASURE PACKING is all about: taking some of the work out of the wilderness so the beauty and happiness are free to shine through.

— Berkeley, January 1972

WHAT'S NEW??
...in the new edition

In the nine years since this book first appeared, a lot has changed. The backpacking boom has brought millions of newcomers out of the cities and onto the trails, swelling our ranks to approximately 10 million, many of them women and families. It has also brought us booms in river running, cross-country skiing, climbing and running—and many of these people have become hikers, too.

The 70s saw radical changes in pack, boot, stove, tent, and bed design—thanks largely to space age concepts, high technology materials and the application of vapor barriers for featherweight warmth, probably the biggest advance of the decade.

The first edition of this book, I'm proud to say, was welcomed by the critics and public alike. With virtually no promotion by its tiny publisher, it sold more than 70,000 copies and came to be regarded as one of backpacking's best books. I'm grateful for the warm response, and I've tried hard to make this revised and enlarged (32 extra pages) edition even better.

Toward this end, during the 70s, I broadened my own experience by hiking in the eastern U.S., New Zealand, Australia and South America, testing equipment along the way. I also wrote a regular column in *Wilderness Camping* magazine, where I frankly reported the often controversial results of my field tests of new gear.

Because there are now hundreds of makers of backpacking gear, it no longer is possible for one man to see, much less test, everything available, but I've probably published critical evaluations of more equipment than any other individual. In this new edition I've written about the gear I actually know, stressing simplicity and taking a hard look at the trends, styles, theories, fads, advertising claims and tipoffs, while explaining and recommending genuine improvements and time-tested products.

Determined to avoid producing "another rehash," I've constructed a totally new first chapter which, for the first time, ties together the body's needs, the various theories of design and the actual (rather than advertised) qualities of the materials, fabrics and insulators employed in gear of all kinds—a highly useful background for the wise selection of backpacking equipment.

In an effort to offset soaring prices, where possible I have pointed the budget backpacker and bargain hunter toward functional inexpensive and make-it-yourself substitutes for high priced gear. Because the backpacking boom has brought millions of inexperienced hikers to the wilderness, pollution, litter and the accident rate have risen sharply—problems I've tried to respond to in this new edition.

But my first responsibility, it seems to me still, is to emphasize and remind that our ultimate goal is simply to have fun, see the country and escape our cares—experiencing the excitement, freedom, peace and contentment that somehow seem so much easier to find when we're walking in the wilds with our homes on our backs.

—Robert S. Wood, Berkeley, January 1981

To Freda

1 NEW BEGINNINGS

Space age technology—new materials and design—offer exciting opportunities for outdoor travelers of the eighties. By taking the mystery and misconception out of both old and new concepts and creations, I hope to enable today's backpackers to go lighter, safer, more comfortable and carefree than has ever been possible before.

By looking closely at body function, theories of design and finally specific fabrics, coatings and insulators, including the very latest creations of science, I hope to enable the reader to confidently choose the very best gear for his or her specific needs.

Along the way I hope to answer such persistent and baffling questions as...Is down better than Polarguard? Do vapor barriers work? Should raingear "breathe?" Is Goretex "the answer?" Can condensation be stopped? Is wool better than cotton? Will 60/40 cloth keep me dry? Do tents need double walls? Should sleeping bags be waterproof? And so forth.

Since long before the dawn of mountaineering, men have diligently searched for ways to shield their highly vulnerable bodies from heat and cold, wind and rain. The quest continues today as modern outdoorsmen—aided by the magic of space age technology—seek comfort and protection in the selection of their clothing, packs, boots, bedding and shelter. Since the walker must carry all he needs on his back, often over difficult, dangerous terrain in uncertain weather, his gear must be light, functional, versatile, compact and above all dependable. Ideally it should also be weatherproof, durable, fireproof and inexpensive. That's asking a lot. No wonder so many travelers in the wilds are still uncomfortable!

Before one can wisely select needed backpacking gear, it is vital to understand the qualities of the materials out of which that gear is made. But to understand materials and how they will function, it is essential to be familiar with the design principles behind them and how they apply, in the wilderness, to the needs and idiosyncrasies of the human body.

The body's peculiarities, sensitivities and strange demands easily double the difficulty of producing gear that works. So the place to begin is the human body—its requirements and preferences and the myths that surround them.

The body is a highly sensitive organism. Meet its complex needs or pain will swiftly follow! Just what does it want, this mysterious creature in which we live but know so little about? For one thing it wants air temperature at the skin to be about 75°F, ranging from 72°F in the hands and feet to about 78°F in the head and trunk. Take away body heat faster than it's generated and the body turns dramatically defensive. To protect crucial head and trunk temperatures it swiftly cuts down blood circulation to the skin by constricting capillaries. If cooling continues, it severely shuts down blood flow to the arms and legs, chilling hands and feet. By allowing skin temperature to drop 20 degrees and reducing blood circulation to the feet by up to 95%, the body can cut overall heat losses by a startling 75%. When the body is threatened it doesn't fool around!

Incidentally, it pays to keep in mind that the body's thermostat is located in the chest area. If you chill the chest while trying to vent excess heat, you're liable to trigger the production (and resultant energy loss) of massive amounts of heat and moisture. So if you want to cool off without threatening the body, keep your front zippers closed and rely on venting at the shirttails, neck, cuffs—and armpits if your garments have underarm zippers.

The head is the only part of the body in which the capillaries do not contract, because the body knows survival depends on continued alert functioning of the brain. So when your skin turns cool and your hands and feet grow cold, pay attention. The body is trying to warn you that heat production can't keep up with heat loss. No mittens in the world will keep your hands warm if the body believes trunk temperature is threatened. So if your feet get cold, put on a hat and jacket—especially when sleeping with the head exposed.

Body heat loss occurs in five different ways: (1) radiation (heat pumped out through the skin like warmth from a stove); (2) respiration (the steady exhaling of water vapor—visible as steam in cold air); (3) conduction (by skin contact with a good heat conductor, especially water); (4) evaporation (as water evaporates it takes massive amounts of heat with it, and (5) convection (heat stolen from the skin by moving air).

Almost as important to the body as maintaining an average 75°F temperature is the maintenance of moist—but not wet—skin. Comfort, to the body, is a surprisingly high relative humidity of 70-95%, despite the mind's belief that comfort means dry skin. This isn't the contradiction it seems. What the mind calls dry skin, really isn't. Truly dry skin quickly turns chapped, stiff, cracked and flaky. Open sores and bleeding follow. Properly moist, humid skin, on the other hand, isn't wet, either. What the body wants is a quarter inch thick cushion-

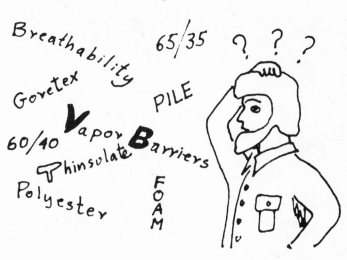

ing layer of moist warm air, like an invisible second skin, shielding and lubricating but not wetting the skin. Humor the body by providing 70°F air with a nomal 50% relative humidity, and it will easily maintain this suit of invisible armor with as little as a pint of water a day. Destroy this protective layer by exposure to a harsh environment and the body goes wild in an effort to restore it. Sweat glands open wide and the body goes all out to pump heated water vapor through the skin. Until the layer is rebuilt, heat and water loss from the body will be a terrific 6-800% above normal—though at the time the mind may notice nothing because evaporation is immediate. But after hiking in dry or cold air for several hours you'll suddenly discover an insatiable thirst. Your body is signaling dehydration and demanding replacement of water—by the quart!

From the body's standpoint, water vapor and heat production are inseparable. It won't produce one without the other (to the distress of clothing designers).

When the skin is below 75°F water vapor passes off unnoticed as "insensible perspiration"—after doing its job: keeping the skin moist. But when skin temperature climbs much above 75°F the body reacts to what it considers uncomfortable overheating by opening the sweat glands wider and pouring out heated water to wet the skin with what we regard distastefully as sweat. So in reality there are two kinds of sweat: the one you don't feel or see that keeps your skin comfortably moist and alive, and the wet one produced by overheating.

The insensible perspiration rate jumps dramatically under a variety of conditions commonly encountered outdoors. When relative humidity drops much below 40%, for example. It isn't widely known that the colder the air the less water it can hold. From the body's standpoint winter ski touring conditions are as dry as those in the desert: it's a struggle to get enough water. At 30°F the relative humidity on bare skin is an arid 15%—even though there's nothing but frozen water (snow) in sight! And liquid water can be just as hard to come by as in the desert. The body may need a gallon a day!

Though dry air sucks up ample moisture (and with its body heat), the two greatest threats to body heat are wind (convection) and water (conduction) because each has the capacity to swiftly obliterate that layer of moist warm air that shields the body. Water's great conductivity—20 times that of still dry air—instantly destroys the air layer and enormous heat loss follows. Ten minutes exposure of the body to 34°F water (if you fall through thin winter ice on the pond) means likely death by freezing! But the water doesn't have to be frigid to chill you. Air temperature of 68°F in a heated home is comfortably warm, but the same 68°F in a swimming pool water feels freezing. Why? In the house the body easily maintains its cushion of moist 75°F air. In the water it can't, and the sudden 7° drop on bare skin is a shock.

Slicing it even finer, if you work up a sweat jogging and return to that 68°F house after you've cooled down, the dampness of your clothes and skin produces chilling evaporative heat loss that will make the house seem chilly, no matter what else you do. But take a shower and put on dry clothes and presto! the 68°F house is warm again.

Wind chill may be even more threatening to the exposed body because the danger is less evident. Most deaths from hypothermia (brain and body core chilling) occur in deceptively mild (above freezing) air temperatures which have been drastically lowered (in chilling effect) because wind has blown away the body's protective layer of still, warm air, permitting rapid heat loss by convection. And it doesn't take much wind. On a 30°F day with mild 10 mph wind, the effective air temperature on bare skin is a chilly 16°F. If the wind freshens to a moderate 25 mph, the effective temperature drops to zero. And on a zero winter day a 30 mph wind is equivalent to a dangerous 50°F below on bare skin!

Combine the threats of wind and water and you multiply the danger by adding the terrible cooling power of evaporation. Although water has 20 times the conductivity of dead air, add evaporative super cooling and that exposed wet skin loses heat more than 200 times as fast as dry protected skin! Stand wet and naked in the wind after a swim on a cool summer day and you'll experience severe chilling in a matter of seconds. Even after you dry and dress it will take a long time to get warm. Sweat up your sleeping bag on a warm autumn evening and you're headed for trouble in the cool before dawn.

When you climb into your bag at night, in any season, insensible perspiration and respiratory water loss continue. Most of that water is driven by body warmth into your bed, and all of it enters your tent, if you have one. Though few campers are aware of it, it isn't uncommon for the weight of your sleeping bag to mysteriously jump 1½ to 2½ pounds in the space of a single summer night from accumulated condensed water vapor given off by the sleeping body.

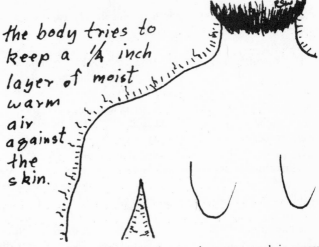

the body tries to
keep a ¼ inch
layer of moist
warm
air
against
the
skin.

But the cooling effect of evaporation can be put to work in warm climates. Soak your hat and shirt (or everything but your boots) every time you pass a stream, for blessed relief. If water is scarce, take advantage of what's known about blood circulation to the head and neck. Veteran desert travelers know the most effective use of precious water to combat overheating is repeated wetting—for evaporative cooling—of the back of the neck and the forehead.

The body's ability to generate heat when needed is far from constant. Since vigorous production is vital in cold, dry or wet conditions, body comfort, if not safety, is dependent on the ability to produce heat at least as fast as it's lost. It is therefore important to be aware of conditions that sabotage heat production. Such stresses as fatigue, wet skin, altitude, poor health, hunger, anxiety and lack of adequate prior conditioning will all make it harder to get warm once chilling occurs. So if the body is under stress or conditions are extreme, take extra precautions against chilling and pay attention to the body's warning system.

Just what is body comfort? The definition I like is "a blissful unawareness of unpleasant sensation," which means the body is content with conditions—for the moment.

The body's great sensitivity, wild fluctuations and varied responses —all the while pumping out troublesome water vapor—have posed staggering problems for designers of clothing, tents and sleeping bags. Small wonder they've been largely frustrated in their attempts to meet the exacting needs of modern hikers. Most of their serious efforts can be broadly classified under three different design principles: breathability, vapor barrier and temporary moisture storage.

Breathability seems to have its roots in a backlash against the sweat and condensation that so often soaks clothing, tents and bags from within. Condensation is defined as the reduction of water vapor by cooling into liquid water. Since it seems to be worse beneath sealed (waterproof) fabrics, designers decided—with more hope than science—that open porous fabrics (being the opposite of closed sealed fabrics) would somehow let body vapor escape before it could condense.

Manufacturers began to advertise "breathable" equipment, people bought it, and before long this shaky thesis had been elevated to the level of fact. Water vapor from the body, it was flatly declared, can be satisfactorily dispersed, before it condenses simply by putting porous (i.e. breathable) materials next to the body and by avoiding sealed (waterproof) fabrics. The theory depends on four assumptions: (1) sweating means wetting and occurs at a constant rate, (2) for comfort the skin must be dry, (3) sealed fabrics inevitably produce condensation, and (4) the volume of water vapor produced by an active body will find its way through the pores in unsealed fabrics.

Since all four of these assumptions are false it's not surprising that breathability has never worked—except under ideal conditions when it's not needed. In wet, cold or humid conditions it fails badly. And when it does work, severely high convective and evaporative heat loss is overlooked or ignored. Even its most feverish adherents admit rain is a problem. Obviously, fabrics porous enough to let body moisture out will let rain in even faster.

Over the years a succession of miracle fabrics have been developed to solve this problem. In recent times we have been offered 60/40 cloth. Reevair, Airweave, Ventile, Bukflex, 65-35 cloth and now Goretex. All of these have failed to live up to their makers' claims. Goretex has given breathability a lift, but even it has severe limitations, as will be seen when fabrics and insulators are individually scrutinized. The fact is, no fabric is capable of "breathing" out the amount of water vapor generated by an average person doing moderate exercise under normal conditions. Not even with the help of "vapor pressure," which is supposed to actually drive water vapor through porous materials. Under field conditions where breathability would be useful, vapor pressure is so faint it can barely push water vapor through the gaping quarter inch holes in a fishnet shirt.

In stark contrast to the breathability myth, which steadfastly ignores the workings of the body and the physics of water vapor diffusion, the vapor barrier approach takes clever advantage of body function. Instead of unrealistically trying to rid the body of moisture while ignoring accompanying heat loss, vapor barriers contain body moisture and reduce its production while stopping heat loss. In short, breathability tries in vain to keep you dry. Vapor barriers aim to keep you warm and comfortably moist while your clothes and insulation stay dry.

A vapor barrier is simply a sealed or water proof fabric *worn close to the skin* to keep body moisture in instead of trying to drive it out. Don't groan with visions of steamy streaming skin. That needn't happen. Though sealed garments worn *away* from the body over clothing (like waterproof parkas) *can* cause oceans of condensation, sealed fabric

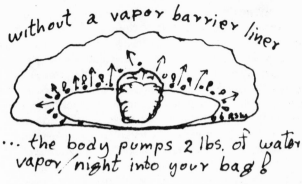

without a vapor barrier liner

... the body pumps 2 lbs. of water vapor/night into your bag!

worn *close* to the skin produces a startlingly different effect. Body heat makes the difference. Because the fabric is warmed by the body, condensation does not occur. Because it protects that moist layer of water vapor covering the skin, optimum humidity is easily maintained with minimal vapor output. Given ideal conditions of moisture and heat, the body gratefully closes sweat glands and shuts down vapor production up to 85%.

It's ironic that striving for dry skin only makes it pump more moisture, while permitting skin humidity shrinks production of perspiration! Not only does the wearer escape the steam room condensation associated with sealed garments, clothing worn over the vapor barrier stays completely dry. The severe heat loss that always accompanies sweating is prevented, and the body's water needs (thirst) are proportionally reduced. With the efficient retention of body heat, the outdoor traveler enjoys remarkable warmth with far less of the heavy, bulky, expensive insulation we've come to think is vital in cold weather. In fact the colder it is, the better vapor barriers perform. And there isn't the slightest reduction in efficiency when conditions turn wet and humid. It isn't until the weather grows warm that vapor barriers begin to lose their value, and that's simply because they're so effective at retaining heat.

Radical as the vapor barrier principle sounds, informed consideration of body behavior shows it to be perfectly logical. Not only is the principle scientifically sound, there is proof in the form of practical application. The vapor barrier principle is precisely what keeps well designed houses warm and comfortable in winter: a plastic or aluminum vapor barrier on the inside of the insulation seals in heat and humidity, and an indoor humidifier adds needed moisture to dry inside air. And during World War II, ski troops were heavily afflicted with trenchfoot and frostbite from continuously wet, cold feet—until both problems were spectacularly solved by providing vapor barrier socks. Furthermore. Mickey Mouse boots employed vapor barriers to solve the frozen foot problem in the Korean war.

Skeptics, I know, will insist that vapor barriers just *have* to produce massive condensation and dismiss the idea without trying it. But there's a very simple experiment the open minded reader can conduct to see for himself. If you suffer from chronically cold feet, you won't even have to go outdoors. Simply take a large plastic Baggie from the roll in the kitchen (or the market produce section) and slip it over one bare foot when you get up in the morning. Fold the top around your ankle, put on normal socks and shoes, and in the course of the day subject your feet to conditions that normally chill them. Not only should your Baggied foot stay dramatically warmer than the other one, at the end of the day instead of the bagfull of sweat you expect there will be nothing more than faint dampness, and your sock will be totally clean and dry! (If the thought of damp plastic on the skin is too repulsive, thin socks can be worn underneath with scant loss of efficiency.)

Extraordinary as it sounds, properly used vapor barriers will increase body wamth by 20°F. I recently went off for an all day climb in the January Sierra at 8-9000 feet with Baggies on my feet and nothing to protect my torso but a 6-ounce vapor barrier shirt, a 6-ounce fishnet shirt and a 7-ounce nylon windshell—no sweater, wool shirt or insulated parka. Though it was after sunset when I returned to the cabin, by staying relatively active and carefully controlling my skin temperature by ventilation, I had managed to stay comfortable and warm all day.

Sound too good to be true? The only catch, as already mentioned, is that a vapor barrier must be kept close to the skin, with no more than one thin layer underneath. If the fabric is not kept comparatively warm, the temperature differential will invite condensation, as with waterproof outer garments. Because the vapor barrier principle contradicts all we've been told about keeping dry it takes some getting used to in the field, and when temperatures are mild the system's great efficiency makes overheating easy. But that's not the sodden problem it is with breathability. When you cross the line from water vapor to sweat, you know it instantly inside a vapor barrier. But since coated fabrics absorb no moisture, ventilation quickly dries both fabric and body, and outer clothing remains perfectly dry.

Not only do vapor barriers work best when conditions are worst, they are featherweight, cheap, low on bulk and versatile. The best applications are socks, shirts, sleeping bag liners, gloves and pants, most of which can be made at home. No commercial sock works any better than a Baggie. And while marvelously adjustable VB shirts can be bought, a plastic dry cleaning or garbage bag (with appropriate holes snipped for head and arms) will work wonders beneath a sweater when skiing in the wind. A VB shirt will double as a windbreaker and even triple as raingear in an unexpected shower, and I know of no more valuable emergency or survival garment.

The role of ventilation in breathability and vapor barrier principles tends to contrast them further. Ventilation is essential to the escape of any significant amount of moisture in breathable fabrics, but it does so at the expense of body heat and dampened insulation. The colder it is,

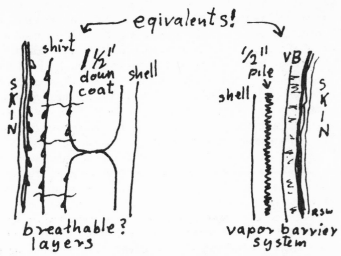

the more insulation and ventilation are needed, and the greater the heat loss. Vapor barriers, on the other hand, require ventilation only in mild weather or when exertion raises skin temperature near the sweat level. But at no time does this ventilation cost needed body heat or dampen insulation.

The third strategy employed by clothing designers is temporary moisture storage (the blotter). Materials have varying capacities for storing the water vapor continually exuded by the body. In order of increasing capacity, cotton, wool and open-celled foam can sponge up considerable quantities before saturation occurs and body wetting takes place. This capacity is often represented as an asset, ignoring the fact that the fabric must be dried and water weight must be carried in the meantime. It is likewise overlooked that once saturation occurs the slow drying that follows (especially in wool and cotton) can mean severe evaporative chilling with enormous heat loss. The chief applications of temporary moisture storage, aside from cotton and wool, are in fabrics lined with foam (foambacks) or the condensation-blotting nexus employed in Bukflex and sometimes Goretex fabrics. Instead of dealing with the sources of condensation, this approach merely conceals it, making it easy to pretend it isn't there.

Having observed the body's needs and its strategies for self-protection, as well as the principles devised to cope with them, it should now be easier to understand and evaluate the fabrics and insulators out of which outdoor clothing and equipment are made.

Fabrics

COTTON is without doubt the most comfortable fabric on the skin, and the most popular and familiar. But part of its appeal comes from its gradual absorption of sweat, and the comfort only lasts until the fabric is wet. Unfortunately cotton's water holding capacity is low and when cotton becomes saturated it sticks wetly to the skin, loses all its insulating value and is slow to dry, often chilling the body for hours by evaporative cooling. Cotton is comparatively heavy and weak, tears easily and rots or mildews readily if allowed to stay wet. Although it sews easily and accepts most water repellents, it is usually a poor choice for either clothing or equipment where the climate is difficult or conditions demanding.

VENTILE cloth is a tightly woven cotton designed to take advantage of the yarn's tendency to swell when wet. Gaps in the weave close tightly when yarns swell, making the fabric fairly waterproof, but open when dry to permit some escape of body moisture. Unfortunately, Ventile must be imported since no U.S. mill weaves it. The resulting high price, combined with cotton's relative heaviness and weakness, makes Ventile gear rare.

WOOL is best known for its warmth and springiness. The stiff, resilient fibers resist crushing and compaction from wetting, giving wool a reputation as a good insulator even when wet. It absorbs more water vapor before saturation than cotton or any other fabric, but when finally wet (like cotton) its comfort drops and its extremely slow drying can mean a long period of uselessness or chilly evaporative cooling. The net result is negative as far as wool's value for outdoor clothing (except socks) is concerned, except in moderate and dry climates (or over vapor barrier shirts). Compared to other insulators, wool is heavy and bulky to carry.

NYLON has become the premier outdoor fabric because it offers great strength, toughness, light weight, elasticity, permeability and freedom from mildew. Its smooth uniform fibers makes possible tight weaves that are windproof and downproof without coatings. Nylons chief drawbacks are slipperiness and smoothness which makes it less pleasant against the skin than wool or cotton. Its smoothness makes it hard to sew, it is subject to quick unraveling if edges are not heat sealed, it resists repellents, and even tight weaves pass rain quickly. But since the fibers are non-absorbent, nylon dries quickly with minimal heat stealing evaporative cooling.

RIPSTOP NYLON is a weave designed for increased tear resistance. Every 200 threads a group of larger, stronger fibers make a ridge to somewhat inhibit long tears, accounting for the characteristic checkerboard pattern. NYLON TAFFETA, now more common than ripstop, is used where light weight and tight weave are most important. Most light nylon fabrics are either ripstop or taffeta, and the minor differences between them are insignificant. NYLON DUCK or PACKCLOTH is a heavier weave fabric, often with a waterproof coating, for tent floors, pack bags and gaiters. It has largely been replaced by CORDURA in recent years, a nubby nylon weave designed to look like cotton duck and resist abrasion. Cordura's success is due mostly to its cosmetic appeal since it is weaker than duck and harder to waterproof. TASLAN is a new light fabric of kinky nylon fibers designed to look

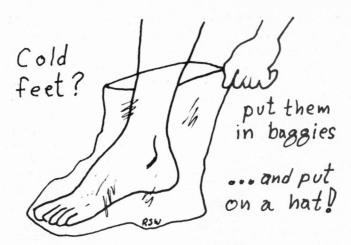

Cold feet? put them in baggies ... and put on a hat!

and feel like sueded cotton and thus improve nylon's image and comfort. TRICOT is still another nylon weave, used mostly as a liner.

BLENDS of cotton and nylon have repeatedly been tried in the somewhat naive hope that the virtues of each could be combined while avoiding the drawbacks: 60/40 CLOTH is the best known. Its cotton yarns run in one direction, nylon fiber in the other. This strategy was supposed to produce a breathable fabric like Ventile cloth with nylon's strength and lightness. The result, while pleasant, leaks badly. Beware any manufacturer who so much as hints that 60/40 cloth is water repellent. The latest blend is 65/35 CLOTH, which is woven in *both* directions with a yarn made up of 65% Dacron and 35% cotton. It's better but still useless in heavy rain.

POLYESTERS (like Dacron) are nearly as strong as nylon and their lower elasticity makes them ideal as a mildew proof thread for stitching all types of fabrics. They are also used in various forms and blends to produce fabrics of all sorts, most of which have basically the same properties as cotton but with rot resistance and greater strength.

Fabric Coatings

GORETEX is a film, not a fabric. Because it is thin and fragile it must be laminated (sandwiched) between two conventional fabrics for protection in most applications. This makes the laminates comparatively stiff and heavy, and the glue inside sometimes makes them crinkly. Because claims for Goretex are extravagant and because it's being sold for everything but underwear, it merits a close look. To obtain the magic film, all manufacturers must purchase the fabrics to be sandwiched and ship them to the Goretex factory in Maryland for lamination. By the time it's shipped back and made into gear the cost has risen 2-300% above that for conventionally coated fabric! And the weight has doubled! Goretex in a parka commonly adds $50 to the price and a pound to the weight.

The claim for Goretex is that it's impervious to liquid water's large

molecules, but readily passes the much smaller water vapor molecules. And as various tests demonstrate, it does exactly that—in the
lab. The mistake is in projecting this level of performance to clothing
and equipment used by humans in the outdoors. It's one thing to say
Goretex film *can* pass water vapor; it's quite another to say a significant portion of insensible perspiration from the body *will* find its way
through. As far as breathability is concerned, Goretex is no better than
the fabrics it's glued to, in fact it's usually only half as good. Since
none of the fabics we've examined is really breathable to begin with,
Goretex cannot pass significant amounts of body-generated water
vapor. And neither partial nor diffusion pressure have a fraction of the
force necessary to help it along. The sad truth is that so-called
breathable fabrics often pass moisture in a cruder fashion. Vapor
condenses to water on the inside of the fabric, wicks its way through,
then evaporates on the outside, stealing considerable body heat in
the process.

Fabrics worn well beyond the range of body heat are generally cold,
causing water vapor to condense. Which means Goretex (like vapor
barrier clothing) must be worn close to the body to stay warm enough
to prevent condensation. Put several layers of clothing (or several
inches of insulation) between Goretex and the skin and all the problems of breathability are magnified, not solved. Goretex also fails to
breathe when wet. Those tiny pores which won't pass water are (not
surprisingly) sealed closed when the fabric is covered by a film of
water in hard rain, trapping body water vapor inside.

The claim that Goretex is waterproof stands up better. Goretex
made before 1978-9 often leaked like a sieve for no apparent reason,
and many kinds of contamination (food, dirt, bug dope, sweat and
sunburn cream, etc.) also caused it to pass water. But a new improved
product (unofficially known as Goretex II) apparently has solved the
contamination problem, though at the expense, it is reported, of a
further decrease in the porosity of the film.

Despite these limitations, Goretex laminates generally shed water,
are exceptionally windproof and permit the passage of some water
vapor under ideal conditions and in reasonable applications. A com-
peting product called ''Klimate'' appeared on the market late in '79.
Since its makers (Kenyon & Howe-Bainbridge) sell their film for
slightly less and don't require pre-purchase and shipment of fabrics,
Gore's monopoly on what is essentially a film of stretched, glued
Teflon may be at an end. Goretex and Klimate are especially suitable
for bivy sacks, gaiter tops, unlined mild weather rain and wind shells
and waterproof protective coverings for down sleeping bags and
garments—providing the buyer is willing to accept the substantial
extra cost and weight.

SEALERS (fabric coatings) such as urethane, polymer fluoro-
carbons and neoprene do not claim to breathe. Their continuous films
are tougher than Goretex and therefore do not need to be sandwiched

between fabrics. They are largely waterproof until punctured or abraded. Double coated fabrics are better sealed and tougher, but half again as heavy. REPELLENTS clog but do not seal fabric pores—much like Goretex—allowing some water vapor to pass (and usually some water, too). Unfortunately, the best repellents (like Zepel) which are applied at the factory, will survive only 2-3 washings, and aerosol silicone-based spray-ons (like "Campdri") last only a few weeks in heavy weather.

Insulation

While fabrics have various functions, insulation has just one: prevention of body heat loss in the cold. Since motionless air effectively prevents conductive and convective heat movement, all insulating materials for weight-conscious backpackers are built on the principle of small dead air spaces (since both the weight and price of air are low). It has been accurately determined that each pocket of air should have no dimension greater than ¼ inch. Larger pockets in materials that flex permit detrimental convective air circulation. (The quarter inch rule explains why air mattresses, which allow free air circulation, transmit ground cold while foam pads don't.) Except for Thinsulate and closed cell foams, the effectiveness of any insulation is determined by its thermal conductivity and thickness. The declining order of efficiency is: dead air, foam, polyester, down and finally wool, but since there is little variation between these materials, effective thickness is what counts, with the emphases on "effective."

Using a rough rule of thumb, at 20°F it takes a quarter inch of insulation to keep a laborer warm while working. When he's loafing it takes an inch, and when he's sleeping he needs 2-3 inches. WOOL we've already looked at as a fabric. Its weight and bulk prevent it from being seriously considered for more than medium weight clothing. DOWN, however, has long been the standard of excellence in backpacking beds and parkas, a position it has gradually been relinquishing as prices soar, quality drops and synthetics improve.

While synthetics are largely uniform, down varies widely. Carefully refined goose down from mature European birds might fill 900

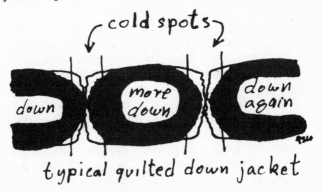

typical quilted down jacket

cubic inches per ounce, while commercial grades are now closer to 500 inches. Quality is determined by down pod size as well as filling power in cubic inches, so since duck pods average smaller, duck down is generally inferior, although good duck down is better than low grade goose down. Down quality is state regulated and bedding labels on every bag give a vague idea of filling quality, but the best measure of quality is loft/weight. On clothing, the buyer should rely on feel and weight.

When it comes to lightness, compressibility, resilience and bulk, down is unexcelled as an insulator. But the drawbacks are not limited to quality and price. Down's great compressibility, a virtue when cramming a sleeping bag in a stuff sack, is a huge drawback in practical applications. Just the weight of light sleeping bag fabric cuts filling power and therefore insulation thickness by 15-50% on the top layer of a good bag. Because fabric pressure in clothing is far greater, down must be packed so tightly to produce insulating thickness (loft) that it often loses its weight advantage to the more resilient synthetic fills. And that part of a down sleeping bag underneath the body is squashed so flat, thanks to down's compressibility, that insulative value is virtually nonexistent.

But down has other disadvantages. Besides providing zero cushioning, it is difficult to clean, mats when wet and becomes dangerously useless as insulation, is extremely hard to dry, collects dust, leaks through all but the most tightly woven fabrics, and tends to migrate if not carefully contained, producing unsuspected thin or empty places in the insulating layer. The small enclosures (5-9 inches maximum in any dimension) required to keep an insulating layer even halfway uniform, involve complex construction which increases weight, and cost. Because of down's sensitivity to weight and tendency to migrate, bag design and construction are often more important to sleeping comfort than the quantity of fill or total bag weight. A 20°F degree slim mummy may need only 20 oz. while a semi-rectangular bag requires 34 oz. for the same temperature rating.

POLYESTER fill (better known by such trade names as Dacron, Kodafil, Polarguard and Hollofil) has made steady inroads in down's markets in recent yeas for a variety of reasons. Polyester is cheaper, more uniform, water resistant and more cushioning than down. It retains substantial insulating value when wet, dries faster, is easily cleaned and non-allergic. Since it comes as sheet batting it doesn't migrate, and it's far less sensitive to weight loading. However, in most applications, it takes 2-4 times the weight of polyester to match down in loft, and polyester has only three quarters of down's compressibility (making bags bulkier—but warmer and slightly more cushioning on the bottom).

Polyester batting tends to be better than down for clothing but troublesome and weak in sleeping bag construction. Down pods, by comparison, are individual and free. Down is easily blown or stuffed

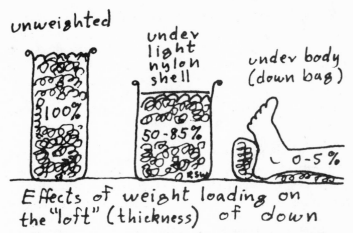

unweighted

under light nylon shell

under body (down bag)

100%

50-85%

0-5%

Effects of weight loading on the "loft" (thickness) of down

into pre-formed sleeping bag tubes but is difficult to manage in garments, suggesting why down is more effective in bags (on top, at least) while polyester is often superior in insulated clothing. Though polyester's history is still short, there is solid evidence that its effective lifespan is short. Bags are often returned after only a season or two of use because the filling has matted and flattened to a uselessly thin layer that refuses to expand; and the price of polyester moves steadily upward.

In the early 1970s down's drawbacks stirred sleeping bag makers to seriously investigate two synthetic alternatives: polyester and polyurethane foam. When the time came to tool up they put their money on polyester. I think they made a mistake, but foam may yet have its day. This spongelike material (which has largely replaced air mattresses because of its excellent cushioning and insulating characteristics), springs back to its original loft more quickly than polyester or down, and is virtually unaffected by fabric weight loading. Weight for a given loft is comparable to polyester, even though existing foams are far from the materials' potential. Foam is cheap, ridiculously simple to fabricate into bags and it's insulative value is unaffected by wetting. When soaked it wrings out easily and evaporation completes the drying process rapidly. But foam's greatest virtue is its uniformity. Combined with its stubborn springiness this provides dependable insulation without thin or cold spots. I have slept in the snow without a tent, in the wind, in perfect comfort in a foam bag no more than one inch thick, top and bottom. Veteran winter travelers know that a better bag can be made at home from one inch foam, plastic sheeting and glue than the most expensive down bag on the market! See Chapter V, BEDS.

Why did bag makers choose polyester? Foam's drawbacks are its considerable bulk and stiffness. Style and fashion conscious Americans, it was felt, would resist a bulky bag that destroyed the slim profile of their pack. And foam does not nestle cozily around the sleeper like down. It tends to stand out stiffly from the body, and like a vapor barrier shirt it takes some getting used to. New and unfamiliar concepts are often rejected, even if they work, because their great difference promotes insecurity—and wilderness travel provides more than enough of the unfamiliar for most people. Foam's short life is a minor consideration because of its cheapness.

One of the newest insulators, appearing in the late seventies, is FIBERPILE (technically "needlestacked fiberfill"), an imitation sheepskin of completely non-absorbent synthetics (acrylic and poly-ester). Actually, pile is the same stuff used in the cheap winter jackets we wore as kids, but in those days it was made of wool. Climbers and North Atlantic commercial fishermen have been using the synthetic version for years, in preference to wool, because it won't soak or hold water. Shake a fiberpile sweater dry and you can put it on immediately with no discomfort. In 15 minutes it's completely dry.

Although pile is three times the weight and bulk of a down garment of similar loft, it has characteristics that make it competitive in the lightweight world of backpacking. Its ruggedly resilient uniformity provides dependable insulation thickness, even at sewn-through seams. There are no gaps or cold spots in this half inch thick layer. Unlike down or polyester batting, it can be sewn into a garment without inner or outer nylon shells. Pile garments may be bulky and far from light, but they're 100% insulation. Without the cold nylon shell, fiberpile offers instant luxurious warmth on bare skin. (Of course, without nylon, pile is no more windproof than wool.) In addition pile is durable, tough and drapes nicely. Best of all it is comparatively cheap. Unlike polyester batting, there is no liability to matting.

The newest entrant in the insulation derby, as the eighties begin, is THINSULATE, a new polyester from 3M that is claimed to break the insulation barrier. Just when we understand that insulation efficiency is strictly a function of thickness, no matter what the material, we are told that Thinsulate provides nearly double the insulation of down, wool, fiberpile or other polyesters for a given thickness of insulation. And it does. The fibers are so small and closely packed that a "vacuum bottle effect" is produced and there is a big drop in heat conductivity.

But where fiberpile's virtues are magnified when applied to back-packing gear, Thinsulate's are diminished, or so it seems. It's still too early to tell. Having been burned by the failings of other polyester batting, clothing makers are wary. Thinsulate is expensive and it remains to be seen whether it will prove more durable than its poly-ester cousins. It has no weight advantage despite its greater insulative value because it is comparatively dense and therefore heavy and bulky for its loft. It comes in three batting weights, all of them thin. Bag makers are skeptical of its use in beds for backpackers.

Ironically, there is consumer resistance, despite the verification of insulation claims, because Thinsulate jackets are so thin. They look skimpy and chilly to a public that has come to equate warmth with

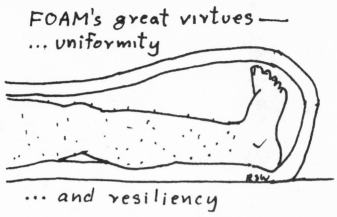

FOAM's great virtues ──
... uniformity

... and resiliency

bulk. And this isn't entirely irrational. Bulky jackets nestle cozily against the wearer, blocking unwanted drafts. Thinsulate jackets, no more than a quarter inch thick, are highly vulnerable to excessive "bellows effect" ventilation unless they are carefully designed and snugly fit. So while Thinsulate is largely windproof, water resistant and almost twice as insulative as its competition, its future is thought to lie in the stylist world of downhill skiing where slim, sleek clothing is the fashion. Its weight, cost and unknown durability seem to make it inferior to other insulators for backpacking gear, although it may have a future in gloves and socks.

Being a booster of foam, I cannot overlook the "wet suit" foam clothing introduced as the eighties begin in skiwear, even though it may be too heavy for backpacking use. This thin closed cell foam (like ensolite) sandwiched between two bonded nylon layers insulates better than Thinsulate, is completely wind and waterproof and dependably uniform, resilient and tough. Though stiffer than Thinsulate it is stretchier and provides greater compression resistance. Like Thinsulate its thinness makes it vulnerable to unwanted ventilation, but a comfortably snug fit can overcome that. Being snug and watertight, foam clothing functions as a vapor barrier as well as providing insulation. With all these virtues, wet suit foam may well be valuable to the backpackers of the eighties.

As fiberpile and Thinsulate have demonstrated, the qualities of fabrics and insulators can be deceptive. What at first seems a virtue may turn out to be a liability when materials are made into backpacking garments and sleeping bags for use on that temperamental humid furnace, the human body. Specific application is what counts. Theoretical results become meaningless unless they result in effective comfortable gear in the field—as will be seen in the chapters that follow.

2 CLOTHES

The latest clothing for wilderness travel is better and more versatile than ever before, but the seasoned buyer will pick and choose. Many clothing manufacturers know more about style and buyers' tastes than they do about the relationship between body function, fabrics and proper design. Hopefully, the reader, armed with the information in Chapter I, will now be able to evaluate both his (or her) needs as well as the clothing available. But before examining individual garments, we need to consider an often overlooked design consideration—clothing ventilation.

Ventilation is by far the most effective way of getting rid of unwanted heat generated by the body. It is far easier to get rid of warm air and excess humidity by causing it to flow out apertures in garments (from an open neck, for instance) than it is to hope for diffusion through porous clothing. As we have seen, when there are several layers of fabric and one or two of insulation, chances are that very little if any warm humid air will escape—especially since the outer layers are cooler than the inner ones. Smart designers like Jack Stephenson of Warmlite employ vapor barriers and rely on ventilation, not breathability, to carry off excess heat and moisture. Jack is a former aerospace engineer who turned mail-order manufacturer to produce unique and original equipment that is available nowhere else—except when copied.

Instead of ignoring body function or trying to fight it, Jack takes advantage of it. The body generates heat, but heat rises. So if air is permitted to flow vertically through a garment, cool air will enter at the bottom and warm air will escape at the top. That's what carries smoke up a chimney so it's called the "chimney effect." To experience it, simply put on a pullover shirt or sweater that fastens tightly around the throat and tuck it into your pants. Then exercise until excess body heat is generated. Now untuck your shirt and open the collar and note how much cooler you rapidly become. You can feel the cool air entering at the waist and the warm air flowing up around your throat.

Far more heat has escaped through chimney venting than could ever be dissipated through even a single layer of the most breathable of fabrics.

In a somewhat different test, Jack discovered there was no noticeable difference in sweating inside chimney vented jackets of Goretex and conventional waterproofing, when both were open at the neck. When venting was prevented the Goretex performed better, but when both jackets were vented the breathability of the Goretex was too negligible to be a factor. This suggests that clothing manufacturers of the eighties should make controllable vertical ventilation a prime objective in their garment design.

The first consideration when selecting backpacking clothing, is protection against cold, wet, windy weather. In my experience, for harsh conditions, vapor barrier clothing is unexcelled. In the early 1970s Jack Stephenson provided me with a vapor barrier shirt and an explanation of the theory that made it work. I was then a columnist and editor of Wilderness Camping magazine (now merged with Backpacker). After exhaustive testing of vapor barrier applications of all sorts, I wrote a series of articles, the first published on the subject. As a result of my experiments I have come to rely heavily on vapor barriers for warmth. They keep me so warm that I now wear them almost everywhere in the winter. I don't even own a big parka anymore.

As was seen in Chapter I, vapor barriers work because they utilize rather than ignore the body's continual water vapor production. They aim to keep you warm and comfortably moist while your clothes and insulation remain dry, completely free of condensation. The warm water vapor generated by the body turns to water when it strikes a cold nylon parka. But if the same garment is kept warm, condensation does not occur. To keep the garment warm, it must be worn close to the body, not as an outer garment exposed to the cold.

The body works to maintain a relative humidity of 70-95% and a skin temperature of about 75°F. Allow the body to maintain a moist layer of warm air next to the skin and sweat production will be minimal. Remove that layer and the body will open sweat glands wide and strive to restore it, pumping greatly increased quantities of vapor through the skin. So, ironically, the way to avoid heavy sweating (with its excessive heat and water loss) is to conserve that layer of moist warm air against the skin. And that's exactly what vapor barrier clothing does. That's why a single thin layer of coated nylon can keep you 20°F warmer than you would otherwise be. And that's why vapor barrier clothing is the biggest technological advance in light weight warmth since the down sleeping bag. And it's dependable under virtually all outdoor conditions. I've bet my life on it innumerable times.

Readers still skeptical can easily conduct three impressive tests without spending a penny. All that's needed is cold and a little household plastic. Probably the easiest and most dramatic test, mentioned in Chapter I, is to take an ordinary plastic bag and slip it over one bare foot when you get dressed in the morning. Then put on your normal shoes and socks and set forth into conditions that normally chill your feet. Not only should the foot in the bag stay dramatically warmer all day long, at night when you undress, instead of the bagfull of sweat you expect there will only be faint warm dampness and your sock will be clean, warm and dry. The other sock (and foot) will probably be just as damp, but it will also be cold and clammy.

Another easy test, this time for your torso, will crudely preview the virtues of the vapor barrier (VB) shirt. Take a clothing bag, the kind in which your clothes come back from the cleaners, or a big plastic trash or garbage bag, and cut holes for your arms and another for your head. What you want is a plastic vest. Put it on next to the skin (preferably) or over something snug and thin. Tuck it in your pants and then put on a relatively snug shirt or sweater that will bring the vest close against your body. Put on a light jacket if you wish, but don't bundle up, then go out in the coldest, windiest spot you can find and notice how amazingly warm you stay with low to moderate activity.

Jack Stephenson has a sneaky and amusing way of "spreading the word" about the effectiveness of vapor barriers. When he goes downhill skiing he takes with him a pocketful of his polyethelene gloves. To the people he meets on the slopes and the lifts he gives just one of these plastic gloves to be worn under whatever ski gloves or mittens they happen to be using, inviting them to see if they notice a difference. Invariably, they search him out later in the day to beg for another glove, amazed at how much warmer it kept their hand.

There you have three easy ways to test vapor barriers for yourself and discover how, properly used, they will increase body warmth by an extraordinary 20°F.

Assuming you've experimented and want something better than a garbage bag vest, it's time to look at commercially made vapor barrier shirts. There are two designs, and both originate with Jack Stephenson, modern day father of the vapor barrier. Jack's "Vaporbarrier shirt" can be vented at adjustable cuffs, the neck, front and bottom, but it has no underarm zippers. He advocates wearing it directly against the skin. At least one layer of clothing is needed on top of the shirt to keep it snug against the body and to protect it from wind and cold.

Jack uses no underarm zippers in his shirt (although he pioneered the idea) because he believes they are unnecessary and defeat one of the basic purposes of the shirt: to prevent moisture loss. He recommends limiting ventilation to the clothing worn over the vapor barrier shirt. This should be easily removed or chimney vented to prevent overheating. The important ingredient in Jack's system is "wearer awareness." Most people, he finds, tend to overdress in winter. It is better to be comfortably cool than to overheat. The aim is to keep the skin pleasantly humid and warm, but never hot and wet, whatever the outside temperature or level of exertion.

Jack strongly believes (and I wholeheartedly concur) that gear

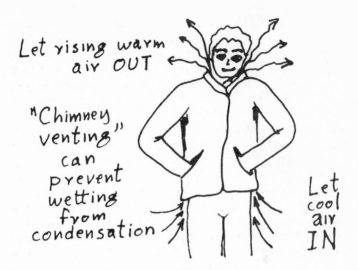

Let rising warm air OUT

"Chimney" venting can prevent wetting from condensation

Let cool air IN

should simplify life in the wilds, not make it more complex. Vapor barriers have a great deal to offer in this respect if one thinks of them simply as a thin substitute for one thick, bulky layer of insulation. They simplify outdoor cold weather living by reducing the wearer's water needs, reducing the weight and bulk of his clothing, eliminating the need for extra clothing by eliminating sweat in clothing, and eliminating the need for special clothing over your VB shirt. Just think of this new garment as a magic undershirt that lets you leave your heavy jacket home.

The late Synergy Works approach was more complicated, more expensive, less efficient and involved greater heat and water loss. But it deserves consideration because it provided easier ventilation and a somewhat wider comfort range. The Synergy "system" involves a series of four layers of clothing with coordinated ventilation. It begins with a fishnet shirt worn next to the skin. Next comes a VB shirt with zips under the arms. Then a fiberpile sweater with matching underarm zippers. The final layer is a wind and waterproof urethane coated parka shell, again with matching zips. The zippers made it possible to quickly adjust heat and ventilation levels as sunshine and exertion changed torso temperature, without removing clothing or taking off your pack.

Although Synergy is no longer with us, its system lives on. Moonstone provides underarm zippers in their VB shirts, and a large and growing number of garment makers offer pile sweaters with zips and/or parka shells with zips. Jack agrees that zippers in outer garments can be useful, although they may short circuit chimney venting, but they should not be viewed as essential to good ventilation.

Which approach do I use? Both, and I sometimes combine them. I almost never wear fishnet under a VB shirt because (like Jack) I'm quite hairy. My pelt holds the humid layer of warm air next to my skin and minimizes the nylon/skin contact which some people dislike. Besides, the fishnet can become unpleasant when it grows damp. On the other hand, I like underarm zips, particularly in a sweater and parka because I can regulate ventilation without undressing or taking off my pack. I know the VB isn't working when the vents are open and I'm losing valuable water and heat, but when I need maximum warmth and efficiency, all I have to do is zip up. I rarely use the zips in the shirt itself, but it's nice to have them when they're needed.

For instance, when I'm cross-country skiing with a pack in bright spring sunlight across a frozen lake at the bottom of a snowbowl, it can be unbearably hot, I need all the ventilation I can get. On the other hand, when I spent a week camped in snow in the bottom of a shady, windy canyon at 15,000 feet in the Bolivian Andes, I never thought of opening a zipper, much less taking off my VB shirt. I wore it day and night, with varying amounts of insulation on top, and never sweated. I stayed warm, my clothes stayed dry and I was more comfortable with less clothing than any of my companions, some of whom were nearly hidden by the bulk of their expedition down parkas.

When it's really cold, as this application illustrates, ventilation is academic and zippers become superfluous. Sweating is unlikely and cold air inside the VB shirt itself would be painful. The question is simply how many layers of clothing over the shirt are necessary. It is only in marginally cold weather, with the likelihood of strenuous activity, that zippers have some utility—and then at the expense of body heat and humidity.

Now for a closer look at the shirts themselves. Jack's is very soft flexible sheer nylon with a zipper front and adjustable velcro and cuffs and neck. The early shirts (like mine) had underarm zips that run part way down the trunk. But after several years Jack concluded that zips are only marginally effective at ventilation, encourage overdressing, defeat the VB principles and increase the cost. So the current shirt, which weighs a featherweight four ounces and costs $22-25, depending on size, has no zippers.

The Moonstone VB shirt is made of stiffer, heavier nylon, has velcro front closure and underarm zippers which run far down the arm. It weighs seven plus ounces and costs $30. Vapraflect also makes VB shirts. The proven success of vapor barrier clothing has caused other manufacturers to experiment with VB shirts of their own. In time there should be a number to choose from. In the meantime, take a look at your gear collection. If you have a light nylon rain shell or coated nylon wind shirt, you've already got a perfectly serviceable VB shirt.

As this suggests, the VB shirt can triple as both wind and rain protection. Weight and bulk conscious bicyclers love them. And there is no superior emergency survival garment. One is nearly always in the bottom of my daypack. I regularly day hike into the wilderness in nothing but shorts and boots, confident that my VB shirt will bail me out if there's a sudden change in the weather. More than once I've been caught by snow or rain or high wind while following some ridge far from home. My flimsy little shirt stops heat loss instantly. When I cover it with a six ounce hooded nylon wind shell to protect it from chilling it immediately begins to function as a vapor barrier to keep me warm. With my torso toasty and protected I can then make my way home safely in comparative comfort. In fact I feel more secure with my two nylon shells (totaling 10 oz.) than I would with a bulky three pound down parka. You can carry the same sort of backup survival protection at no cost and less weight by simply stuffing a big plastic garbage or cleaning bag in the bottom of your pack.

Under-arm zips help.

No one has yet offered VB trousers, as such, but a pair of coated nylon rainpants work admirably, especially if they have zippers for ventilation control. Two pairs, with fiberpile pants in between and perhaps polypropylene underwear next to the skin, will almost keep you warm standing still in a blizzard! And a single pair, over the long johns or under the pile pants, are more than warm enough for cross-country skiing in the wind.

REI Zip Rain Pants, with 2-way outseam zippers (10 oz., $25) make ideal VB pants. Because your legs are generally moving, they are usually warm enough without VB trousers except in sub-freezing conditions. But VB pants are marvelous sitting around a chilly camp, and a VB suit is even better in bed than it is on the trail. Put plastic bags under wool socks on your feet and plastic gloves under mittens on your hands and, dressed head to toe in vapor barriers, you have added at east 20°F to the capability of your sleeping bag! (See Chapter 5, BEDS.)

Finally, for those people who can't afford to buy vapor barrier clothing but don't want to settle for garbage bags, consider a plastic Storm Suit. It's a pullover shirt with snap closing neck and simple pants with a drawstring waist, both of heavy duty polyethelene. It comes compactly folded in a plastic pouch, altogether weights 20 ounces and customarily costs $2-3. I often see them in surplus, sporting goods and variety stores rather than backpacking shops. These cheap compact plastic garments are low on fashion and durability, but they're terrific as multi-purpose emergency and survival gear. I often throw one in my pack when I'm heading into the wilds and skimping on rain protection.

And worn against the skin they function admirably as vapor barriers. They're exceptionally good when sitting around a cold camp and as VB sleepwear, and of course they offer leakproof rain protection during an unexpected cloudburst. You can even carry two suits, one for vapor barrier warmth, the other for rain. Add plastic bag socks and throw-away plastic gloves and you're fully equipped for only pennies. The only thing cheaper is going naked! Basically the same suit is available in far more durable coated nylon from EMS for $30-35.

The fishnet shirt (also known as Norwegian net or string) is probably my favorite backpacking garment. I wear it almost anytime temperatures are moderate, i.e. when it's not cold enough for vapor barriers or warm enough to go shirtless. Net shirts are probably the only garments that deserve the term "breathable," but it isn't hard to get condensation in them, too, if conditions are right. Their quarter inch holes provide admirable ventilation, yet help maintain that layer of warm moist air on the skin that keeps the body content. Fishnet's bulk provides a spacer between the skin and its covering, and its ability to soak up sweat gives the illusion of dryness without permitting the wholesale evaporative chilling rendered by a sweat-soaked t-shirt.

Because of the balance between insulation and ventilation, fishnets actually help warm you in winter and cool you in summer. They come in cotton and wool. Some people like the wool because it's softer after washing, but it's heavier, costs considerably more and if you toss it in with the family wash, as I did, it will shrink to unuseable doll-size. Wool fishnet shirts cost $12-14 and weigh half a pound, while the cotton equivalent costs $7-8 and weighs only six ounces. Actually, the cotton shirt is often 50% polyester.

I object to models with a solid fabric yoke over the shoulders. The purpose is to provide a soft smooth surface for pack shoulder straps to dig into. Unfortunately, the fabric continues into the armpit where it grows as wet and soggy as any t-shirt—and stays that way—defeating the shirt's prime purpose. I buy only all-net brands like L.L. Bean and Scandinavian Knits because the shoulder problem for me has been nonexistent. Additional fishnet shirt advantages are ease of drying when washed on the trail, and their usefulness as sleepwear on mild nights. But their chief value is as a warm but well-ventilated undershirt in moderate temperatures.

Warm and moderate weather underwear—or lack of same—is largely a matter of personal preference. Warmth, protection and ventilation are usually the prime considerations. String jockey shorts are now available from Allen-A and perhaps others, but for good crotch ventilation boxer shorts are better than the jockey variety, and nothing at all is better still in the opinion of some.

An increasing number of clothing manufacturers are now offering backpacking clothes cut specifically for women, although many smaller ladies are pleased with the prices they find in the boy's department of large clothing stores. New small firms are emerging like QP-Pants which offers both trousers and shorts designed exclusively for women. All have velcro fastened vents in the crotch for comfort and privacy when nature calls, plus excellent ventilation. In the late seventies there emerged a mail order catalog called Outdoor Gal to collect offerings for a female audience. Included are Woolrich, Duofold, Trailwise, Lee, QP-Pants, Vasque Boots and Outdoor Bra. (See List of Suppliers.)

The newest backpacking garment in widespread use is the fiberpile sweater, not to mention bibs and pile pants. Styles vary from baggy-

Make a "magic" VB undershirt by snipping holes in a big trash bag and wearing it next to the skin ...tucked in.

TRASH KING

outer shirt

looking sweatshirts to sleek models with under arm zippers (only Moonstone and Mark Pack Works). Most have crew or turtlenecks, zippers down the front and elasticized cuffs and waistbands. They commonly weigh a pound and a half, which is heavy for only half inch thick insulation, but worn between a VB shirt and a good shell parka they provide all the warmth most active outdoor people need, even in winter.

People accustomed to bulky down or polyester padded parkas will find the pile sweater startlingly different. Though it's comparatively thin, it won't compress very much and you'll find it harder to stuff in your pack than a down parka twice its size. There is no hood so you'll need a wool watch cap or balaclava for your head. Like all sweaters, it really isn't designed to be worn as an outer garment, except under mild conditions, because the wind blows right through. If it didn't, the snug waist and cuffs would seriously inhibit ventilation. But when you need heat retention the pile sweater can provide it. Zip it up tight, put a wind shell over it and a VB shirt under it and you begin to cook. It doesn't seem possible that only half an inch of insulation can keep you so warm—or provide such a wide comfort range.

Helly Hansen is the oldest and best known maker of pile clothing, but a number of firms like Chouinard, Lowe, Mark Pack and Forrest make increasingly refined designs for backpackers, and most clothing manufacturers have pile garments on the drawing board. Demand grows monthly as buyers discover the toughness, durability, comfort and dependability of this soft synthetic sheepskin. You can soak it in icewater, shake it dry in seconds and put it on immediately without discomfort. Instead of babying it, as so often is necessary with fragile backpacking gear, you can treat it rough and count on its near foolproof indestructability. Sweater prices average $45.

As the eighties begin, Goretex parkas are all the rage, and it's hard to find shells coated with the far lighter and cheaper urethane, despite its superiority when ventilation is provided. One garment maker told me he reluctantly makes only Goretex parkas, despite their obvious shortcomings, because he can't afford to make an item that might not sell. But Marmot "Nightrider," designed for bicyclers, may help reverse the trend. This urethane coated parka shell of nylon taffeta comes with underarm zippers and sells for $110. Other manufacturers are ready to switch to urethane coatings when demand picks up, as it should when it's discovered that well vented sealed jackets don't have to get you wet.

In the meantime, garment makers are giving the customer what he asks for: Goretex coated nylon jackets and parkas of every description. Following Synergy Works' lead (and before that Stephenson's), an increasing number of manufacturers now provide underarm zips. The customer can choose from Kelty, Banana, Marmot, REI and so forth. It seems only a matter of time before the word is out that, with underarm zips, you don't need Goretex and its extra weight and cost. Goretex in a parka adds $50 to the price and a pound to the weight, in return for which you hope your body vapor will somehow find its way out through the film's microscopic pores.

Unfortunately, Goretex's breathability is so negligible under critical field conditions that it can't prevent condensation. And when wet its pores are sealed and cannot breathe. Under ordinary conditions Goretex performs well, which impresses people who don't realize that under ordinary conditions *all* parkas perform well, provided there's reasonably good ventilation. As a waterproof covering for highly vulnerable down jackets and sleeping bags, Goretex makes slightly more sense, despite the considerable extra weight and cost. As a practical matter, truly adequate breathability in a waterproof garment under critical conditions is an impossible dream.

Another disappointment is 60/40 cloth, but it's still being offered and advertised for parkas. This impossible dream was supposed to combine the best qualities of cotton and nylon. Instead, it combines the worst features. It is heavy, leaks like a sieve and holds onto water. Beware any manufacturer who so much as hints that 60/40 cloth garments are rain repellent. The truth is they'll completely soak through in the shoulders in only five minutes of moderate rain. The only good use I can imagine for 60/40 clothing is bushwhacking through heavy brush in the dry season. And 60/40, though uncoated, permits only negligible breathability through its tight, windproof weave. It's a pleasant, good looking fabric and still sells well to people more interested in fashion than outdoor travel.

When it became apparent that 60/40 was a failure, the mills created 65/35, hoping that if both natural and synthetic fibers were woven in the same direction something wonderful might occur. It didn't. The result is another handsome, tough, heavy fabric that's hopeless in real rain. I much prefer parka shells of lighter, stronger cheaper ripstop nylon or its smoother cousin nylon taffeta to any cotton/synthetic blend. I have probably hiked more miles in the spring, summer and

expeditionary parkas are rarely needed.

fall Sierra in my old olive green six ounce hooded nylon taffeta shell than I have in all other garments combined. It shouldn't be assumed that all outerwear must be waterproof just because it could conceivably rain. One rain garment is ample in dry climates, and even that might be left home under certain circumstances.

Having considered all the fabrics of which parkas commonly are made, let's now consider the virtues and drawbacks of the various insulations with which they are stuffed. Down, long the standard, probably deserves first consideration. The attributes of any material, as we have seen, are neither good nor bad—until judged for a specific application. Considered as parka insulation, the balance sheet looks like this. Down's chief virtue is lightness, followed by bulk (the way it snugs gently against the body) and compressibility (when being stuffed in your pack). But bulk also defeats ventilation, and excessive compressibility is a liability in clothing. Because of the fabric pressure in clothing, down must be packed so tightly that its weight advantage often disappears. Down is the least uniform of insulators. Because of the fluidity of its unconnected pods, it must be contained in small pockets, usually formed by quilting with sewn-through seams. Insulation thickness is great in the middle but often non-existent near the seams. Because down pods are reluctant to work themselves into tight places, the gap in the insulating layer at the seams is far wider than the billowing quilt hints. Infrared cameras measuring heat escape have shown a shocking volume of loss through the grid of seams in many an impressively thick, expensive down parka. This great heat loss in so thick a garment is what makes fiberpile seem so remarkably warm for its half inch loft. Pile is pure, uniform, continuous insulation, while down is pockets of insulation with gaps in between. The rare and expensive exception is the expeditionary down parka engineered so that the pockets of down overlap and baffles over the seams. While these gigantic coats are warm, the vast quantities of nylon they contain (often four layers) make them heavy and incompressible.

If down's unsuspected cold spots are disconcerting, its vulnerability to wetting is positively dangerous. Increasing numbers of veteran hikers, climbers, snow campers and long distance travelers are relying on synthetics in critical conditions because wet down is worse than useless; it's a positive liability. When wet it weighs a ton and it simply cannot be dried in the field. If down clothing is worn day after day, it gradually grows heavier and less effective as it absorbs body moisture —unless a vapor barrier shirt is being worn, in which case bulky down clothing probably isn't required. I like the cozy bulk and quick warmth of down on cold winter days in the city, but I find myself increasingly reluctant to carry it on the trail. Having long since switched to vapor barrier warmth, I find I simply don't need it.

If I'm less than enthusiastic about carrying down clothing, it's not because I'm crazy about polyester batting. Far from it. There are dozens of trade names used by clothing manufacturers, but nearly all of them originate at Eastman (Kodasoft), DuPont (Hollofil) or Reliance-Celanese (Polarguard). Hollofil and Kodasoft are chopped fibers that rely on a silicone coating to make them repel one another and thus resist the matting that kills resilience and loft. Polarguard relies on the crimping of a continuous filament fiber to resist matting. The sad truth, however, is that these strategies don't work for long in the field.

After 6-8 years experience, gear makers have discovered to their sorrow that polyester batting "dies" in a comparatively short time. The fibers gradually interlock or align with the friction of use aggravated by compression and heat. Matting occurs, resilience disappears and the loft that yielded insulation is permanently lost. Infrequently used parkas kept cool and never compressed may appear to last for years. Heavily used or abused garments can "go flat" (lose half their loft) in six months. Unlike down, polyester batting has a very short life.

Nevertheless it has virtues which make it worth considering, especially since it's become the favored insulator for many manufacturers. The batting of all three makers is far more uniform, when used in garments, than down. It doesn't migrate so it doesn't need to be quilted into a series of small pockets. Not only are there fewer seams, the seams aren't as cold because the batting has far higher resistance to compression than down. Polyester is much cheaper than down and more cushioning, and it doesn't absorb water which means garments soaked by rain or condensation retain useability and can be dried in the field. In this regard it lies about halfway in between hopeless down and easily dried fiberpile.

Unfortunately polyester has another drawback: weight. It takes two to four times the weight of polyester to achieve the same loft as down.

In summary, parkas insulated with polyester batting may be worth buying when weight is less critical than the hazards of wetting and when the shorter life is reflected in the garment's lower price. Down parkas may be justified when weight and compressibility are vital, long life is essential, liability to wetting is minimal and cost is not a limiting factor.

As the eighties begin, down, polyester batting and fiberpile account for probably 95% of outdoor garment insulation, but two others, foam and Thinsulate, though largely untried, show great potential. Urethane (open cell) foam offers unbeatable uniformity and resilience. It is cheap, competitively light, unaffected by wetting and as easily dried in the field as fiberpile. Its short life is adequately offset by its cheapness. Foam's virtues outshine those of all three major insulators combined, but it has yet to enjoy success because of two problems. Despite its softness and stretchiness, foam has poor "drape," i.e. it stands out stiffly from the body instead of nestling cozily like down. Foam's other drawback is bulk, but in that respect it's no worse than fiberpile.

It's easy to make a foam hood

I have owned several foam parkas and found them exceptionally warm, if somewhat stiff. I also found the ease of ventilation an asset that greatly increases the garment's comfort range. Quarter inch foam sandwiched between loose nylon facings performs insulating miracles in a well-cut jacket. The only maker I know of foam parkas, jackets & vests is Cosy Quip (formerly Ocaté). If clothing (and sleeping bag) makers would spend half the time and money on foam that they've squandered on polyesters, I'm convinced they could develop a soft, large-cell, superlight, resilient, stretchy, uniform insulator that would clearly excel all other materials in all vital respects. The reluctance stems largely from anxiety over public acceptance. See Chapter 5 BEDS for more on foam.

Closed cell foam (like Ensolite) laminated between nylon skins is being used in skiwear as "wet suit foam" for racing suits. Like Thinsulate (see Chapter I) its insulating qualities transcend mere thickness, utilizing a "vacuum bottle effect" to supply nearly twice the efficiency of the same thickness of down, pile, polyester batting, etc. Thicknesses employed are in the neighborhood of only one eighth inch. As with any layer this thin, excess ventilation is a hazard. Closed cell foam laminates are heavy, expensive and a trifle stiff, despite their great virtues of uniformity and resilience. Thinsulate's prime qualities are super warmth, softness and good drape. Its drawbacks are weight, expense and the fact that its life and durability are unknown. Thinsulate insulated jackets are being offered by Sierra Designs, North Face and others outside the ski industry. One or both of these new products could make it big if manufacturers take enough of a chance and public acceptance materializes. Or both could quietly disappear, like many a miracle fabric before them.

One final material that shows promise for the eighties is "fleece," another synthetic (acrylic and polyester) that resembles heavy flannel crossed with pile. This dense, woven material has a rich, warm soft feel that is sure to have appeal because it's both warm and good looking, though heavy. Many manufacturers are experimenting with it, but few garments are yet on the market. Chouinard offers a 22 oz. pullover fleece sweater for $45 and a zip front model at 24 oz. and $48. And Moonstone sells fleece sweaters in several styles.

Insulated parkas, jackets, vests and sweaters can be vital—if it's cold enough. By using vapor barriers, however, which add 20 degrees of warmth, I often find it possible, even in winter, to leave home the insulation (or most of it) if I carry a well designed lined parka. Two layers of fabric, thanks to the trapped air in between, offer more than twice the insulation of a single layer or shell. For years I wore a lined Synergy urethane-coated parka that was so warm when shut tight that I rarely wore anything heavier than a moleskin cotton shirt (and vapor barrier) beneath it.

Having thoroughly discussed parkas, it's time to return to shirts. When it isn't quite warm enough to go shirtless I favor short-sleeved Ben Davis pullovers ($8) with zipper necks. For mosquito or sunburn protection in hot weather I like a light, long-sleeved button-up denim work shirt ($7). For cool but active summer days I choose a heavier cotton pullover Ben Davis Hickory shirt ($10). This, as all my friends know, is my favorite shirt, and I wear it alone, or over a string shirt or VB shirt, and sometimes under my six ounce nylon wind shell ($10-20), or a urethane parka shell if rain is likely. I like the hickory shirt because the cotton feels so good and because the pullover design is warmer and more easily chimney vented than button-front models. If the weather gets too raw I wear an even softer cotton flannel moleskin or chamois shirt ($15-20 from a variety of makers), over a VB shirt and under a good windshell.

As the weather gets colder I may wear a Pendleton wool shirt over the VB ($30), but probably I will reach for a fiberpile sweater with underarm zippers. I never wear wool except when protected from sweat by a VB shirt, and I never wear wool pullover sweaters at all. They're too hard to take on and off and provide no ventilation control. Wool, once the essential insulator for backpackers, is now third or fourth rate. It provides an illusion of dry comfort as it soaks up sweat or rain, but when saturation is reached your wool garment has become a heavy sponge that is very slow to dry. Only soaked down is worse. There's no reason to wear wool when fiberpile is so cheap.

Two other fabrics used for parkas and jackets should be briefly mentioned. Ventile cloth, made by just one mill in England at last report, is a tightly woven long staple cotton that swells when wet and seals the fabric from most water penetration. Parkas made from it are extremely heavy (3 lbs.) and expensive ($200). They are no more condensation-proof than a urethane coated parka with good ventilation, and they're considerably less waterproof.

The highly advertised Peter Storm Bukflex jackets utilize sealed fabric laminated to a spongy liner that absorbs condensing body

wax
rubbed on
where
the rain hits
Keeps
legs dry
without
sweating.

moisture, producing an illusion of dryness (not unlike wool). The hope is that this moisture will have a chance to evaporate between wearings or before saturation is reached. In the meantime, you carry condensed and heavy but invisible water with you, and the liner is rather fragile and short lived.

Vests, usually down-filled, but increasingly available in polyester, pile and even foam, can be highly versatile garments. Because they are open in the armpit, they permit ventilation while keeping the trunk warm. They likewise recognize a lesser need for insulation on the arms. (Reflecting this need is an admirably designed sweater by Mark Pack Works: the torso is half inch pile while the arms are quarter inch fleece. Underarm zips would make it perfect.) MPW also offers an unusually good-looking pile vest for less than $30. Such a garment can be worn over (or under) a pile sweater in winter as an inexpensive and invulnerable alternative to carrying a heavy parka, if the sweater alone isn't quite warm enough.

When it comes to protection from heavy or continuous rain, a waterproof parka shell may be insufficient. The easiest improvement is the addition of rain chaps, 4-6 ounce tubes of coated nylon that are meant to be worn over regular pants and under a hip length parka. They begin at the crotch to provide maximum ventilation. Rain chaps start at 4 ounces and under $2 for the plastic pants in my Storm Suit. For $10 at REI you can get chaps in 6 ounce coated nylon chaps which tie at the waist and fasten under the instep.

The next step up in rain protection is the Anorak (the name given to a pullover, rather than a zip up, unlined parka) that comes a little below the hip. Such garments weigh 10-24 ounces and cost anywhere from $15 for the simplest urethane coated shell to $70-120 for fancy Goretex models. Companion to the Anorak for rainy country travel are rain pants with full length zippers down the outside seam. They weigh

10-16 ounces and range from under $30 in urethane to $100 in Goretex. This combination is the durable, fitted nylon equivalent of the 20 oz. plastic Storm Suits for which I customarily pay $2.67. Which one you buy depends on whether you expect to live and travel in it under dependably cold wet conditions, or whether you want temporary backup or emergency protection for unexpected bad weather. In either situation, I do not recommend Goretex.

The other garments for rain protection are the poncho and the cagoule. Ponchos tend to offer more ventilation but are so vulnerable to wind that they become virtually useless in anything but the quietest drizzle. Their advantages: they can double as ground cloths or emergency sleeping bag shelter. The cheapest are heavy army surplus, or superlight but short-lived plastic. Most come with snaps on the side. Adjustable ventilation at the neck is vital. A common coated nylon poncho will weigh 7 ounces and cost $20. One big enough to cover a pack and fitted with a hood might weigh 20 ounces and cost $30. Don't ever count on a poncho to keep your hands or legs dry, even in a quiet drizzle. And be prepared for condensation unless you're just sitting in camp.

The garment most likely to keep you dry in wind driven rain is the cagoule, a hooded anorak with a full skirt that comes below the knees. Usually there's a drawstring at the hem so you can retract your feet and bivouac inside in an emergency. And there ought to be hand-warmer pockets, sorely missed in a poncho. Neck ventilation should be better than in a poncho, and cagoule hoods are better cut and more adjustable. The great drawback in cagoules is that condensation is often massive if you exercise at all because ventilation is poor. Underarm zippers could transform this sweatbox into a valuable garment, but so far there are none on the market. Coated nylon cagoules commonly weigh 14-20 ounces and cost $40-50, but I've bought plastic models for under $5. And rain chaps or pants will still be needed if you expect your trousers and socks to stay dry.

The alternative here is gaiters. These coated nylon leggings which fasten under the instep come in two sizes: shorties with elastic tops designed to cover only ankles, boot tops and socks, and high gaiters which zip and snap up to a drawstring or elastic band that fastens just below the knee. Once used exclusively by climbers and skiiers, gaiters are increasingly being used by backpackers who find them invaluable in spring snow and slush or as a substitute for rain pants or chaps in mild summer storms. I rely on Sierra Design shorties to keep my feet dry as long as puddles and snow last in the Sierra, even though I'm wearing shorts. Gaiters offer a legitimate application of Goretex to keep down condensation while keeping out mud and snowmelt. Shorties (more common in ski shops) weigh 2-6 ounces and cost $10-15. High gaiters, in a variety of styles, may be found in mountain shops and outdoor catalogs, weighing 6-10 ounces and costing $12-30.

Cunningly designed long underwear that claims to keep you warm

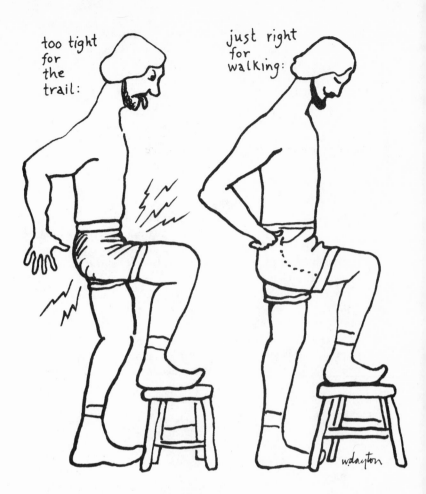

too tight
for
the
trail:

just right
for
walking:

w.dayton

and bone dry is advertised heavily in the magazines and catalogs, but
I'm skeptical. Most claims seem to defy what we know about the
body's heat and humidity generation. Breathability has to be negligible in tightly woven long johns of the sort offered by Allen-A,
Duofold, Janus, etc. Where do you suppose the moisture goes? I
realize I'm atypical, having a comprehensive layer of hair, but for
three-season hiking and camping I get all the warmth I need from
fishnet long underwear, and I rarely use that, even in the snow. Pile
sweaters and pants make super underwear—if it's cold enough—to
wear beneath nylon storm pants and over a VB shirt. That's the
combination most of the veteran winter climbers and cross-country
skiiers I know like best.

For slightly milder winter conditions the favorite as the eighties
begin is long underwear made of polypropylene. This single layer,
totally non-absorbent weave doesn't itch or cling. It's featherweight,
cheap, stretchy, comfortable and remarkably warm. Like other under-

wear it wicks away moisture that has to go somewhere, but outer layers of insulation can be effectively protected by wearing vapor barriers. Made by Odlo-Termic (best) and Lifa, it comes in crew-necked shirts, pants and bibs costing about $15 each.

The trouble with most trousers made for backpacking is that conventional belts and buckles, beneath a tightly cinched hipbelt, not only serve no purpose, they dig into the body. Even belt loops and buttons may mark the skin uncomfortably. Suspenders, which compete with pack shoulder straps, are no better. Another problem is the lack of ventilation in the crotch. After skiing one bright spring day across a frozen lake in reflected heat so great that my crotch was soaked, I prevailed upon friends at Synergy to alter a pair of $10 loose cotton work pants for me. They removed the zipper fly and replaced it with a double opening coil zipper that ran all the way from my navel through the crotch and up the back to my waist. And they removed belt loops and button and installed an elasticized waistband of the sort found on golf slacks, with an adjustable velcro-closed tongue.

The trousers have proved entirely successful. The waist is so adjustable that I can tuck in several bulky layers for ventilation control without discomfort. I save the weight and bulk of a belt and buckle, and when I cinch my hipbelt tight there is nothing beneath it to dig in. Perhaps best of all is my ability to open both zippers wide and let the cool breeze blow through instead of overheating and sweating in the crotch. And it's amusing to see the puzzled look on people's faces when they see that zipper in the rear—especially if it's open! They tend to think they've met a man who's put his pants on backwards!

At about the same time, Jack Stephenson put on the market a version of the pants he's been personally testing for the last eight years. Called Converta Pants, they are designed for maximum versatility and ventilation. Full length coil zippers in the inseam permit varying degrees of ventilation. Zipped all the way open the pants can be tucked into the waist band to form adequate shorts. A stem to stern zipper, as in my pants, permits crotch ventilation. The waist is fastened shut by a velcro tab and a separate velcro half belt is adjustable. Adjustable velcro closed cuffs permit snug closure around the ankle for added warmth. The fabric is a synthetic called Aramid with the feel of cotton and the toughness and windproofness of nylon. Converta pants are good looking, custom made to your measurements, weigh 20 ounces and cost $80. I've tested them thoroughly and found them great, though I prefer separate lightweight shorts for extensive hiking.

There are other trousers which merit consideration for extreme conditions. Rough Rider and Sportif, Sunbuster and Woolrich all make tough trousers, but they are considerably more expensive and not necessarily better than the pants, like those I had modified, to be found in the workingman's section of any sizeable department store. L.L. Bean's Chino pants offer extra warmth in the cold thanks to a

Chouinard's
"Shants"

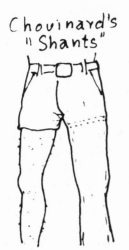

Stephenson's
"Converta Pants"

lining of thick-napped, soft cotton flannel. They weigh 28 ounces and cost $21. Wool gabardine makes a tough, warm trouser, and so does wool whipcord. And some people swear by heavy cotton corduroy.

A majority of backpackers probably still wear jeans, despite the fact that they are uncomfortably tight, heavy, hot and water absorbent. Back when I wore them regularly I overcame their tendency to soak up rain by rubbing the front of the thigh and the back of the calf with the cake of wax in my fly tying kit. The surfaces most exposed to wetting were thus effectively waterproofed while most of the fabric remained free to breathe, thus preventing condensation. Though few will admit it, most backpackers wear jeans because they're in style, not because they are comfortable.

When it comes to choosing clothing, wilderness travelers who want to maximize comfort and hold down cost should not limit themselves to the stylish offerings of backpacking shops and catalogs. Work clothes and skiwear are worth considering too. And a lot can be learned from our cousins, the climbers. For mountaineers the priorities are different. Dependability and ruggedness are vital when you're counting on your gear to help keep you alive. Weight and even fashion become secondary.

One of the leading outfitters of the climbing fraternity is Yvon Chouinard's Great Pacific Iron Works. I'm impressed with its climbing pants and shirts which come in heavy duty corduroy, canvas, pile and polyester fleece. There are double-seated trail pants (21 oz., $25), rugged canvas and twill shorts and stretchy wool and polyester knickers. When it comes to pile, no one offers more: there are vests, anoraks, zipfront sweaters, crewnecks, hoods, pants, socks and two styles of mittens. There is even a sleeping shell (see Chapter 5, BEDS). One of the most interesting and useful offerings are combination shorts and long trousers, called "Shants." Concealed velcro strips on tough cotton-poly shorts permit the easy secure attachment of matching pant legs. These versatile, convertible trousers should be a boon to backpackers. Price is $35.

Except in mid-winter I do almost all my hiking in shorts. I like the feeling of freedom, the breeze on my legs, the ventilation in the crotch. As a consequence I wear shorts when almost no one else does: in rain, snow, wind, brush, and mosquitos—because I'm happier that way, thanks partly, I'm sure, to the fur on my legs. But I've got lots of company, worldwide. The Swiss hike in shorts if they possibly can. In Switzerland I learned that if you are careful to keep the torso warmed, you can hike all day on snow or ice without chilling your legs. In New Zealand's rainforests it was explained to me that shorts are best in the rain because it rains every day and legs dry more quickly than trousers. I was also right at home in Australia where everyone wore shorts to combat the heat and humidity.

But the culture may be more important than the climate. In South America the custom is long trousers, even when it's sweltering. In hot, humid Buenos Aires, people gaped at my shorts and sandals as though I'd come from outer space. Here in America many people wear heavy, hot long pants for no reason beyond habit, or a vague anxiety about exposing their legs to bugs and scratching. While I rarely go day hiking in anything but shorts, when I backpack I always carry the appropriate long trousers needed for protection against the cool of evening in camp.

As the seventies began it was hard to find good shorts, but now there is a wide selection to choose from. Tastes differ, but beware a snug fit. It's far better to be baggy and comfortable. I like heavy cotton, the shorter the better, with a conventional pocket arrangement. When trying on shorts be sure seams and hems in the crotch are not bulky enough to cause chafing or you'll be painfully raw in a couple of miles. A slit up the outer seam can further increase comfort. Good shorts are where you find them, and most of mine do not come from mountain shops. Because I don't like belts or belt loops, I look for elasticized waists. As a consequence I often set forth into the wilderness in two ounce running shorts of parachute cloth or boxer-style swim trunks. Their lightness, freedom and comfort more than offsets the lack of pockets. A fanny pack can easily be swiveled to the front for access to the small items usually carried in pockets. Besides, bulging pockets are no aid to comfort, and lifting a pocketful of knives and gadgets with every step uses energy to no purpose. Veteran outdoor travelers know the value of headgear, even if, like me, they don't particularly like hats. When it's cold or windy, head coverings are vital for the simple reason that since capillaries in the head and neck don't contract when chilled, heat loss can be enormous. Protecting the head's warmth can make the difference between overall comfort and dangerous chilling. Remember the old axiom: if your feet get cold, put on a hat. The best all-purpose hats for warmth are thick synthetic (or wool) watchcaps or Balaclavas, widely available at ski and mountain shops

felt hats
become cooler
after a little
judicious snipping.

and clothing stores. One or the other will be indispensible as sleepgear in all but the mildest summer nights. The warmest weigh 4-6 ounces, while light knitted stockingcaps for summer use may weigh as little as 2-3 ounces.

For really harsh weather, like ski touring in the wind, I have devised a sort of crude helmet out of half-inch open celled foam which I call the "Wood Hood." Anyone can make one by draping a square yard of foam over the head from shoulder to shoulder so that you're looking out a tunnel that extends slightly beyond the nose. Have a friend mark the back appropriately for cutting. Cut with scissors and glue together with rubber cement. Glue a scrap across the front to bridge the tunnel somewhere between chin and nose. Be sure foam extends down onto the torso on all sides. Although my design impairs lateral vision, the increased protection from raw winds more than compensates, and in lighter air the tunnel can be folded back for better vision. The Wood Hood converts a shell and sweater or jacket into an insulated parka. Weight is negligible, compressibility is great when not in use and cost is so low that experimentation is cheap. The tunnel will keep your face surprisingly warm in deep cold. It is even more impressive in your sleeping bag at night.

The only manufactured equivalent I know of is Chouinard's pile hood, a medieval-style cowl of fiberpile with a drawstring to close the face opening. It weighs 4 ounces and costs $8-9.

Hats are also worn for protection against sunburn, glare, light rain, wind and bugs. Probably the most popular summer trail hat is the 3-ounce hobo or rollercrusher with 3-inch brim. The back of the brim needs to be turned up, perhaps fastened with a safety pin, to avoid constant rubbing when a pack is worn. These felt hats become cooler and lighter when scissors are used judiciously to cut holes for ventilation. Since there is no perfect hat, most people carry what they like. Some of my hiking partners stubbornly wear baseball caps, others insist on tennis hats, hunters caps, straw hats and wool berets. All but the snuggest fitting hats should be equipped with nylon cords that can be tied beneath the chin on windy days.

Since I dislike the restrictive feel of a snug hat when all I need is sun and glare protection, I generally wear one of my collection of sunshades, usually one of straw. I also like a tennis visor which incorporates a useful and cushiony sweatband.

Gloves and mittens, as mentioned in Chapter 1, get a tremendous boost in efficiency when worn over vapor barrier liners. Disposable plastic gloves sold in drugstores and paint stores are fine, so long as they don't bind. I've tried dozens of different models without much success. Now I rely on Jack Stephenson's poly gloves which sell for 15¢ a pair. I carry a pair or two wherever I take gloves or mittens, secure in the knowledge that my hands will be both warm and dry. I like them best under acrylic knitted mittens for autumn chill and under Chouinard's pile mittens (3 oz., $9) if it's colder. With a Goretex shell the price jumps to $18 and 4 oz. For real cold I'll take heavy wool Dachstein mitts at $10-16 and 6 ounces. For the deepest cold of all I use huge CosyQuip mittens of nylon-covered, unlined urethane foam. They're too clumsy for many tasks but the warmth—on the trail or standing around camp—is unbeatable, even without VB liners, because the thick foam nestles snugly against the skin to prevent convective heat loss.

Bandana handkerchiefs, available in most mountaineering shops at three for a dollar, are so endlessly useful that I sometimes take two. Extremes of temperature, wind and cold, cause noses to run, and Kleenex is extremely impractical on the trail. Besides their usefulness as handkerchiefs, bandanas often serve as hot pads, dish towels, neckerchiefs for protection against sunburn and insects, compresses, hand towels, large bandages, napkins, slings, wash cloths, etc. Since they dry very quickly, I often include them in the afternoon wash along with my string and denim shirts and socks.

These are the clothes that have proven themselves best adapted to backpacking. Some are found only in mountaineering shops, but many are best hunted for at the back of the closet, in surplus and discount houses and at the workingman's store, where discovery of the perfect garment at a reasonable price can bring considerable satisfaction.

3 FOOTWEAR

The eighties began, surprisingly enough, with a buyer revolt against heavy, costly traditional boots that sent worried bootmakers back to the drawing board. The result of their efforts to create new appeal has been a genuine revolution in outdoor footwear, a long overdue breakthrough in boot design.

Back in the mid-seventies, sales of conventional boots topped a million pairs. By 1979 the total had shrunk by an alarming 70-75%! Backpackers had simply stopped buying the great leather dinosaurs they had once believed were essential for travel beyond the sidewalks.

What prompted this unexpected revolt? A combination of price and fashion. Skyrocketing leather prices and inflation have pushed the cost of good medium weight (4 lb.) top grain leather boots past the $100 barrier. And the running boom has spawned featherweight jogging shoes that are so comfortable and unbelievably light that your grandmother now regularly wears them to go shopping. The better-than-barefoot feeling has become addictive, and lightweight comfort has produced a new fashion in footwear.

And after running like the wind in their magic slippers, hikers understandably rebelled against putting on huge, stiff heavy boots to go backpacking. It just didn't seem right any more to encase the feet in great unbending blocks of rubber and stiff leather—especially when they cost more than $100 a pair! Once you've tasted caviar, it's hard to be content with catfish again.

People were tired of boot break-in programs that bordered on masochism—enduring the chafing and pinching of new boots a little longer each day in hopes that maybe next summer they might not have their feet chewed to hamburger on the first day of their annual hiking vacation. People were tired of worrying about crucial fit: if it wasn't perfect, they knew, the pain might never stop, even after the purgatory of break-in. People were tired of trying to remember whether to use Sno-seal on oil tanned boots and Neatsfoot oil on vegetable tanned leather—or was it the other way around? (Yes.) And how could they be sure they were getting top grain leather rather than a cleverly doctored split? People were anxious about the conflicting claims of superiority for Norwegian welts, Littleway stitching, injection molding and Goodyear welts. In summary, people were just plain tired of heavy boring boots, and I'm tired of writing about them!

Given the unbelievable lightness and comfort of running shoes, it's little wonder that people started wearing them into the wilds. They worried at first about destroying their feet, but when nothing awful happened they discovered they could hike miles further without tiring than they ever did in the old clodhoppers. Their feet weren't pulverized or overheated, and it didn't really matter if they got wet because running shoes dry quickly. Just splash across that creek and keep on going.

My first glimpse of the revolt came a few years ago when a friend came to visit wearing outlandish Nikes he had whimsically colored with green and orange felt pens. When I remarked on his wild footwear he told me he had worn these same shoes for more than a hundred miles on high Sierra trails and cross country while carrying 60-80 pound loads to stock a series of caches for next winter's ski tour. They'd been great, he insisted, and he was through with big heavy boots forever.

The point I'm trying to make is that the builders of antidiluvian boots were wrong. We don't need to wear the same basic boots our grandfathers hated, every time we go into the hills. We don't have to encase our feet in thick leather armor just because we're leaving the pavement. Having made the point let me hasten to add that I don't really believe today's running shoes are ideal, or even satisfactory, for hiking with a pack in rough terrain. But they point the way to new superlight, space age, high technology footwear that is lightyears ahead of the boots we've been buying. The revolt against big boots has hit bootmakers so hard where it hurts that they've finally begun to reconsider. As the eighties begin there are totally new concepts in boot design emerging. Imagine a pair of sturdy hiking boots that require no break-in, no waterproofing and no special care. They cost well under $100, weigh just 2¼ lbs., and the fit isn't even a matter of life or death. Buy them one day, go backpacking the next. And rejoice!

It's hard to overemphasize the importance of weight. It's well known that a pound on the feet is equivalent to five on the back, but think what that means on a ten mile walk. If you take an average 2000 steps per mile, it means you lift five tons in ten miles for every pound of boot on your feet! So every pound you save—going from four to three pound boots, or three pound boots to the new two pounders— saves the energy needed to lift five tons. Think what that energy saving could mean to your enjoyment of a trip, or how it might extend your range? Instead of collapsing in camp to soak and patch your swollen red feet you might actually enjoy a stroll after supper.

More and more of the people I talk to have forsaken the big heavy boot that seemed so essential only half a decade ago. In the mid-

mail·order boots

rarely fit the way

they should.

seventies the blocky, bulky Lowa typified the fashion. Heavy massive mountain boots were a badge of style. Big was good and bigger was better. But times have changed. Sales are so poor as the eighties begin that Lowas are no longer being imported. Some of my friends are wearing basketball shoes, others have turned back to light and inexpensive work shoes. My heavier boots have been gathering dust because I no longer feel the need for such heavy, stiff protection. For a really rugged walk or climb through scree and talus I have been wearing lightweight Vasque or my lightest Pivetta boots, but for day hikes, mostly on trails, even in high country wilderness, I have been wearing sandals because I love the ventilation and am willing to take a few precautions to minimize vulnerability. Though I sometimes wear huaraches, I much prefer Mobes because the cushioning is marvelous and protection is maximized in this exceptionally adjustable Velcro fastened footwear.

The revolt has even reached the institutional level. Mountain Travel, the world leader in launching treks and expeditions to the world's wildest places, has recently been recommending that its clients on long Himalayan marches wear running shoes where terrain permits, letting porters carry their heavy hiking boots until they're really needed.

It's hard to say which contributed more to the revolt against big boots: the breakthrough to running shoe lightness or the approximately 300% incease in the price of hiking boots during the seventies. Thanks to huge increases in the price of leather in 1974 and again in

1978, a boot selling for $35 in 1972 was up to $105 in 1979, and about to rise again. In any case, 1979 boot sales, compared to those of 1975, were down 40-80% for the major manufacturers, and such popular big boots (in the mid-seventies) as Raichle and Lowa were not even being imported as the eighties began. Myriad lightweight, high-tech fabrics, glues, rubbers and non-organic materials make nineteenth century construction (laboriously sewing heavy leather uppers to even heavier midsoles) as obsolete as the dinosaur. Now that the buyers have revolted, it's only a matter of time before revolutionary space age footwear largely replaces the old leather workhorse.

The first tentative attempt to bridge the gap between the running shoe and the hiking boot was the Inter "Ranger," an inexpensive "hiking shoe" made in Korea. It was a heavy canvas 6-inch high top with a padded scree collar to keep out dirt and a reassuring lug sole of light gum rubber. The sole has half the life of Vibram but it's also half the weight, and it will easily outlast the upper. Although it offers no real support and has a decidedly short life, the Ranger looks a lot like a trail boot, is attractive, weighs just over two pounds and costs a mere $20-25. It's even machine washable. Sierra Designs first offered them in the summer of '79 and they sold like crazy—while sales of conventional hiking boots slumped lower than ever.

Donner Mountain Corp. (DMC) of Berkeley, sole agent in the U.S. for Pivetta, made arrangements with Ranger's makers to add a steel shank to improve protection and support. DMC calls this improved version the "Trail Tread." It's suitable for light trail hiking, not substantial backpacking or cross-country travel, but it makes a great hiking boot for kids. And if you want to take your lady on her first-ever walk in the wilds but don't know whether she'll ever go again, a shoe like this would be an ideal purchase, and not just because of the price. Almost as important—if you want to keep her happy—are the super-light weight and total lack of break-in. But don't expect more than a month or two of hard use from this first hybrid featherweight running shoe-boot.

The next creation to surface in the boot revolution was the "Tred II Walking Shoe" (no relation to the Trail Tread), a more serious attempt to provide support that came out in late '79. To quote the REI catalog it "combines the comfort of a running shoe with the support of a hiking boot." Available in two models—one all leather, the other with a nylon and leather upper—the shoe provides a shock absorbing raised heel and a steel shank. Though a low shoe, not a boot, there is reassuring stiffness, support, and protection from the good counter, toe cap and heel cup. Because the midsole is light and a running shoe sole is used, weight is only 1¾ pounds per pair, with a cost about $40. This shoe is less a response to the demands of backpackers than it is to a belief that the jogging craze is subsiding into a less strenuous trend toward walking. Nevertheless, the Tred II Walker was extremely popular at REI in direct competition with conventional boots (where it

city footwear does poorly in the wilds.

was displayed) until supplier difficulties caused it to be discontinued. It remains available elsewhere.

Convinced by its experience of the need for lighter footwear, REI arranged with Danner, a well regarded bootmaker, to produce a 3½ pound hiking boot featuring a Goretex upper. Since I am far from a fan of Goretex, the idea seemed crazy to me at first, particularly since Goretex has been vulnerable to soiling which causes leakage. But seasoned hikers will agree that any increase in boot breathability, however slight, would be a welcome improvement, and the heaviest nylon, though non-supportive, is far lighter than any boot leather. There's nothing holy, after all, about leather for boot uppers. Its only real virtue is abrasion resistance.

The REI Goretex boot is relatively conventional, except for the upper, which is made of two layers of heavy nylon oxford cloth and foam, with a film of Goretex sandwiched in between. The upper is fully leather lined, and on the outside there is top grain leather over the toe, around the perimeter and up the back for stiffening and abrasion resistance.

There is a heavy duty full grain leather midsole, a Danner stitched down welt, half steel shank, toe cap, gusseted tongue and sturdy heel counter, with a Vibram Montagna lug sole. Rubber filler between the midsole and insole is further protection against leakage around the welt. Fastening is by grommet and hook lacing. Price is $85-90 a pair. The chief advantages of this boot are the breathability of its upper and its comparative lightness. The move from leather to Goretex is a major advance and highly commendable, even though the rest of the boot is conventionally heavy and stiff.

The first boot maker to use Goretex, however, was DMC, when, about the same time, it introduced a far more original and exciting boot and walking shoe, totally new and scientifically designed for maximum support and protection at an absolute minimum of weight.

The upper is a Goretex sandwich with heavy duty nylon pack cloth on the outside and nylon tricot inside. The rest of the boot also utilizes space age, high technology materials and a cunning design that combines the lightness of running shoes with the support required in a backpacking boot.

First the boot. Instead of heavy leather or rubber, the midsole is made of Duralight, a special high strength blown (expanded) microcellular rubber material used in running shoes that saves half a pound per pair while providing improved flexibility, cushioning and the necessary stiffness. The insole is featherweight Texon, an absorbent fiberboard that won't harden or crack. The sockliner is Airpore, a breathable poromeric that cushions, absorbs perspiration and won't stiffen or flatten. There is a steel shank, a nylon tricot lining, and the toe cap and heel counters are made of thermoplastic, a hard but lightweight material that will not soften or crack.

DMC covers the vulnerable parts of the Goretex upper with leather in much the same pattern found on running shoes, but instead of using expensive top grain it uses a lighter, less expensive silicone treated split. It reasons that since the leather is only present for scuff and stretch resistance, not waterproofing, split leather is entirely adequate. The silicone treatment is merely to prevent the leather from sponging up and holding water which would add to the weight of the boot. Seams in the Goretex upper are twice hand sealed and completely covered by leather. The life expectancy of Goretex boot uppers, of course, is still unknown. The one conventional element is the sole, a yellow label Vibram Roccia, because the majority of backpackers seem to believe (incorrectly) that "it can't really be a hiking boot without a Vibram sole." The upper is inside (Littleway) stitched to the midsole. The tongue employs a sophisticated bellows design found on fine hiking boots to keep out moisture and dirt and prevent tongue movement. The boot is called the PTF 1000, PTFE being the initials of the scientific name for Goretex and 1000 being the weight in grams per pair—about 2¼ pounds. The boot sells for $65-70.

The PTF 800 Walking Shoe is low cut, designed somewhat differently, weighs 800 grams (1 lb., 12 oz.) per pair and costs $55. As in the 1000 there is a spring steel shank, Texon insole, Airpore sockliner and upper of Goretex laminate with sealed seams and wear points covered with an abrasion resistant split leather. Thermoplastic toe caps and heel counters provide support and protection, and a boot style bellows tongue keeps out dirt and water. But the midsole is cushion crepe, the fastening is cement rather than inside stitch, and the sole is Vibram Morflex (expanded rubber with a light ripple tread), rather than the much heavier conventional lug. While this sturdy shoe is built for walking, it provides a level of protection, support, durability and cushioning that is far above that of running, tennis or basketball shoes. In fact it is only inferior to the 1000 in its lack of a high top which

more than 1/8 IN.
Lift means
trouble
in
the
heel.

protects the ankle against scrapes and bruises and keeps out dirt and water.

Don't dismiss the PTF 800 for backpacking just because it's low, classed as a walking shoe and doesn't have a lug sole. That's the kind of tunnel thinking that kept us in 4-5 pound boots so long. The 800 is probably better than any other low shoe made in terms of ankle support and lightness. It's certainly superior to all the running shoes currently being worn in the back country. Under conditions where entry of loose dirt and gravel, or ankle bruising aren't a problem (or low gaiters can be worn), this shoe might be regarded as a low-cut boot. I certainly intend to test it as such.

The notion that a high top provides ankle support is a myth, despite appearances to the contrary. The vast majority of sprains, twists and related injuries occur well below the ankle bone in the sub talar region of the heel. Even the most rigid high top boots do not always provide protection against such hazards. Strong, durable, tight-fitting heel counters offer the best security. As evidence of the fact, many professional athletes now wear low cut shoes. DMC has taken pains to equip both its models with the strongest such counters on the market, so do not fear that a Goretex upper must be loose and floppy and incapable of providing needed support. Envision instead footwear that will let out water vapor before it soaks up your socks and also keeps out rain (though not very effectively at the same time). Fit is important but not the matter of life and death it becomes in stiff leather boots, and the long, painful process of break-in we all grimly associate with new hiking boots becomes a fading memory. Support, protection and comfort, we discover with delight, do not require subjecting the feet to blisters and battering after all.

DMC sees its boot as a transition model on the way to even better footwear. The PTF is far from the ultimate. The present technology can take us much farther when customer acceptance is assured and expensive machinery is procured. (At present the latter is only found in Europe.) For instance, says John Schelling, DMC's president, boots are stitched as well as cemented to reassure the buyer as to durability. The stitching really isn't needed, and injection molding would be superior to cementing because of its speed, greater uniformity of adhesion and waterproofing. A polyurethane midsole would also be an improvement, but the biggest potential is in the sole. Because design of the PFT 1000 is radical to say the least, the conventional Vibram yellow lug sole is employed to help reassure buyers that this indeed is a hiking boot and will provide needed traction.

Actually, the lug design has as many drawbacks as it does advantages for wilderness travel, especially when the lugs become rounded with wear, which they do rather quickly because their surface area is so much smaller than that of the sole. Lugs are good on forest paths and gravel, not so good in mud because they clog quickly, and inferior on some slick surfaces like bare rock. Because of the high carbon content (for wear and hardness) Vibram is distinctly heavy. Resistance to wear of any material is measured in a standard manner and given a Durometer rating. To qualify for the yellow label, Vibram must achieve a Durometer rating of at least 150. One of the biggest rubber companies has developed a lightweight racing tire synthetic rubber that has a Durometer rating of 3000! Imagine its potential in a boot sole. DMC envisions using a thin strip of it to produce an injection molded boot that would last longer than Vibram and weigh in the neighborhood of 1¼ pounds a pair—a third the weight of yesterday's middleweight leather boots! And in the boot of the future, fit will be no problem. Fit is only crucial when you put the flexible foot in an inflexible boot.

Speaking of molding, there's another new technique that got its start in ski boots and promises increased comfort for the hikers of the eighties. It addresses a subtle but important defect in boot construction: the fact that tightening laces causes a decidedly inward (not upward) pull on the upper, producing a wedge shaped profile (see drawing) that causes pinching. Blisters, bunions, chafing and even wedge shaped callouses can result after hours in tightly laced boots. A somewhat more common problem is the sideways slipping of the foot that causes it to ride up on the boot upper. This will result in pinching, blisters, bunched socks and great discomfort, as well as poor weight distribution, especially for skiers.

Both problems are solved by a patented process called Ski-Thodics. The customer sits in a specially designed throne and impressions are taken of his feet. From these are made molded cork-like insoles that wrap around the feet. Like the sole of a Birkenstock sandal, they cup the ball and each toe and support the heel and arch. When this customized insole is slipped into your ski or hiking boot, your foot is locked securely but comfortably in a customized fit. Your feet are dead level and can't slip or slide. Some people benefit more than others, depending on how closely their feet resemble the lasts used at the factory for making their boots, but the increase in comfort and reduction in fatigue have made Ski-Thodics wildly popular, even at $40 a pair. Life expectancy of this new product is still unknown, but it can be used in running and walking shoes, as well as for hiking and skiing.

Despite the miraculous emancipation of enslaved feet brought about by development of the DMC boot and hybrid running-walking-hiking shoes, there remains—for the present at least, a definite need for conventionally built leather hiking boots. Mercifully, there has been a decided trend toward lightness and improved design here, too, as makers increasingly make use of new materials and concepts. The 180 degree change in fashion—from the Lowa-look of the mid seventies to the silk slipper running shoe look—has likewise had a profound effect on new designs. So has customer resistance to price! Bootmakers of the eighties, it may be said, are trying harder to please.

Before looking closely at the offerings of the six boot makers that most deserve a buyer's attention, it might be helpful to briefly define the important terms and labels used to describe leather boots. Boots are fastened together in four basic ways, and they are then classified according to the construction technique used.

LITTLEWAY (or McKay) construction means that the leather upper is turned under (inward) and one or (better) two rows of stitches inside the boot sandwich the upper between the insole and the midsole. The stitches, being concealed within the boot, are protected from abrasion so that badly worn midsoles can readily be repaired and the boots resoled. Soles can be trimmed more closely (of particular interest to climbers) since there is no welt to break, and waterproofing is easier. Since the innersole is stitched down, the edges are not subject to curling when wet. Inside stitching has become increasingly more popular during the seventies as boot repairmen and their customers have loudly protested against welted boots. This is clearly the best way to build most leather boots. The vast majority of Littleway boots are imported from Italy.

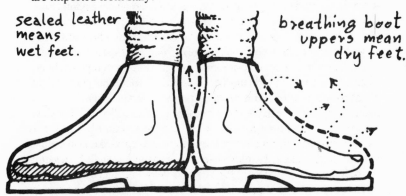

sealed leather means wet feet.

breathing boot uppers mean dry feet.

NORWEGIAN WELT construction is second in popularity. The upper is turned outward and a line of stitches in the gutter connects it to the insole. Then the midsole and turned-out upper are sewn together in an exposed line of stitches on the flat shelf (welt). Larger boots are traditionally fastened in this manner, partly because heavy boots are hard to inside stitch and partly because the shelf is needed for the attachment of ski bindings and crampons. Norwegian welt boots can only be resoled easily as long as the shelf has not been worn away—and the shelf at the toe often wears quickly. A still more vulnerable variation is the Goodyear welt, the method used to make most men's shoes. Welted boots, generally, require more care and are more expensive to repair and resole.

CEMENT BOOTS are the cheapest to build and buy but they usually cannot be resoled. Since they are essentially disposable, workmanship and materials tend to be inferior. The upper is turned under exactly like a Littleway boot, but there is no stitching. The upper is glued to a combination insole-midsole. In order not to be deceived as to the construction being offered, the buyer must peel up the shoeliner down to the instep (the heel is not stitched down in many Littleway boots), to determine the means of construction.

INJECTION MOLDING is a comparatively new construction technique in which the heated liquid thermoplastic which is to become the midsole is forceably injected into a mold where it bonds directly to the upper and insole. The result, when cooled, is securely fastened and dependably waterproofed without stitching of any kind. If the upper is molded solely to the midsole and the outer sole is glued on—as it is in all the above processes—the boot is resoleable. In the cheapest boots there is no midsole, the upper is bonded directly to the outer sole and resoling is impossible. Thus injection molding is found in both good quality boots and very cheap ones. This modern method seems likely to be the preferred means of making the boots of the future.

Leather may be classed as "top grain" or "split." Top grain refers to the layer on the outside or hair side of the hide and is naturally water-repellent and easily sealed. Splits are layers from any other part of the hide. They are not waterproof and cannot be made so by any kind of dressing. Needless to say, top grain leather is needed and used in good (and better) boots while splits, though common and much cheaper, are decidedly inferior and only suitable for dry trail use. Top grain leather may be smooth (hair side) out or rough-out, while splits are always rough-out. But beware imitation smooth-outs. Unless the maker's catalog clearly states "top grain" leather, the buyer must assume that a split has been used. Hides are tanned by one of two means, or a combination. Chrome tanning gives the leather heat and abrasion resistance, while vegetable tanning provides moisture resistance.

The "last" is a plastic plug, designed to resemble the average

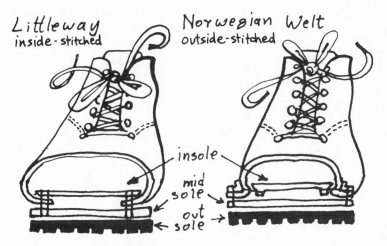

human foot, around which the manufacturer builds his boots. Not surprisingly, there is no standardization of lasts since boot makers are independent and have different ideas of ''average.'' Your ability to find boots that fit depends almost entirely on your luck in having feet that closely resemble the lasts on which a given brand is built. Shanks are built into boots to provide needed rigidity. A half shank stops short of the toes and permits the boot to bend. A long shank stiffens the entire boot from end to end, providing the rigid support needed only for technical climbing. Never buy a ''mountaineering'' boot for trail walking unless it has a short shank and you're sure you need a big boot for carrying extra heavy loads.

I hope I have already made clear the need for strong, long lasting heel counters that grip and socket the heel firmly, and hard toe boxes that will not soften or collapse. Theories of tongue design are endless, but the chief aims are comfort and protection from water and dust. Although interior padding often causes problems when it wears out or becomes tattered prematurely, its absence makes still more trouble because unpadded leather boots tend to brutalize the feet. And padding can be essential where the foot is hard to fit. The scree collar design is important: it needs to be flexible and snug without abrading the foot, but the collar itself must be protected by the upper from outside abrasion and from excess rubbing from within. The top of the boot should never be rigid or the wearer will suffer unduly.

Now for the best six bootmakers.

ASOLO boots, made in Italy, are relatively new to America, but already they are well known for superb design, top grade materials and comfortable fit. There may be no better line of boots, judged as a whole. The three general hiking boots, the Trail, Ridge and Allegro, are all of Littleway construction with top grain rough out one-piece uppers, short shanks, impressive Celastic toe box and heel counters, and Vibram soles. The Trail is lightest, the Ridge offers Galluser leather (probably the world's finest), and the Allegro provides no padding, to give hikers a choice of styles. Weights for such strong boots are respectably light (3.3-3.6 pounds) and prices run $115-130. For heavier use there is the Yukon K, a rugged Norwegian welt boot with short shank and Galluser rough-out leather, made for mountaineering, that weighs less than 5 pounds and costs about $140. Also, superb lasts and three different widths makes this one of the easiest lines of boots to fit.

FABIANO, also from Italy, offers a wide range of well made, extremely light boots. Their only drawback (for some people) is that the Fabiano last is rather straight, so fitting can be a problem. The three best, lightest boots are the Madre, Padre and Ria, all inside stitched. The first two employ splits, but the Ria ($95) has full grain leather. These boots, while not in the same class with their Asolo counterparts, are a little lighter and considerably less expensive ($75 for the Madre). Heavier Fabianos tend to be lesser values.

GALIBIER, from France, has slipped a little in quality while greatly inflating prices. For years the Vercour was one of the finest heavy-weight backpacking boots available. It's still good, but others are better built in the toe and heel, provide superior leather and better fitting. (Galibier offers only one width.)

KASTINGER, from Austria, is another relatively new boot to Americans. And like Asolo it offers top quality and decent price and weight throughout its line. The Horizon offers a one-piece rough out top grain upper, superb scree cuff (from a design by Steve Komito also employed by Asolo), Littleway construction, a narrow backstay with recessed stitching and Vibram sole—at a very impressive 2 lbs., 14 oz. and $90 price tag. The bigger Kastinger boots for heavy backpacking may be even better. The Tarn (4½ pounds, $120) and Cirque (5¼ pounds, $130) both come with uppers of unexcelled Galluser rough-out leather.

PIVETTA, from Italy, probably is unexcelled in dependability and performance. having offered a full line of uniformly fine boots for more than a decade in this country. Pivetta is the only major boot-maker to offer big boots as well as lighter models with Littleway construction and distinctive smooth-out uppers on their top grain leather boots. And few other bootmakers provide five different widths to choose from to ensure a good fit. The Eiger and Pivetta #5, both at 4 lb. 6 oz. and about $150, are fine full grain backpacking boots, while the Muir Trail, a pound lighter and made with split leather, is a long time dry trail favorite at $90.

VASQUE boots probably outsold all other brands during the seventies, and I have doubtless hiked more miles in them than in any other boot. Vasque was one of the first to offer a variety of truly light, Italian made Littleway stitched boots featuring one-piece full grained leathers at truly modest prices. I have owned a number of different models over the years and they have proved durable enough to survive hard wear after resoling. Thanks to improved lasts and as many as six

when the boot is firmly anchored the fit is easily checked.

widths, Vasque has always been an easy boot to fit. The company offers Italian-made light Littleway boots, and larger American-made welted boots.

There are, of course, many other bootmakers, some of them offering excellent boots, but the six companies discussed above stand out above the rest.

It's impossible to overemphasize the importance of fit. The greatest boot ever built will be useless if it isn't comfortable on your foot. The stiffer the boot the more crucial the fit. While some people have successfully bought boots by mail for years, the practice is more often unsatisfactory. The buyer usually needs more help than he can get from a catalog in choosing the right model and getting a good fit. Drawn patterns and shoe sizes are not really reliable; buyers often fail to discover the poor fit until too late, and exchanging boots for 'the next size larger' does not always solve the problem. As a consequence, I strongly urge against buying boots by mail. Most people are better off with the best model and the best fit that a competent salesman can provide than they are ordering a perfect-sounding boot by mail.

Boots should be fitted over whatever sock(s) the buyer expects to wear, or, if there is doubt, over a single heavy rag sock. In general, a hiking boot should be a little less roomy than a street shoe—comfortable, but snug. It should be remembered during fitting that the weight of a pack causes feet to flatten out, and vigorous hiking causes the feet to fill with blood and expand. At the same time, it must be remembered that loosely fitting boots will generate painful friction and lessen badly needed support.

Boots being fitted should be firmly laced, especially across the instep. Since leather is certain to stretch, one must be sure that the bands holding the laces remain half an inch apart when the boots are firmly laced or it may be impossible to lace them snugly once they are broken-in. With the boots firmly laced, the toes should have room to wiggle, but neither the ball of the foot nor the heel should move perceptibly when the salesman anchors the boot rigidly and the buyer tries vigorously to twist the foot.

Generally speaking, boots should be snug in width and generous in length. It is vital that the heel be socketed down within the cup formed by the heel counters so that it lifts no more than an eighth of an inch off the innersole when the heel is raised at the end of a step. A small allowance can be made for the stiffness of new boots, but the buyer should be convinced that the boot will fit snugly enough to keep his heel from lifting. Misery and blisters are the alternative. Foam padding around the ankle helps somewhat to socket down the heel. So does an inward taper of the boot's heel profile, but the principal grip comes from the construction and stiffness of the heel counter.

If the boot passes stationary tests satisfactorily, it is time to take it walking. (Any reputable boot salesman will be agreeable—providing his boots come back promptly, clean and unscuffed.) If the heel remains socketed on the level, one should walk briskly uphill or climb stairs. If the heel lifts more than a little, the boot is too large, at least in the heel. Next, one should walk briskly downhill for at least fifty yards. If the foot slips forward far enough for the toes to hit the front of the boot, it means the boot is too wide or too short, or not laced tightly enough. Patience and thoroughness during the fitting will reward the buyer with many miles of comfortable walking.

A great many hikers pay far too little attention to their socks. People who will spend a fortune on the finest gear will perversely refuse to spend $5-8 on the best in boot socks, prefering to take old or cheap cotton work socks camping. Seasoned hikers don't cheat their feet. They know the right socks can make the difference between comfort and misery on the trail.

Socks serve four vital functions: (1) they cushion the feet against the shock of each step; (2) they absorb perspiration from the feet; (3) they absorb friction between boots and feet; and (4) they insulate the feet from extremes of heat and cold. Socks that can do all four jobs well tend to justify their immodest price tags.

There is no single best sock or sock combination. Too much depends on the fit of the boot, the temperatures expected, the terrain, the tendency of the feet to sweat, skin sensitivity, etc. But it is generally true that too many pairs (too thick a layer) of socks reduces boot support and increases friction, and too thin a layer diminishes all four of the above vital functions. For trail backpacking in the summer Sierra the choice is generally between a single heavy sock by itself and the same sock worn over a light inner sock.

Generally, less sock is needed on easy terrain in well broken-in boots. Two heavy pairs of socks may be advisable for stiff boots or cross-country hiking likely to be hard on the feet.

As the realization of the importance of socks grows, so does the selection and sophistication—and price. Once dismissed as unimportant, socks now occupy pages in the mountain gear catalogs. For years, the Norwegian wool rag sock set the standard. Nylon reinforcing improved it and Spandex made it desireably stretchy. Probably the finest reinforced wool stretch rag sock is the North Cape, sold by Marmot as Norsocks and guaranteed by Early Winters for 1000 miles of walking. It's made by spinning a thread of nine parts Merino wool and two parts nylon around Spandex elastic—which may explain the $8/pair price tag. Knicker length socks cost $13. But these socks are cushiony, comfortable and wear like iron. I have five-year-old pairs that still look and feel like new.

Foam boots can't be beat

The Janus Lumberman, made from 92% wool and 8% nylon is another thick, soft, long-wearing expensive ($7) sock, although it doesn't stretch and therefore will not hold its shape so well. In addition to these ribbed knitted socks there is a popular style, pioneered by Wick-Dry, in which thousands of tiny terry cloth springy loops inside a smooth outer sheath provide excellent cushioning, insulation and moisture absorption. Whereas moisture absorption is to be avoided in most garments, in warmer weather it is the aim in socks to sponge up sweat and hold it as far from the skin as possible. Since wool is unexcelled in absorbing and holding moisture without matting or losing resiliency, it is the preferred material for socks, even though damp wool socks are slow to dry. Synthetic fabrics absorb no moisture, and cotton, though highly absorbent, collapses into a hopeless, shapeless soggy mess when wet. Avoid it like the plague and half your socks problems are already solved.

... for snow

Inner or liner socks are popular with many people, and for a variety of reasons. With new boots or difficult-to-fit feet the layering reduces painful friction. Many people find wool scratchy and need something softer underneath. Then there is the school of thought that insists nonabsorbent synthetic liners keep the foot drier because they transmit moisture to the outer wool rather than holding it. Inner socks need to be snug or stretchy so there are no bags or wrinkles to generate blisters. Olefin liners are probably most popular, but some people prefer soft wool and a few insist on silk although it tends to be cold because of the hard finish, and clammy because it absorbs water.

The important thing is to be kind to your feet by taking pains to obtain good, strong, cushioning wool socks that fit without wrinkles. Brand, number of layers, and even fabric (avoiding cotton) will not matter if your socks are comfortable and protect your feet. People allergic to wool will need Wick Dry all-synthetic socks. Other good wool socks include Marmot's ToeToasters ($14), Hi-Riders ($6) and Wool Inner socks ($3). Wigwam, Klondike and Ripon are also good brands. For many of us machine washability without excessive shrinkage is vital. My stretch rag socks have survived many washings while Wigwam socks, even those advertised as shrink resistant, have been a total loss. And once you've found the socks that suit you, don't forget to take them along when you go shopping for boots—or you may be forced to make a change. Speaking of fit, Spenco insoles of cushiony, cooling closed cell foam can help a lot with hard-to-fit feet, as well as providing added comfort (2 oz., $5/pair).

When it comes to really cold weather, nothing will keep your feet warmer than vapor barrier socks. The colder it is the better they work. Since they take up no room you can wear them beneath your favorite socks without tightening your boots. Since they protect your socks from moisture, they never get damp or dirty and a change of socks becomes unnecessary. What's even nicer is that they're weightless and virtually free (if you use bread or produce bags). Because plastic bags are cheap, weightless and bulkless, you can take along plenty without concern for the fact that they puncture or wear out. Or if you want more quality you can order VB socks from Stephenson's at 15¢ a pair. Rumor has it that Wigwam plans to market a VB sock. Friends of mine heavily involved in winter camping, climbing and ski touring who depend on VB socks absolutely for frostbite protection and cannot stop and change bags every time a cold foot suggests failure, obtain needed security by sewing their own crude but durable socks out of the lightest sealed nylon fabrics they can find. An alternative is to use 2, 3 or 4 bags, although the foot may be inclined to slip around in your boot. Many people put the bag over their bare foot, but if you can't bear the thought of plastic on your skin it's perfectly okay to wear it over a thin inner sock, which will probably grow no damper than it would if you weren't using a vapor barrier. The only way to discover that a baggie on your foot will keep it unbelievably warm and not fill up with sweat is to try it—on just one foot—and compare. The price is right!

Speaking of bare feet, the warmest footwear I know on snow is the CozyQuip (formerly Ocaté) unlined foam boot which is worn bare-foot. Like the VB sock, it has to be tried to be believed. A bare foot in raw open celled urethane foam is not only sensuously free and comfortable, it's snug and warm. These calf-height Mukluks cost about $25, are bulky but light and rated to −20°F. Add a VB sock and they'd probably keep you warm in forty below. As the revolution in footwear gathers momentum, there are sure to be exciting designs in store for us—light comfortable footwear with unbelievable durability, and some of it may even be cheap!

4 PACKS

The bewildering profusion of new pack designs that burst upon the scene in the mid 1970s has left a good many pack buyers scratching their heads, wondering what they need. Early in the decade, when the backpacking boom was still young, the choice was simple. For back-packing on trails there were tubular metal frames (hopefully with hipbelts). For cross-country, climbing and skiing there were a variety of torture devices that could be classified as either framed rucksacks or floppy knapsacks.

Of course a good many travelers staggered to the wilderness bizarre-ly burdened with duffel bags, suitcases, pillow slips, satchels, baskets, cardboard cartons, hampers and ice chests. On the heavily-traveled trail that passes near my cabin I have seen families pushing wheelbarrows, ladies dragging shopping carts, Boy Scouts toting laden stretchers. And hikers still load themselves down in strange ways—often because they simply don't know what they need. The array of available packs is bewildering, even intimidating.

There are wraparounds, terraplanes, a huge selection of frame packs, a wild assortment of internal frame packs, fanny packs, day-packs, rucksacks, softpacks, kid packs and dog packs. To further complicate matters there are all sorts of special features, options, extras, innovations and departures. The prospective buyer is often buried under an avalanche of new terms: compression straps, stays, struts, quick release buckles, ski sleeves, detachable pockets, crampon patches, telescoping frames, double bottoms, hold-open bars, zip out dividers, sternum straps, leather lash points, detachable this and convertible that. Where once there were a dozen pack makers to consider, nowadays there are closer to a hundred, all clamouring for the prospective buyer's attention.

To escape the maze and sort out all these offerings requires some organization and classification. First of all, I divide packs into (1) overnight (2) daypacks and specialty packs. Overnighters are further divided into (a) external frame (b) internal frame packs and (c) frameless softpacks. Though there are notable exceptions, external frame backpacks are still the best choice for trail travel. Carrying capacity and comfort are maximum because the frame is unlimited in size and holds the load away from the back, permitting welcome air circulation. Where the terrain is difficult or the footing tricky, the size and high center of gravity of an external frame becomes a liability. In dense vegetation the pack rails catch on brush and limbs and the hiker is easily thrown off balance. Similar difficulties are found in skiing, snowshoeing and climbing.

For all these rigorous activities, where the body must twist and turn, and balance is vital, it is generally agreed that frameless or internal frame packs are superior and safer, even though (generally) they are less comfortable and carry less, because the load is carried comparatively close against the back. Instead of being suspended away from the body where it can swing disconcertingly, it snugs tightly against the back, becoming an extended part of the body and greatly improving balance.

The ski-snowshoe-climbing boom of the early 1970s demanded improvement in the shoulder killing rucksacks (like the Bergen) or knapsacks (like the Duluth). As usual, necessity was the mother of invention, and makers began offering sophisticated softpacks (like terraplanes) that spread weight to the hips, and ingenious internal frames that provided surprising comfort with only a fraction of the metal found in traditional external pack frames.

Until the terraplane (or Jensen Pack) appeared, softpacks were only bags that hung on the shoulders. The distinctively shaped terraplane takes the shape of an inverted ''T.'' The bottom is a single horizontal sleeping bag pocket that wraps around the hips, tapering into a hipbelt. The vertical section is divided down the middle into two separate columns. When packed so tightly that they resemble two bulging vertical sausages, these columns become structural members which are supported by the horizontal sausage hipbelt. In theory the load becomes a frame, enabling the wearer to carry the weight on hips or shoulders or both. In practice, it isn't generally possible to pack the vertical columns tightly enough to take much weight off the shoulders.

The terraplane has been eclipsed by the development of marvelous internal frames, but it remains the best of the frameless packs, unbreakable, light, clinging closely to the back, capacious and comparatively inexpensive (around $50). Many climbers and ski tourers, despite sweaty backs, swear by it. Casual backpackers tend to swear *at* it. Most other softpacks, because all the weight must be carried on the shoulders, are inferior to framed packs for overnight sized loads and therefore will be examined no further.

Though virtually unknown in the early 1970s, internal frames, thanks to cunning new designs, have enjoyed a surge of popularity that has in many cases propelled them ahead of conventional external frame packs for climbers, winter campers, cross country trampers and experienced backpackers. The appeal: generally lighter weight, lower

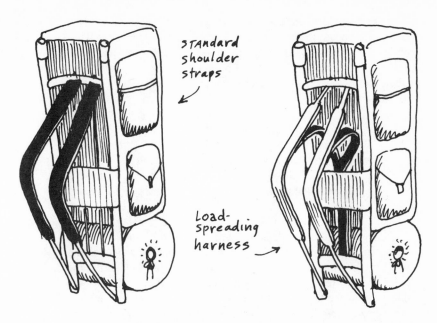

sTAndard shoulder straps

Load-spreading harness →

price, all terrain capability, flexibility, simplicity, versatility and much improved comfort and freedom of movement.

Structurally, the internal frame consists of two vertical aluminum stays, usually connected by one or two horizontal braces, or two stays in the form of an ''X.'' Either way, the stays run to the pack's four corners. Shoulder straps attach to the bag at the top two, while the hipbelt is hung from the bottom two. The stays, usually of low temper soft aluminum that can be bent to custom fit the individual spine, permit the wearer to transfer pack weight back and forth between the hips and the shoulders at will, as with a good external frame pack. There are still internal frame packs on the market that cause supreme discomfort, thanks to poor or antiquated design, but the best of the new offerings are marvels that deserve consideration for use in all seasons.

Much of the appeal of internal frame packs stems from the fact that the stays tend to flex and move independently, minimizing transference of shoulder torque to the hips and vice versa, as encountered in most rigid external frame packs. The lack of jarring means added comfort. Being on the inside, the frame takes up space and gets in the way somewhat, but internal frame packs are low on bulk, and many of them collapse nicely for storage or transport. In use, the bags tend to be a bit floppy, like softpacks, lacking hold-open bars and the neat compartmentation found in their external framed brothers. Ideally, stays are encased in sleeves (although this increases price and weight), and the bag must be heavily reinforced at the four points where stays end and hipbelt or shoulder straps attach. Armouring leather or fabric patches and the sewing at these critical wear points are the chief index (along with fit) of pack quality.

The best shoulder suspension on an internal frame pack involves straps that come up from the back in a harness arrangement and wrap around the shoulders. Adjustable lift straps attached to the tops of the stays actually support the load and permit cinching the load snugly against the back. A back band or mesh panel attached to the pack's four corners can likewise be cinched tight like the string of a bow to keep most of the pack away from the back and permit badly needed air circulation. This was the arrangement that made the late lamented Synergy Works pack the most comfortable of internal frame models. All others of this breed rely on strategically placed, built-in closed cell padding to cushion the body. They do a better job each year, but there is no escaping the fact that a pack against your back makes for a sweaty shirt.

It isn't generally known that the best new internal frames are designed with belts that ride significantly higher than do the belts on any external frame packs. Snugging down around the waist and the tops of the hips, instead of hanging low on the hips, they permit the wearer greater freedom to twist, and bend without being thrown off balance. And the higher ride offers more support by bone and less from working muscle, which more than offsets the slight curtailment of deep breathing—especially with big loads or in dangerous terrain.

Some of my friends who are expert four-season campers insist that the very best 3-4 internal frame packs make external frames obsolete. They claim (1) greater comfort with large (50 pounds plus) loads, (2) better balance with any load, (3) vastly superior versatility (ski-touring, climbing and cross-country capability), (4) far greater durability in the face of rough handling, (5) the pack's lower and closer center of gravity fits the body better, (6) far greater adjustability (because the stays can be bent) means a custom fit for every wearer, and finally (7) greater safety in difficult terrain, on skis or snowshoes or where the footing is poor or dangerous.

I cannot disagree. People who plan to use a pack more off the trail than on and spend much of their time on truly difficult terrain (like my friends) are probably better off with a superb internal frame—especially if they can afford only one pack. As internal frames become more sophisticated and comfortable and more and more people go camping in the snow, there is a definite trend toward these new creations.

Meanwhile, external frames have undergone changes, too—some of them major, some minor. Early in the 1970s 4-5 pack makers introduced a radical departure in hipbelt suspension. Instead of hanging the belt from the back of the frame, it was hung from metal arms extending about eight inches forward from the frame around the hips. The intent of this design was to put the weight of the pack squarely over the legs, in direct line with the body's center of gravity, hopefully increasing comfort and carrying capacity by spreading the weight more evenly. I field tested four of these ''wraparound'' or ''hipwrap'' frames and my findings were published in a 1972 *Wilderness Camping* article entitled "THE WRAPAROUND FRAME: breakthrough or gimmick?" To my surprise, the story polarized the entire pack industry and launched a controversy that lasted for years.

In summary, I discovered that putting the weight of the pack in line with the *body's* center of gravity rather than the *pack's* center of gravity caused the pack to pull backward on the shoulders and push forward on the hips with something like three times as much force as when the hipbelt was fastened in the traditional manner. To neutralize this push-pull it became necessary to lean about 30 degrees forward while walking! But this push-pull was only half the problem. The other half was bruised hips. Since no hipbelt is rigid, the weight of the pack is actually concentrated at the point or points where the belt attaches to the frame. On the conventionally hung hipbelt, weight is concentrated on the outward swell of the sacral promontory, a broad shelf of bone at the base of the spine that is admirably suited to bearing weight.

On the wraparound, however, the attachment points are centered on the sides of the body, concentrating weight on vertical flexing muscle instead of flat sloping bone. The hipbelt, I soon found out, must be worn abnormally tight, and even then it worked its way downward over moving muscles unable to support it. After several miles I became aware that my stomach muscles were also under strain, both

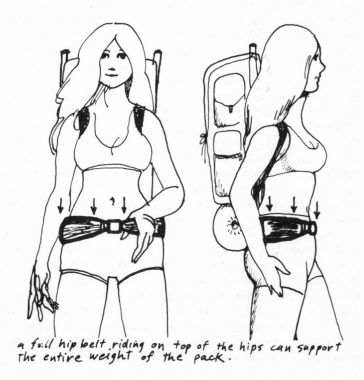

a full hip belt, riding on top of the hips can support the entire weight of the pack.

from the abnormally tight belt and the subtle push-pull that I experienced with every step. I tried every possible adjustment on all four packs, but if I loosened the shoulder straps, the pack pulled away from my back—unless I walked doubled over. If the belt was snug enough to support a large share of pack weight, my hips became chafed and bruised.

Wraparound pack makers, unaccustomed to criticism, insisted I must be obese or a hipless freak. It's true that I am slim in the hips, but not abnormally so. Others tested the wraparound, and some gave glowing accounts of its performance, but many shared my complaints. Half a dozen years have passed, and a few wraparounds are still made and reportedly sell well, particularly the Alpenlite. I do not wish to argue with satisfied customers—although a good many of them are likely first time pack buyers with little basis for comparison.

While preparing this revision I tried another wraparound, and my results were the same. While I have no reason to change my conclusions, it is clear that wraparounds serve admirably for some highly knowledgeable hikers. An independent pack tester wrote in 1978 that hipwraps don't fit everyone, that if your hips are narrow the belt may not stay up, that if your hips rise and fall when you walk they are likely to grow sore, that hipwraps limit side to side torso movement, affecting balance, so where the footing is precarious they could be dangerous. Be warned.

Two minor hipbelt changes in the mid 1970s brought definite improvements. Instead of hanging the hipbelt loosely from the back of the frame, Kelty and Antelope (independently) came out with hipbelts rigidly fixed to the bottom of the frame. The slight improvement in fit caused other packmakers to follow. Differentially cut hipbelts (and shoulder straps) have reduced the bunching of fabric which often led to chafing, and contouring hipbelt shape to match the curves of the body has permitted belts to be worn a shade looser without slipping down. These decided improvements are increasingly found in high quality packs.

The biggest advance in external frames since the hipbelt, in my view, is the completely new design of the North Face Back Magic, in which shoulder suspension is entirely independent of hip suspension. That may not sound like much, but the difference in performance is tremendous. Until I carried this pack I simply wasn't aware of how much torque the swing of my hips transmitted through the hipbelt to the shoulder straps and vice versa. I wasn't aware of how much discomfort (theretofore attributed to the weight of the pack) this needless torque transmission was producing.

This small miracle is accomplished by hanging the hipbelt from a sort of flexing universal joint of tough plastic recessed in the center of a radical figure eight aluminum frame. The joint flexes easily from side to side, but only slightly from back to front, permitting the hips to roll and swivel without making the frame bounce. Until I tested this frame, I never realized how much tugging and rubbing on my shoulders came from the action of my hips. Now I can swivel my hips like a lady of the night and my shoulder straps lie perfectly still.

Wearing the Back Magic, I'm inclined to carry more of the weight on my hips because I can do so more comfortably. The belt can be worn looser without working its way down. The pack performs well, not surprisingly, hiking steeply downhill where hip swing becomes accentuated, and because it is easy to keep the body in balance this is the best external frame cross-country pack I know, despite its high center of gravity. Weight is five pounds plus with a full length divided bag and cost is $135 for the most comfortable external frame pack I know.

The trends in pack design may or may not be helpful when it comes to choosing what pack to buy. As with all other gear, what you need depends on how you expect to use it. And as with choosing boots, nothing is more important than fit. The best available pack that suits your purposes will be superior to the world's greatest pack that just isn't comfortable. People are built differently and they walk differently. What's comfortable for you may not suit your twin brother. Don't buy a mail order pack unless you (and the manufacturer) are prepared for you to ship it back for a refund.

Keeping availability and fit in mind, the field can be narrowed by considering intended use, size (capacity), weight, durability, price and cosmetic appeal. (Packs are impressively styled and many people buy on the basis of name, fashionable profile or the profusion of clever compartments, unfortunately.)

To be any good, a frame has to fit.

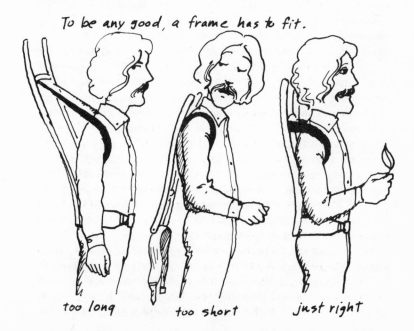

too long   too short   just right

In terms of use, external aluminum frames carry the largest loads, provide the most comfortable ride (in terms of ventilation) on trails, cost most, weigh most and usually provide the most accessories and conveniences—generally speaking. Internal frame packs are second in comfort, capacity, cost and weight. They bring the load closer (partially against the body) flex with the body to some extent and are therefore less apt to throw the wearer off balance as he climbs, skis, bushwacks or boulder hops. They are hotter and usually carry less, but they're decidedly cheaper, lighter and safer when balance or footing are tricky. The soft pack (terraplanes, frameless rucksacks, climbers' sacks) is too uncomfortable for overnight travel because all weight is hung on the shoulders, except for specialized difficult skiing and climbing conditions.

As both internal and external frames are refined, the area of overlap between them grows, so that many snow campers are happy with huge capacity external frame packs, and an increasing number of clever internal frame packs are being successfully used for summer back-packing, even on trails. Of course not everyone who packs under a wide range of conditions can afford two packs! Once the choice is made between internal or external frame, pack capacity should be considered.

There has been a tendency in recent years, with the influx of newcomers, for packs to get larger and larger—because people buy them. They then proceed to fill them up with gadgets, extra protection, spare this and essential that, no matter how far they're going or how long they stay out. Not surprisingly, they feel like pack mules on the trail. I can't tell you exactly what to take, but most people could get along with less. And many would enjoy their trips more if they simplified their wilderness lifestyle. Just because you admire a devilishly clever design doesn't mean you need it. Unless you plan long distance trekking or expedition travel, you may be better off if you're limited financially. The simpler packs also weigh less. Packs have gotten steadily heavier because very few manufacturers worry much about weight—chiefly because their customers don't.

When you've made the appropriate decisions on use, size, weight and cost and are ready to scrutinize the models actually available, there are a number of ways you can evaluate quality, durability, features and other attributes. With an external frame pack, the place to begin is with the frame itself, especially the joints.

Joints have always been the weakest, most vulnerable parts of aluminum frames. Some makers have chosen to bolt or clamp their frames together, but most represent their frames as 'welded.' It can make a big difference whether they are eutectic welded (also known as soldering or brazing) or heliarc gas welded. Brazing is quicker and easier and cheaper, but brazed joints will break under stress. Heliarc welding is slower and more difficult, but the bond is as strong or stronger than the members it joins. Other methods of securing joints can be as strong as good welds, when done properly, like Antelope's nuts and bolts and Stephenson's adhesive bonding.

To test joint and frame strength, tilt the frame to one side so just one rail is on the floor, then push down. The salesman may turn pale but you'll get a real sense of the strength and rigidity of the tubing and connections. Another useful test involves setting the bottom ends of both rails on the floor and holding them rigidly in place with your feet while attempting to twist the top ends of the rails. Of course a few frames (Jansport, Coleman, Alpine Designs) are meant to flex.

Next in importance is the frame's suspension system: shoulder straps and hipbelt. Shoulder straps on good packs are fairly standard: about two inches wide, padded with ensolite or other closed cell foam, encased in differentially cut rough finish nylon duck or Cordura. Avoid slippery finish nylon that will slip with every step. Straps should be one-hand adjustable for length as you walk, so weight can be shifted easily from shoulders to hipbelt without breaking stride. On most good frames the attachment points at one or both ends of the straps are adjustable so the spread between them can be changed and also raised or lowered for an ideal fit.

While most shoulder straps hang from the highest crossbar, a few pack makers offer a harness arrangement wherein the straps continue down the back of the shoulders and meet in a yoke above the middle of the back. A short adjustable strap joins the strap to the upper crossbar. The harness, designed by Trailwise and later copied widely, effectively spreads pack weight over the entire shoulder instead of concentrating it on a comparatively small area.

To distribute pack weight against your back and provide ventilation, there are four main kinds of backbands. Best for warm weather are the full frame mesh panel or the mesh backband. The old standby is one or two 6-inch nylon back bands, and a few makers pad them with foam. Beware the suspension system in which a low padded backband doubles as the back section of the hipbelt.

The hipbelt, the biggest boon to carrying comfort since the invention of the aluminum frame, is now standard equipment on all decent overnight framed packs. But there is considerable variety as pack makers experiment and refine. They range from two web straps from

— how to put on a heavy pack —

the lower pack rails (primitive) to gigantic floating belts of complex construction. Functionally, the aim of all belts is to allow all or part of the load to be transferred from the shoulders to the buttocks, pelvis and legs.

On conventional frames (the vast majority) the belt is rigidly attached to or hung from the bottom rails. On wraparound or hipwrap frames the belt is hung from two hinged or rigid arms that stick forward from the bottom of the frame. As mentioned earlier, my testing of hipwrap frames produced mostly negative results. I found they tended to push forward on the hips and pull back on the shoulders excessively, and the vertical muscles at the hips supported weight poorly, necessitating a tight belt and often producing bruising.

Pack-frame joints:

Brazed is poor

arc welded is better.

As also mentioned earlier, there are two schools of thought on mounting conventional hipbelts. Free floating belts are commonest, but the newer rigidly attached belts (Kelty, Antelope) have considerable appeal. The former may be more comfortable; the latter provide more control and support. Any hipbelt, however hung, should offer a velcro closure (increasingly popular) or quick release buckle that allows the pack to be instantly jetisoned with one hand during a fall to minimize the chance of injury. Belt tightness must be easily adjustable as you walk to facilitate the weight shift between hips and shoulders that prevents premature tiring. Hipbelt padding, once a luxury, should be regarded as essential for carrying comfort.

Before discussing packbags, let's return to the crucial criterion for pack selection: a comfortable fit. When you go looking for a pack, wear the trousers you'll use on the trail—for the same reason you wore trail socks when shopping for boots. The waist needs to be snug, without a bulky belt (beltless is best, providing the working of the hipbelt won't gradually pull your pants off). You might also bring along your favorite hat, to make sure the pack won't prevent you from wearing it. If you have a choice, favor establishments that offer more than one brand and that provide experienced, patient salesmen who feel a responsibility to see that you get a good fit. Don't be bashful about asking for help. You need it and you're paying for it! Beware a pack seller who doesn't have a supply of sandbags with which to load his test packs. He also needs rocks, slopes or stairways or the like to simulate going up and down hill.

In a properly fitting loaded pack, the shoulder straps should meet the frame on a level with the shoulder top or slightly above it, and you should be able to hunch your shoulders high enough to lift the unfastened hipbelt easily into the ideal position for tightening. Conversely, when the hipbelt is snugged moderately tight it should accept the full weight of the loaded pack when all weight is taken from the shoulders. Bend over as you lift one knee toward your forehead to test for hipbelt pinch on your stomach.

If the frame is too short, it will either be impossible to get all of the weight off the shoulders, or to do so will drop the crossbar well below the shoulders, causing the pack to ride low and away from the back. If the frame is too long it will be impossible to fasten the hipbelt high enough to support weight unless the shoulder straps are abnormally tight. Fortunately, most manufacturers make their frames in three or four sizes and one of them can probably be adjusted to fit.

While wearing the loaded pack (try several different weights) test every adjustment and all sorts of positions. Does the frame gouge your back when you bend double? Try long strides and short, uphill and down. The pack should move with you, with your rhythm, not its own. Internal frame packs should snug against you and become part of you, but are you satisfied with the comfort, and will the ventilation be adequate? On hipwrap frames be sure the comfort and fit are superior to traditional frames before you buy, remembering that push-pull fatigue and hip bruises don't develop until you're miles down the trail.

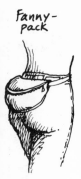

Fanny-pack

Compared to pack frame selection, choosing a pack bag is almost inconsequential. The fit, strength and suspension of the frame are vital. The selection of the bag has far less bearing on carrying comfort, even though the best bags cost as much or more than the best frames. Backpackers on a tight budget are advised to put their money in a really good frame and buy a cheap bag or improvise with a tarp.

When I first went backpacking, I owned an excellent frame (for those days) but no pack bag. Keeping weight distribution in mind, I positioned all my gear in a rectangule in the middle of my waterproof nylon ground cloth, folded over the edges to form a neat package, then lashed it to the frame. The resulting pack was as neat, compressed, compact and well centered as any that can be loaded in today's fancy bags.

Belt-pack

Do not imagine that I scorn the modern pack bag. I don't. I'm as much a slave to their endless conveniences as anyone. But don't be so dazzled that you forget your rational criteria for choosing a pack. There are basically two bag styles: the full frame bag which is a single compartment of maximum size, and the three quarter bag which leaves room at the bottom of the frame for your sleeping bag. In external frame packs nearly all are three-quarters length, and most are divided horizontally into two separate compartments, not to mention 2-6 pockets. Internal frame packs tend to have fewer compartments.

Bags are conventionally top loading, which means you stand them up to load them and cinch down on the covering storm flap to compress the load. The lower compartment is front loading of necessity, and the trend is toward horseshoe shaped zippers (which produce their own flap) for maximum opening and access. The trend in internal frame packs is toward front loading, which means the pack must be laid down flat (messy in mud or snow), and toward compression straps to bring the load closer to the body.

As far as I am concerned the most important bag design consideration is its depth. The best bags keep the load as close as possible to the body. My rule of thumb is that, to keep the center of gravity close, the bag should be no more than nine inches thick at any point. Higher and wider is far better than thicker. I therefore take a dim view of packs with large pockets on the back because they tend to pull the pack backward. In this case, the fashionably slim profile makes perfect sense. The other important feature in top loading packs is a large storm flap that will cover everything you could ever stack on top of the already stuffed pack. The buyer will have to make up his own mind about the value—in ounces and dollars—of such myriad accessories as pockets, hold-open bars, lash points, leather reinforced bottoms, ski sleeves, hauling loops, compression straps, sternum straps, camera rings and the like. Like the blades on a Swiss Army knife, a few are handy, but most are unnecessary. Aside from sleeping bag straps, laces or shock cord, little is really essential.

Despite all the clever features built into packs, sometimes it will be necessary for the buyer to improvise his own innovations, perhaps to carry a coat that won't fit inside, to dry wet socks while you walk, hang a camera, keep a map handy, carry an oversize foam mattress, etc. I generally carry a two or three piece fly rod with the reel attached and the line and leader threaded through the guides to my fly. The best method I have found for attaching this rig to my pack is an aluminum film can taped flush with the bottom of the right hand rail, into which the rod butt and additional section(s) fit snugly. At the top crossbar a piece of nylon line is secured to lash the rod sections against the rail. The rod, of course, is somewhat vulnerable in this position, but I have never broken or damaged a section, even during the many years that I carried split bamboo. And the danger, for me at least, is more than offset by the fact that I can be ready to fish within thirty seconds of stopping.

Nearly all good pack bags are made of coated nylon (usually Cordura or duck). Antelope makes a notable exception. To check bag quality be sure to examine such stress points as seams, corners, attachment and lash points. Stitching should be 5-10 to the inch and reinforcement should be impressively evident. Zippers should be nylon coil or plastic tooth and covered with tight fitting storm flaps. Be sure there is no pucker in hipbelt or shoulder straps. Examine how floating hipbelts are fastened to the frame because this area gets maximum continuous stress.

Closely check all moving parts because these wear fastest, along with the points where body meets pack. Bag mounting is a good index to quality. Clevis pins are most common and dependable. Individual pins are far superior to the long wire cotter pins that rattle, bend and get caught on things. Snaps need to be tested because some are undependable. Straps and lashings are effective but sometimes cumbersome and heavy. Sleeves are generally cheap and flimsy and deserve a skeptical appraisal.

I am a little dismayed at the way packs have been growing in both weight and size—not to mention price, because the growth seemed based on fashion (demand) rather than genuine need. While 2500

Backpacking -
the hard way.

cubic inches should be enough volume for 90% of the trips most
recreational backpackers take, bags of 3500 and even 4500 are being
made because they sell well. And average pack weight has crept up to
over 4½ pounds for external frame and 3½ for internal. A few weight
conscious pack makers, however, can save you 1-1½ pounds. Thanks
to size growth and inflation, decent packs for under $50 are decidedly
scarce; the average good pack tops $100 and an increasing number are
pushing $150.

With this general background, the reader should be better able to
evaluate both the packs he has to choose from and the dozen or so with
which I am familiar.

ALPENLITE is probably the ruggedest and most popular of the
hipwrap frames. People generally love it (if it fits) or hate it (if it
doesn't). To maximize the chances of fit adjustment is unusually great,
and there are several bag styles to choose from. Weight and cost are
about average.

ANTELOPE BACKPACKING makes a very large line of adjustable
packs that are well-engineered, strong, inexpensive and innovative.
The rigidly attached hipbelt permits weight to travel with you, not
follow, and concentrates pack weight closest to the body's center of
gravity. Frames are securely joined with nuts and bolts, and bags
come in tough waterproof canvas as well as Cordura. Every time I loan
my Antelope pack the borrower wants to buy it!

CAMP TRAILS, like Antelope offers an unusually large selection of
moderately priced packs, many of them adjustable. Camp Trails set

the early standard in big padded hipbelts, and they have continued to refine their designs without getting carried away, except in top of the line models. For years I have been pointing newcomers to the sport and people who want a dependable inexpensive first pack to Antelope and Camp Trails, with no complaints.

GREGORY MOUNTAIN PRODUCTS, a new and tiny firm, nevertheless makes probably the finest internal frame packs on the market. Endless adjustability, superb workmanship and significant design innovation will be found in both the $135, 5 lb. Rock Creek and the $175, 6 lb. Cassin, ultimate packs that custom fit anyone.

JANSPORT has long been an innovator and developer of unusual and generally successful packs, including the first deliberately flexing aluminum frames. The D-3 is a popular flexing, front-loading hipwrap held together with machined couplings of almost 3000 cu. in., and the Mountain Spirit is a capacious touring pack supported by two internal vertical stays. Both are popular.

KELTY has long been justly famous for strong, well engineered, dependable packs, and the product has been improved by Kelty's willingness in recent years to switch to coated fabric, covered zippers, etc. Like Camptrails and Trailwise, Kelty claims to have invented the aluminum frame, and the classic backpack profile is the Kelty silhouette, but Kelty's reputation is built on unexcelled craftsmanship.

LOWE ALPINE makes probably the best vertical stay internal frame packs that are widely available. Adjustability, wide selection, workmanship and dependability are excellent in these constantly refined packs.

NORTH FACE is the maker of the already discussed Back Magic, the new design in which shoulder suspension is mercifully independent of hip suspension for a marvelously comfortable ride. The North Face Ruthsac, one of the first modern internal frame packs, pioneered the front-loading feature and has been continually refined for added comfort and utility.

SYNERGY WORKS, alas, has folded its tent, but its exceptional internal frame packs live on, as do its patents for a tensioned mesh back panel that provides unmatched comfort and ventilation, and for an X-stay system rigidly fastened in the middle by two pins. It remains to be seen whether these fine features find their way into other packs.

TRAILWISE like Kelty has a long and well-earned reputation for strength, design and dependability, and Trailwise developed and perfected both the shoulder harness and the full-frame mesh backband as well. The single compartment pack is a favorite with expeditionary trekkers. I have put more trouble-free miles on Trailwise frames than any others and heartily recommend them.

There are a good many other fine packs with which I'm less familiar. A-16 makes a rugged adjustable hipwrap. Stephenson offers one of the lightest and most innovative packs available. EMS makes soundly designed, well-built internal and external frame packs, as does Cannondale, Hine Snowbridge, Mountain Equipment, REI, Universal and Wilderness Experience. Coleman and Alpine Designs offer flexing frames made of plastic. And there are doubtless fine packs that I have yet to encounter.

Packs designed for day hiking are so numerous and similar that probably no one has cataloged them all. The tear-dropped shape has for years been most popular because it keeps the load close to the back and provides decent ventilation, but there are excellent rectangular designs, too, which offer more capacity. The things to look for in a daypack are padded, adjustable shoulder straps, quality sewing, reinforcement of stress points, effective zipper covers and coated nylon fabric. As with overnight packs, a flat profile is greatly to be preferred to a deep pack which will tend to pull you backward. There are a variety of ways the bag may be divided and zippers placed, none of which is best for all occasions, although two compartment bags are preferred by most hikers.

Load up the dog.

Because I sometimes need to hang a bulky jacket on my pack, I find an attachment point on top essential. And a carrying loop is useful for times when I want to dry off my sweaty back and pack but keep on moving. Most important of all, of course, is a comfortable fit. Don't buy a daypack without trying it, loaded. Because some have poorly designed shoulder straps, even a lightly loaded daypack can be irritatingly uncomfortable. If you want those dayhiking miles to be pleasant, and if you're going to pay $20-40 for a good pack, you'll have to exercise some care in making a choice.

Don't buy a daypack if what you need is a child's pack for overnight travel. If you want your children to enjoy the trip, you have to make them comfortable on the trail. Antelope, Jansport, Kelty, Wilderness Experience, Cannondale and Camp Trails all make good child-sized frames and softpacks with varying capacities for different age ranges. Fit and comfort are even more important in kid's packs. Take the trouble to make sure that shoulder straps don't rub or chafe and that hipbelts will stay up and support. Adjustability may be important for a good fit. A decent pack can make the difference between your child's loving the trip and wanting more, and hating the outdoors. Decent packs that fit well cost no more than good daypacks and may be an even better investment.

The less I have to carry, the more I enjoy the country, so I day hike whenever possible, sometimes from a backpacking basecamp. In recent years I have developed an affection for fanny packs because they sit closer to the body, do not swing like a daypack, leave my shoulders free and my back sweatfree. The pack's center of gravity is lower and the minimal weight is so easily supported by the scaral promontory that I'm scarcely aware I'm wearing a pack at all. Another plus is that I can lift the pack until the belt is loose and slip it around to the front to get at whatever I need without taking it off or even loosening the belt.

In fact it's perfectly feasible to wear two fanny packs, one in front and one in back to increase capacity, or one or two belt packs or pouches can be worn in front. Since fanny packs have been growing in popularity, the selection has been increasing, designs are being refined and larger volume models are now available. Especially if it's warm enough to go shirtless, I enjoy a day outing far more with a compact fanny pack than I do with a pack I wear on my shoulders.

When I first took our St. Bernard, "Rafferty" backpacking, I had to make, by trial and error, a pack in which he could carry the considerable quantity of food he required. Nowadays there are probably half a dozen commercial dog packs on the market that do a considerably better job than the primitive rig of harness, old towel and handsewn saddlebags that I devised. Most dogs love to go backpacking and well-trained animals that don't chase wildlife, disturb others or raid the larder are a joy to take along.

An effort should be made not to change a dog's diet on the trip, unless he is used to fresh meat. I once packed two half-gallon bottles full of fresh cooked meat for a ten day trip for Raff, but after five days it began to ripen and after seven it was all I could do to empty the containers in a hole without gagging. The rest of the trip Raff shared our food; he even came to enjoy small overcooked trout. Dry kibbles and canned meat make the easiest combination; and dogs do not mind carrying out the flattened cans. In fact, Raff regularly carried home a good deal of my more indestructable gear.

If you want to go one step further, get a llama! These docile, friendly, amusing animals can be led like a dog and will cheerfully carry a hundred pounds while you swing along whistling, unencumbered. We enjoyed using them in Bolivia and now they're available in California from Shasta Llama which both raises them to sell and offers summer llama tours. You can even get a space age llama pack from the people at Antelope, illustrating the fact that there has never been a wider selection of packs to choose from. Whether you get help from your pets or go it alone, you can hardly go wrong if you put function and fit ahead of fashion and fancy features.

5 BEDS

Just a couple of years ago sleeping bags were all pretty much the same. A backpacker's bed was simply a rectangular or mummy shaped envelope stuffed with fiberfill or down. Period. Nowadays the common sleeping bag is increasingly being displaced by half a dozen sophisticated "sleeping systems," all different. There's the Down Home Modular Sleeping System with a possibility of perhaps 100 different combinations, the Stephenson Triple bag, the Camp 7 system, the DeWolf System, foam bags, and, perhaps most important, vapor barrier liners. In addition there are new wrinkles in amazing down and foam air mattresses, not to mention bivy sacks and foam pads—everything but waterbeds, and they may not be far away.

Why all the changes? A continuing demand for lighter, more comfortable, more versatile beds. And the availability of new high-tech materials as well as refined designs. The backpacking boom has brought a lot of new people into the wilds, and they've demanded comfort as never before. Probably nothing is more essential to the success of a trip than a good night's sleep at the end of a day of strenuous (and probably unaccustomed) activity. Sleeping on the ground outdoors in the wild (or in a confining tent alongside a companion) is startlingly different from the familiar bed at home. Even if there's no altitude, wind or cold to contend with, it takes some getting used to—every trip for most people. As the old prospector I used to travel with liked to say, "A man's no good for anything if he can't get his rest."

Beds are made today of down, foam, polyester fiberfill and combinations. It is noteworthy that all of the new systems include vapor barriers of some sort. In addition, 3M has commissioned five manufacturers to try and develop a Thinsulate bag. The one I talked to was skeptical. Despite specially made batting from 3M, the best he'd been able to do was a bag 30% heavier than one made with PolarGuard, and the drape was poor. Fiberpile, likewise, seems unsuitable for bags.

Before looking at the systems and the bags themselves, it's important to consider the suitability of the prime insulators for sleeping bag construction.

Down remains the most popular filling for substantial reasons, chiefly because of its unexcelled lightness, bulk, long life, compressability and resiliency. Down pods compress to one seventh their expanded size with virtually no loss in resiliency. And even after a long period of compression, an ounce of good down will expand (if unrestricted) to stop convective air flow in a volume of more than five hundred square inches. Unfortunately, down's attributes have decided drawbacks. Its compressibility, a virtue when cramming a sleeping bag in its stuff bag or your pack, causes the down beneath your body to be squashed so flat that its insulating value is virtually nonexistent. Just the weight of light fabric used to make a good bag cuts down loft by 15-50%.

Because down is made up of individual, unconnected pods, it is the least uniform of insulators. Since it is capable of enormous expansion and compression, it tends to migrate if not carefullly contained, producing unsuspected thin or empty places in the insulating layer. The small (4-8 inch) pockets required to keep its insulating layer even half way uniform, involve complex construction which increases weight and cost. Because of down's sensitivity to weight and tendency to migrate, bag design and construction are often far more important to sleeping comfort than the quantity of fill or total bag weight. Infrared cameras measuring heat escape have shown a shocking volume of loss in impressively thick bags because of poor design, down shift, inexpert filling, etc.

If down's unsuspected cold spots are disconcerting, its vulnerability to moisture is positively frightening—and at times less apparent. Many people know that a down bag soaked by rain, frost, fog, dew or snow becomes sodden, leaden, loses all loft and therefore insulating value. But it isn't understood that in a single night the moisture from body and breath will weigh more than 3½ pounds, and 2-2¼ pounds of it regularly condenses invisibly in the down of your bag! If you don't or can't dry your bag you'll not only carry that moisture, your bag will lose a significant portion of its loft (warmth capability) as a result.

Down's vulnerability to wetting as the facts become known, has been largely responsible (along with price) for the shift to fiberfill for critical conditions. It has also been a stimulus for the use of vapor barrier liners, Goretex covers, bivy sacks and tents. Although the price of down actually dropped in 1979, soaring costs during the seventies made $2-400 down bags prohibitively expensive for many backpackers. And down is difficult to clean, collects dust and odors and is highly variable in quality. So while down is easily the most popular filling for sleeping bags, it is far from ideal, and not necessarily the best insulation for a bed.

Polyester fiberfill, however, is decidedly worse, on balance. First the advantages. Fiberfill is cheaper, more uniform, water resistant and more cushioning than down. It retains substantial insulating value when wet, dries faster, is easily cleaned, non-allergic, doesn't migrate and is far less sensitive to weight loading. Unfortunately, it takes 2-4 times the weight of fiberfill to match down in loft and has only three quarters of down's compressibility, making bags bulkier. It could be forgiven these defects if only it had a reasonable life. But it doesn't. The terrible truth is that fiberfill often "dies" before a buyer can get his money's worth, even at comparatively low prices, unless he babies his bag.

Hollowfill II and Kodasoft are chopped polyester fibers that rely on a silicone coating to make them repel one another and thus resist the matting that kills resilience and loft. PolarGuard relies on the heat crimping of a continuous filament fiber to resist matting. But neither strategy works for very long in the field. Silicone does not stick well, especially to slick surfaces, and when the coating wears off matting begins. The heat crimp in PolarGuard is put in at 140°F. It's like a "permanent wave" in that it's anything but permanent. Compression and heat are its enemies. Store a PolarGuard bag in its stuffsack and you're killing its loft. Leaving it stuffed in the trunk of your car in summer (where temperatures easily exceed 140°F) invites certain death.

By their very nature, fibers pressed together and allowed to move and work will gradually align and interlock. The process is aggravated by compression and heat. Neither silicone nor a heat crimp can prevent inevitable matting. And when matting occurs resilience (the ability to spring back) disappears and the loft that yielded insulative value is permanently lost. After 6-8 years experience, bag makers, to their sorrow, have confirmed the fact that polyester batting dies in comparatively short time. I have participated in the autopsies of a number of bags which have been returned because they "went flat."

this snug sleeper is shaded from the early morning sun and sheltered from the chilly night sky.

When cut open the bags reveal locked, knotted batting that looks more like compressed cotton, wool or Thinsulate than it does the original light, fluffy fiberfill. A continuously used or abused bag probably won't last one summer. A bag infrequently slept in and kept cool and uncompressed may last for years and give the illusion of long life. But it is generally (though not publicly) acknowledged by people who know that, on the basis of actual use, fiberfill bags won't last long enough to pay for themselves. That may have something to do with Celanese's decision to stop making PolarGuard, the most popular fiberfill for bags. And it is certainly reflected in the fact that The North Face excludes PolarGuard, along with Goretex and Thinsulate, from its lifetime guarantees.

But the future looks brighter. Still in the testing stage at this writing is a polyester fiberfill of great promise. It's efficiency (weight/warmth ratio) is 20% better than today's polyesters and so far it has shown marked resistence to matting. When (and if) durability is proven you'll see it on the market in 1981 or 82. And it's entirely possible, as research and development continue, that synthetic fillings equal (or superior to) down in quality and cheaper in price will be available by the mid-eighties.

In the early seventies down's drawbacks and sharply rising price caused bag makers to seriously investigate two synthetic alternatives: polyester fiberfill and polyurethane foam. When it came time to tool up they put their money on fiberfill. I said at the time they were making a mistake, and that was before it was known that polyester dies young. I am still convinced that foam has the potential to be the premier insulator, bar none. Consider its impressive credentials. Foam's resiliency is marvelous: It springs back to 100% of its loft almost instantaneously and is essentially unaffected by fabric loading. Its weight is lighter than polyester, even though existing foams are primitive compared to the material's potential. Foam is cheap, non-allergic, fireproof, impervious to wind, ridiculously easy to fabricate into bags, surprisingly durable, and its insulative value is unaffected by wetting.

When soaked it wrings out easily and evaporation or body heat quickly completes the drying process. But foam's greatest virtue is its perfect uniformity. By comparison both down and polyester are pathetic. Combined with its stubborn springiness, sheet foam's uniformity of thickness provides dependable insulation without thin or cold spots. It's hard to convey what insulation uniformity means because few people have experienced it. Uniformity is what permits me to sleep in the snow without a tent in the wind and stay toasty warm in a foam bag with a total loft of two inches: an inch on the top and one on the bottom! It's what permits me to state that, as veteran winter travelers know, a better snow bag can be made at home out of one inch foam, plastic sheeting and rubber cement than the most expensive down bag on the market!

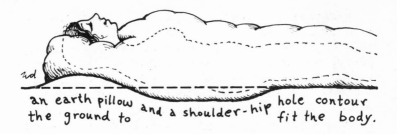

an earth pillow and a shoulder-hip hole contour
the ground to fit the body.

For recreational summer backpackers, however, existing foams present both real and imagined problems. The imagined problem is a matter of style. Foam is bulky, and a big sleeping bag, even though light, looks heavy and destroys the slim silhouette so beloved by the fashion conscious. At least that was the worry of bag makers. Foam's real problem (though it's sometimes a great blessing) is its stiffness, it's resolute refusal to nestle cozily against the sleeper like down. Instead, thanks to its great resiliency, it stubbornly holds its shape.

This attribute of a foam bag provides unparalleled ventilation, permitting comfort ranges unheard of in other types of bags. Of course excess ventilation can be a problem when the cold is intense. Sleeping in and adjusting a foam bag is a totally different experience than sleeping in a conventional bag, and this scares bag makers as well as backpackers. As mentioned in Chapter I, new and unfamiliar concepts are often rejected, even if they work, because their great difference promotes insecurity—and wilderness travel provides more than enough of the unfamiliar for most people.

When I ski into my snow bound cabin at 7400 feet in the winter I sleep in a nearly ten year old Ocaté bag of one inch foam because of its 70°F comfort range. At bedtime, thanks to a roaring fire, the cabin may be 70°, but when I climb into the bag I am perfectly comfortable. The superb ventilation keeps my feet from sweating, a problem for me in down bags on much colder nights. The slight bellows effect produced by my breathing drives out excess warmth. I can feel it pumping out past my shoulders and neck. Sleeping in a foam bag is a little like sleeping in a coffin because the tunnel of foam doesn't drape against the body. It takes a little getting used to, but I find the sensation extremely pleasant and free, now that I know I don't have to bundle up to sleep comfortably and warm.

As the fire dies and the snow-buried cabin cools, I partially close the drawstring that turns the top of the bag into a hood, reducing the volume of escaping warm air. Before dawn, when the cabin is close to freezing, I'll cinch down again on the drawstring to further reduce the opening, maintaining a comfortable degree of warmth inside the bag. When I sleep outside in the snow in the same bag, I begin with the hood closed down to a hole about the size of a softball. As it grows colder I cover the opening with a piece of spare clothing or a foam plug and pull on the two nylon laces I have brought into the bag at my chin.

The bag is equipped with a lacing system much like a shoe. To increase bag warmth at below freezing temperatures, I pull on the laces to draw the whole length of the bag closer against me, locking them in whatever position seems appropriate. This may sound complicated but it's as easy as closing the drawstring on the hood of any bag. By cinching up the bag to the dimensions of a mummy, wearing thermal underwear, using a one-inch foam pad (for luxurious cushioning) and a plastic ground cloth beneath the bag, I sleep comfortably at zero.

One night I awoke with a cold damp foot and discovered the foot of the bag had slipped off the pad and was in direct contact with the snow. When I swung the bag back onto the bed, my foot dried and warmed up with amazing quickness. Thus, this somewhat primitive ten year old bag made of one-inch foam kept me comfortable over a range of 70 degrees, a feat inconceivable in any other kind of bag.

Ocaté is now known as CozyQuip, the country's only producer of production foam bags, mukluks, mitts and a variety of jackets, parkas, vests and anoraks. As the exposure of the foot of my bag to the snow illustrates, foam is breathable to a degree never approached by other insulation, including pile, thought it comes closest. And foam doesn't store the moisture that passes through it. You can hold a foam garment underwater until it's saturated, squeeze it 96% dry by hand, put it on comfortably and let body heat complete the drying in a matter of minutes. CozyQuip jackets made of quarter inch foam sandwiched between loose nylon shells are the official choice of the New Mexico State Police and other state agencies whose men work outdoors in the winter.

Unlike my old Ocaté, the new CozyQuip bags protect the shoulders from cold night air by a pair of half inch foam flaps called "wind baffles." There is also an optional "breathing plug," which functions like a cork in a bottle to seal the top of a bag closed in the coldest weather without inhibiting the sleeper's breathing in the slightest. CozyQuip bags have likewise been reduced in bulk. My old Ocaté was hard to ram into a stuffsack 18 inches in diameter. The new bags are folded in half then rolled and tied before being slipped into 12-inch stuffsacks. And don't forget that a foam bag reduces the bulk and weight of the mattress you need to carry. To clean a foam bag you merely submerge it in bio-degradable soap and warm water in your bathtub, and trample it with bare feet. Rinse the bag, squeeze it out and hang it in the breeze, and it will probably be dry in an hour.

If you wonder how a mere quarter inch thick jacket can keep a man warm in the snow, remember the incredible power of uniformity in insulation, and consider that four inches of CozyQuip foam has an insulative rating of R-54, compared to R-43 for a foot-thick layer of Corning fiberglass insulation! The urethane foam is made from a patented formula with a glycol base that provides elasticity and a high percentage of air cells, but won't crumble, break or crack as most foams will. It's baked like bread in sheets of uniform thickness and consistency which are so easily fabricated into bags that Santa Fe Boy Scouts buy it and make their own.

CozyQuip makes four different bags. The Arctic, rated to -40°F, has 1½ inch foam on top and 1¾ on the bottom. In six foot lengths it weighs five pounds and costs about $120. The Rover, rated from zero to 70°F, has one inch foam on top, 1¼ on the bottom, weighs 3¼ pounds and costs about $90. The Zip-lok has 1¼ inch foam on top, 1 and ⅜ on the bottom, weighs five pounds and costs about $100. Its comfort range is an incredible 90 degrees, from -20° to 70°F. The Summer Bag, rated from 20° to 80°F, has 1¼ inch foam on the bottom, a half inch layer on top, weighs less than three pounds and costs about $85. The other three are four-season bags.

All four bags have the same lacing arrangement as my old Ocaté. It looks a little strange, but I've found it highly functional, foolproof and so simple a child can operate it. The bags themselves are also somewhat different in appearance. Instead of irregular billowy thickness, there is a comparatively thin, absolutely flat smoothness. Only the Zip-lok has full length zipper, and bags can be zipped together. Believe it or not, zippers really aren't needed, except for convenience when getting in. And because the bags are so firm and smooth, one slides easily into foam when it would be a struggle in a conventional bag. The absence of a zipper keeps down cost and weight and enormously boosts warmth because there's no seam to lose heat. The continuous, uniform layer of foam around you is uninterrupted.

In down or polyester bags a double-slider, full length zipper is essential for ventilation (as well as entry) to combat sweaty feet with hoped for air circulation. Because of foam's unexcelled breathability and ventilation, zippers simply aren't needed to keep your feet dry and comfortable, even on the warmest nights! And because you're lying on cushiony, resilient foam instead of crushed flat down or fiber, you have insulation and mattress comfort beneath you. Nothing else is

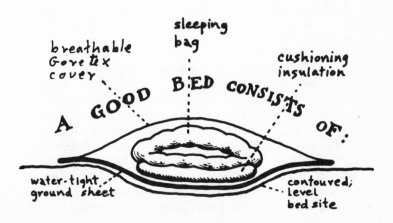

really needed, saving you the weight, bulk and cost of a separate mattress, unless you (like me) want the luxury of additional cushioning. Ensolite-type closed cell foam is more than adequate on snow or any terrain. Anything more is delightfully decadent.

As good as foam is, there is enormous room for improvement (which cannot be said of down or down bags). Foam's two principal problems: poor drape (stiffness) and bulk need to be improved. And I have long envisioned a solution that would likewise greatly reduce foam's weight. CozyQuip's patented foam has 62-64 air cells per cubic inch or roughly twice as much air as the average foam. But those cells are still tiny. What if they were made much bigger? It has accurately been determined that there is no adverse air circulation (convective heat flow) in insulation as long as pockets of air have no dimension larger than ¼ inch.

If a foam could be baked or blown to sponge-like consistency with quarter inch bubbles, it would be far lighter, much less bulky and considerably softer. Such a foam in the top of the bag (the present foam's fine for the bottom) should improve drape and cut weight and bulk. I mentioned my dream foam to CozyQuip president Dave Curtis, a chemist, and he saw no reason why it couldn't be fabricated. He has promised to experiment, see what he can develop and provide me the results for testing.

For years Dave and his friends have tested foam bags and clothing in the snow at 14,600 foot Wolf Creek Pass, Colorado where winter temperatures are commonly -25° to -50°F. Since Dave and his friend Gil Phillips are both scout commissioners, it's not surprising that they often take scout troops to Wolf Creek Pass to teach them winter travel skills. Total reliance on these trips is on foam. Participants usually make their own gear under the supervision of Dave and Gil. They wear foam hats with face tunnels (which inspired the "Wood Hood"), foam mittens and foam mukluks over bare feet, and the arms, legs and torso are wrapped with sheet foam which is held against the body by loose clothing.

Using Dave's foam and patterns they make highly professional bags with only scissors and rubber bonding cement, substituting 4 mil plastic for nylon covers. If time is short, they simply take along sheet foam and sheet plastic and make safe, cozy burrows in the snow. Here's Gil's design for a better snow bed than the finest down bag made. On one half of a 12-foot square of 4 mil polyethelene spread on the snow, position a 4 x 8 sheet of uncoated nylon. On top of that goes your mattress, a simple sheet of one inch foam, without cover. Next comes either a CozyQuip or homemade foam bag, or simply two sheets of 1-1½ inch urethane foam about three feet wide. Now fold the free side of the plastic over the bed and tuck it securely underneath on the far side. Fold the plastic under at the foot of your bed and you're ready to crawl into the open end and go to sleep in your foam clothes, controlling ventilation and carefully maintaining a supply of air to breathe through the open plastic tunnel above your head. Dave has slept comfortably wrapped in sheet foam and plastic at 50 below!

You can snuggle deep into your bag and fold the foam over your head securely because foam is so porous you can easily breathe through it. Moisture given off from your body (and breath) during the night passes out through the foam to condense to frost when it hits the plastic and collect as ice in the nylon sheet beneath your mattress, which is there to act as a blotter-collector. In the morning you "snap" the ice from your sheet and shake the ice dust from your plastic before packing up. The rest of your bed is bone dry. Although it's longer lived and lighter, you don't need CozyQuip foam for your bag. Any light urethane open-celled foam will suffice.

space
rescue
blanket

In the early seventies when I first wrote in *Wilderness Camping* of foam's superiority as an insulator, despite its rejection by sleeping bag makers, I asked readers for their experience. I was surprised to find a number of people had been privately experimenting with foam for some time. Jerry Pournelle, a California novelist with aerospace industry experience, for instance, told me he had built several bags out of one-inch upholsterers foam rubber stitched together with nylon fishing line, sealed with rubber cement and lined inside and out with uncoated nylon. "After several nights at about zero," he reported, "I concluded that it was the best bag I'd ever had. Materials cost me about $20, with an investment of about five hours work."

down
pod:

And Anthony E. Sowers, a New Mexico engineer, built four different foam bags, each in a different design, but all utilizing vapor barrier linings. For extreme conditions he constructed an eight pound bag with 3¾ inches of soft foam on the bottom and four inch loft down on the top, with a VB liner of coated nylon. It was warm and comfortable at -10°F, and he felt confident it could handle much colder temperatures.

It's not surprising that every single one of the "sleeping systems" mentioned at the start employ vapor barriers of one kind or another inside. Even the die-hards who won't try vapor barrier clothing because they're sure they'll get wet, reluctantly admit that it's valuable in a sleeping bag, especially one of down, to protect the insulation from picking up 2-4 pounds of body moisture in the night. But that's just half the problem. The heat lost along with that water, it has been calculated, would be sufficient to melt 27 pounds of ice! That's a tremendous amount of wasted energy. Since it's being generated in an effort to maintain body warmth and skin humidity, why not give the body some help by retaining heat and moisture and at the same time preventing dampness from penetrating your insulation? Much of that wasted energy can be saved by using a vapor barrier, because heat and moisture generation will drop sharply when proper humidity and warmth level at the skin are maintained. But the biggest payoff for many people is that a vapor barrier liner can increase the warmth of any bag by an impressive 20°F.

The application of vapor barrier to sleeping bags is much simpler than it is in clothing because there's no change in the body's activity level and temperatures remain constant or change very slowly. Offsetting this somewhat is reduced human awareness. When you're asleep you're unaware of overheating, chilling or dampness until discomfort is sufficient to wake you.

There are four different ways to apply vapor barriers to sleeping. (1) You can construct a sleeping bag with coated fabric on all interior surfaces. (2) You can use a separate coated fabric liner (VBL) in a conventional bag. (3) You can wear a vapor barrier shirt and a free-floating half sack VB liner, or (4) You can wear a VB shirt and pants, not to mention gloves and socks, in any bag.

The first and most comprehensive sleeping system to utilize vapor barriers, not surprisingly, was Jack Stephenson's Warmlite Triple Bag, available since 1968. The refined version is still revolutionary as the eighties begin. Unique features (or "firsts") include: an integral foam pad or down air mattress (DAM) instead of down on the bottom, reflective fabrics to reduce radiant heat loss, a vapor barrier interior fabric for warmth, down protection and sweat reduction, a removable multi-layer top, a down-filled collar to stop neck drafts and double zippers at the openings to prevent heat loss. Made from 1.2 oz. ripstop nylon, the outer fabric is windtight, water repellant (to dew, not rain) and aluminized on the inside. The interior fabric is coated on the inside, where you can't feel it. If you get wet from sweat it feels slippery instead of sticky. And when it quickly dries (once you ventilate) there is no lingering clammy dampness emanating from damp down.

The bag has two separate foam tops, one twice as thick as the other. Small nylon coil zippers make them entirely removable. In the warmest summer weather you use only the thin top; in colder spring and fall you use only the thick top; in the coldest winter weather you stay warm beneath both. Thus you have three bags in one, with a comfort range unknown in down beds, and four season capability, yet you carry only what you expect to need on any given trip. In the coldest weather a down-filled collar snugs closely around the top of the neck and the hood is formed with zippers and the face opening closed with a drawstring.

The two-inch-thick foam pad replaces a down bottom that was uselessly crushed beneath the sleeper. It also simplifies packing, makes it easy to turn over, reduces rolling and eliminates the need for a separate mattress. Warmlite is one of only three companies that uses the finest available goose down, no matter what the price, because it provides maximum loft/weight and the best possible resiliency and durability. Loft varies with the supply from 600 to 850 cu. in./oz., loaded. Because the inside fabric is coated, the down never gets damp or heavy, the bag never needs washing and the interior can be safely and effectively cleaned with a damp soapy cloth. The Warmlite Triple

3 types of sleeping-bag tubes:

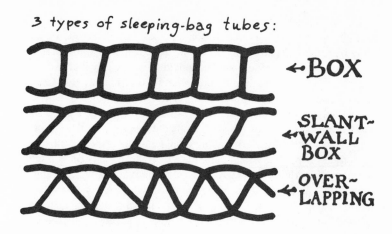

←BOX

SLANT~
←WALL
BOX

OVER~
←LAPPING

bag, with both tops and foam pad costs about $280-$400, depending on size, and weighs 5½ lbs.

Equipped with the Down Air Mattress instead, the cost range is $333-460. The DAM, which is custom made to fit your bag (or your specifications) is $75 separately. When I first heard of this intricate, cunning creation, put together with sewing, heat sealing and glued foam, I thought Jack had gone too far. I should have known better. The DAM is now the preferred mattress because of its reduced weight and bulk and its easy, dependable operation. It must not be inflated by mouth, to keep moisture from the down, but an ingenious adaptation permits easy inflation by using the sleeping bag carry sack as a pump. The purpose of the down inside the mattress is to prevent the convective air movement that has always made air mattresses cold.

A couple of my experiences with my Warmlite Bag will give some idea of how it functions. On the very first night that I slept in it there was still some snow on the ground at the High Sierra campsite and I was using the heavy top to be sure I was warm enough. After an hour or two I awakened, sweating, and groaned at the thought of spending the rest of the night wet and clammy. Then my head cleared and I remembered the vapor barrier lining. I jumped out of bed (naked), zipped the bag clear open (down one side and across the bottom) and waved it in the cool dry air. In no more than two minutes both myself and the bag were thoroughly dry, whereupon I climbed back inside, set the zippers for greatly increased ventilation and slept comfortably dry for the rest of the night.

On a steaming August night in the Pennsylvania woods it was impossible to get cool and I was sweating heavily, even with both sides and the foot of the thin top unzipped. But while my companions' bags were soaking up sweat, mine was damp only on the surface. And sometime after midnight when a tiny night wind slipped into camp, I was the beneficiary of evaporative cooling that also dried both me and my bag. These examples are meant to reassure people who imagine that vapor barriers will get them wet and keep them that way. Just the opposite is true. The nylon interior feels just like the inside of any other bag, but it doesn't pass water into the down, keeps you warmer and reduces your sweat output and dehydration on chilly nights.

Probably the largest bag maker offering a VBL system is Camp Seven. The system consists of a comparatively snug down mummy bag with a flat hood called the Arete, which weighs about 2½ lbs. and costs $160. On the inside goes a separate but attachable VBL of coated nylon ($16) with a drawstring at the shoulders. That's the combination for summer trips. For winter camping the Arete and its VBL slip into an outer, zipperless Polarguard bag called the Pioneer, which weighs about 2 lbs. and costs about $80. The Polarguard bag, of course, can also be used alone or with the VBL, providing a number of different combinations for a wide range of conditions. Total cost of the system is about $256, with a total weight of less than 5 lbs.

Other firms make vapor barrier liners that can be used in your existing bag. Vapraflect, believing that urethane coatings pass too much moisture, adds an additional saran coating to its Polar Pouch. The 1.2 oz. ripstop nylon is also aluminized to reflect back body heat to the sleeper. This free-floating VBL offers a side zipper, comes in regular or long and costs $30-35. Also in the works is a Polar Pouch covered with a layer of Thinsulate to add still more warmth to any sleeping bag. Cost will be about $60, with a weight of 1¾ lbs. Vapraflect also makes vapor barrier shirts.

Down Home, which has its own modular sleeping system, also makes a separate VBL out of 1.5 coated ripstop, that costs $25-30 and weighs about 6 oz. It attaches to Down Home bags but is free-floating in bags without attachment points. Unfortunately, VBLs that aren't secured tend to get horribly tangled and twisted in the night. To solve the problem Moonstone developed a vapor barrier system that consists of an excellent VB shirt (7.3 oz., $30) and a VB half sack (5.7 oz., $13) that fastens snugly over it at the waist with an elastic band. The virtue of this system is that the shirt can be worn during the day, and the half sack is light and does not become easily tangled.

A VBL liner or system can add warmth capability as well as protection to any bag you own. Shortly before I was to leave for a month in the Bolivian Andes all of my bags but one were stolen. What remained was a light polypropylene summer down bag that North Face had given me to test years before. As a further experiment, I took it back to North Face to be fitted with a light custom-made VBL held in place by half a dozen velcro tabs. The liner boosted the bag's warmth about 20°F, so that, dressed night and day in a VB shirt, I was always warm in a bag with much less loft that those used by any of my companions. And when we left the peaks and descended into the Amazon jungle, I stored the bag and slept comfortably in the liner, well protected from the insect population.

The Down Home Modular Sleeping System is ambitious, to say the least. Its options, designed to handle any temperature or condition, are nearly endless. Basically, it starts with the detachable VBL already mentioned and progresses to the Zephyr, a 24 oz. bag that has a 2½ inch loft down top and only a single sheet of nylon taffeta on the bottom. The Zephyr can be used upside down in a heat wave or turned right side up and snapped at the corners to an Evazote (EVA) closed cell foam pad when it's cool. Flaps that wrap around the pad keep out cold air. For winter use the Zephyr (minus the pad) and the VBL are slipped inside any of Down Home's extraordinary down bags.

The "DeWolf System," devised by my friend Bob DeWolf for protracted winter ski touring, goes a step beyond the others. Instead of using a bag with interior coated fabric or a VBL liner, he extends the Moonstone system by substituting VB pants for the half sack liner. Dressed from head to toe in VB clothing, he enjoys substantial advantages over any VBL system. He can easily roll over without moving his bag, he saves the weight and cost of the liner, his VB suit is useable during the day, and he can control his comfort over a wider temperature range by the selection of clothing he wears over his VB suit. But best of all he's fully dressed, which means he avoids the chilling agony of getting dressed on a frigid morning. He doesn't have to wait for the morning sun to warm his bed to avoid the shock of cold air and, even better, he can get up in the night when nature calls without traumatizing his body.

Bob regulates his insulation levels to suit conditions and the bag he's using. Next to the skin he wears Odlo polypropylene long underwear. Over that goes a VB shirt tucked into REI Zip Rain (VB) Pants. On his feet are plastic bags and his hands are protected by poly gloves. If he's winter camping he might wear zipper ventilated pile pants, pile sweater, mittens, down booties and two balaclavas (heavy wool outer over a light silk inner). With this outfit to prevent heat and moisture loss, he can save several pounds by carrying a summer bag instead of one rated for winter—and he still has no clothing that he doesn't need anyway during the day. In fact he recently returned from a 20-day high Sierra ski tour on which he carried only one pair of

foam offers a new alternative:

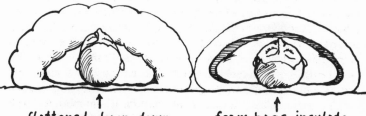

flattened-down down provides no insulation.

foam bags insulate under the body.

socks! Protected at all times by VB (Baggie) liners, they never got dirty or damp.

In the summer Bob might add a pile vest to his wardrobe and leave his sleeping bag at home, relying on his tent for shelter and sleeping inside a one pound bivvy sack, which he carries anyway for climbing. "It's a little mind-blowing," he reports, "just to lie down and go to sleep without anything around you—no covers to pull up, nothing to crawl into—that's where the bivy sack helps." I agree. The bivy sack adds significant (10-20°) warmth by holding heat and keeps off the inevitable chilling drafts, in my experience. Bob finds traveling without a sleeping bag marvelously carefree, in the spirit of the happy hobo or John Muir going into the wilds with nothing more than a big coat.

Many people will find his system too extreme, but it makes perfect sense. Why should a weight-conscious backpacker carry two complete sets of insulation systems, one for day, the other for night? Why not avoid the duplication and save pounds? Even the most conservative outdoor traveler can probably trim his load by re-thinking his needs along these lines. At the most fundamental level, that means carrying a lighter bag and relying on the clothing you have to take anyway to provide some of your nighttime warmth. By using a VB suit you can then reduce the clothing you need, as well as protect it and your sleeping bag from loading up with condensed perspiration. For instance, you shouldn't wear a down parka to bed unless you wear some sort of VB shirt to protect it from sweat—and even then it may get damp from the moisture you exhale during the night. Pile, foam or polyester clothing would escape the wetting problem.

The only drawbacks I can see to Bob's system are (1) slightly more moisture might find its way into your bag than with a VBL, but far less than you're getting now! And (2) sleeping fully dressed will be less comfortable for some—until it comes time to get up in the night! But the price is small for a pack that's pounds lighter, and it's a satisfying feeling to have more functional, flexible and versatile gear—all of it working for you day and night. By relying more on clothing (with VB underneath) than on the narrow comfort range supplied by a down bag, you'll have greater control of your comfort: less chance of helplessly roasting or freezing.

When it comes to more or less conventional down bags (i.e. without VBL) the finest are probably made by Marmot and Down Home—and the latter offers VBL as part of its system. Both, along with Stephenson's Warmlite, use the finest (highest lofting, most resilient and durable) goose down available, whatever the price—in fact all three buy from the same source. (Characteristically this down is 10% loftier, 10% more durable and 10% more expensive.) Both use bilaminate hot-cut 1.5 oz. Goretex ripstop nylon on the exterior for increased thermal efficiency and windproofness, but most of all for vital protection of the down from the various sources of wetting. Although Goretex adds $60-80 to the price and ½ oz./yard to the fabric weight, I have reluctantly been convinced that the dual cost is justified for cold or damp weather conditions because down is so vulnerable to disastrous dampening.

Both firms use differential cut throughout and intricately constructed foot sections (Marmot's has seven baffles) to ensure that your toes will not poke through the insulation layer. (Bags lose most of their heat at the feet and along the zipper.) Marmot uses double offset draft tubes that are forced together when the zipper is closed, a down-filled collar around the shoulders to keep out drafts held in place by an easily-released elasticized drawcord, well-named "Luscious" interior fabric, and a new scoop-cut shaped hood is easier to draw around the head without loss of loft over the forehead.

flat-cut sleeping bag:

Down Home, like Warmlite, provides double zippers to protect against heat loss and a unique form-fitting design that assures full insulation thickness over the shoulders. But its most revolutionary feature is a "Floating Hood" that you wear like a gigantic helmet. Being entirely detached, it permits you to sleep on your stomach or side with full protection without twisting hood or bag.

Almost as unusual is the optional boxed hood, an integral version of the helmet that provides far more warmth than do the hoods on conventional bags which are formed by cinching down on a draw-string. At Down Home every bag is custom made because there are so many options to choose from. Basically, the Hummingbird, rated to 15°F, costs $290 and weighs 3 lbs. plus. The Dipper, rated to −5°F, weighs under 4 lbs. and costs $325, while the Snow Bunting, rated to −20°F, weighs 4½ lbs. and costs $350. The most popular Marmot bags are the Pocket Gopher, rated 0°-10°F, at 3 lbs. and $320, the Gopher, rated −10 to −20°F (3½ lbs., $340) and the Penguin, rated −20° to −30°F (4¼ lbs., $400).

differentially-cut bag:

These two companies offer perhaps the finest production down bags available, but even with Goretex skins they are highly vulnerable to wetting from within, especially if used in winter when storm conditions may prevent vital airing. For instance, acquaintances just came back from a high Sierra ski tour on which the weather was so foul that they made only 18 miles in 7 days. In that time a fine 5 lb. Goretex down bag, used in a tent and aired whenever possible, more than doubled in weight (and lost half its loft) due to condensed body moisture. After barely escaping frostbite, its owner will never be without vapor barrier protection on that sort of trip again.

Needless to say, you don't have to spend $300 to buy a good down bag, but the above described bags provide a standard against which other bags can profitably be compared. The buyer is in no position to judge down quality but he can easily see whether a bag is minimally filled (and highly vulnerable to down shift that creates cold spots) or plump and firm. Dependable down bags are decidedly billowy, but light. And billowy but heavier is far better in terms of warmth than flat and flabby but light. Other keys to bag quality are small stitches (at least 10 to the inch), true differential cut, full length nylon zippers backed by plump draft tubes, a foot section that toes won't penetrate, draft protection at the shoulders and a hood that maintains loft when closed up tight.

Sleeping in a mummy bag on the ground in the wilderness is not much like sleeping in a heated home, but too many people, it seems to me, blame the resultant strangeness and likely wakefulness on the shape or confining nature of the bag. The mummy bag is so much more satisfactory in the long run than its larger relatives that an effort should be made to accept its confines. People shopping for a bag who are skeptical of their ability to adjust to its dimensions would be well advised to rent or borrow one for several trips to give themselves a chance to discover its virtues.

Before selecting a bag, the buyer needs to ascertain whether he sleeps warmly, cold or just about average. This determination, along with intended use, will largely determine the minimum temperature rating required for comfort. A bag to be used in wind and rain at high altitude by an exhausted, hungry climber will need to be warmer than one used by the same person at the same temperature under milder conditions. It is always a good idea to question backpacking friends about their bags.

When buying a bag it is worthwhile getting inside to check length, foot room, snugness and the ease with which the hood can be closed from the inside to a face hole the size of a baseball. Drawstrings should be supplied with some sort of spring loaded clamp that can be operated with one hand.

Although design and down quality vary, Sierra Designs, North Face, Trailwise, Camp 7 and such small companies as Feathered Friends, Western Mountaineering and Bugaboo make dependably good down bags. And there are doubtless other fine down bags with which I am not personally familiar. Only a few of the above offer Goretex outer fabric, and fewer still recognize down's liability to internal wetting by making VBLs, although North Face is seriously considering it. With prices what they are, most people nowadays know better than to put a $200 bag in the dirt, but let me emphasize again that down will sponge up moisture from any available source and will give it up very reluctantly. So, except in dry warm climates, down beds should be protected on the outside by tents, bivy sacks or Goretex, and on the inside by vapor barriers for maximum safety and efficiency.

Where down's vulnerability to wetting is too great a risk in the buyer's mind, or where price is more important than durability, there is still a sizeable market for polyester bags—partially, I fear, because fiberfill's short life is not widely known and because urethane foam's virtues and availability is virtually a secret. Probably the best Polarguard bags are made by Moonstone. Features are almost identical to those in Marmot's down bags, except for the double draft tube.

There's differential cut, a Luscious interior, sophisticated foot section, pre-formed hood and optional Goretex exterior.

Most distinctive is the absence of stitching to fasten batting to shell. Moonstone laminates (glues) the outer batts in place and the rest are "free floating" to minimize the compression of the construction process, thus obtaining an unusually high weight/warmth ratio for fiberfill. There are four models to choose from, the most popular being the Noatuk, rated 0°-15°F (5 lbs., $215) and the El Capitan, rated 30°-35°F (2¼ lbs., $105). Moonstone also makes a unique Polarguard bag that uses an exterior fabric consisting of two layers of aluminized mylar (to cut radiant heat loss) and three layers of nylon netting (to reduce convective heat loss), substantially boosting the effectiveness of the insulation.

North Face, a pioneer in Polarguard bags, uses "shingle" construction to approximate the slant wall baffle system used successfully with down, thus obtaining a high weight/warmth ratio while sewing batts to both liner and shell. North Face offers 11 different variations of six basic bags that are rated from 20° to −25°F, weigh 2¾ to 7¼ lbs. and cost $75-200. Another Polarguard pioneer, Snow Lion, offers six quilted bags in the same temperature range, with weights of 3½ to almost 7 lbs., costing roughly $100-150. A number of other companies make polyester fiberfill bags, many of them doubtless of good quality. The buyer can best determine quality by examining zippers, draft tubes, foot sections, hoods, plumpness and sewing—as well as weight and price.

Bivouac sacks and sleeping bag covers are an important part of the beds that some of us carry, but they are discussed, along with tents in Chapter 8, SHELTER. Because of the success of Goretex bivy sacks and the new lightweight tents, fewer people now entrust their beds to a mere ground cloth, even though it's by far the lightest, cheapest, simplest protection that can be provided—and often all that's needed. Where once we "rolled up" in heavy canvas tarps or army surplus ponchos that weighed more than today's bivy sacks, it's now possible

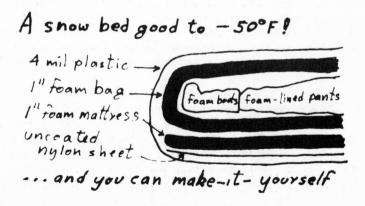

A snow bed good to − 50°F !

4 mil plastic
1" foam bag
1" foam mattress
uncoated nylon sheet

foam body foam-lined pants

... and you can make-it- yourself

to cut bed protection weight to a few ounces. The choice is between plastic of varying thicknesses which is cheap but punctures easily, and coated nylon tailored tarps which may cost four times as much but last four times as long.

What you choose will also be determined by the type of terrain, weather expected, your inclination to baby your gear and the extent to which you prepare your bedsite. Four mil plastic can be made to last if you groom the ground first. Since the job of a ground cloth is to protect the top of the bag from dew and showers, as well as ground moisture, it needs to be big enough (at least 5' × 8' and better 7' × 9') to generously fold over and tuck well under on the open side and ends—ideally with all your gear underneath. To save on the cost of a tailored nylon tarp, you can buy six yards of 45-inch coated nylon off the roll at your local mountain shop (or from a catalog), cut it in half and get your lady to sew the two strips together with a lap-felled double stitched seam down the middle.

Pillows, as such, are traditionally scorned, but anyone accustomed to one—and that means most of us—must find some way to elevate and cushion his head if he wishes to sleep in any kind of comfort. Half the problem is solved during site preparation by making an earth pillow. Cushioning is generally supplied by a down parka stuffed into one of its own sleeves or the sleeping bag stuff bag filled with spare clothing.

The seventies saw a revolution in backpacking mattresses. For years we had relied on ensolite (heavy and short-lived) to provide primitive, minimal cushioning but excellent insulation and protection from dampness. Egg crate urethane foam pads, often with nylon covers were excellent, if bulky and short-lived for drier conditions. And old fashioned rubberized fabric air mattresses, with only one or two compartments, were compact but heavy, vulnerable to puncture, and convective air currents within made them colder at times than a hammock. Plastic air mattresses, though cheap and light, were certain to leak.

Ensolite has now been replaced by a generation of tougher, lighter, more durable closed cell foams like Evasote (EVA). Egg crate urethanes are still with us, somewhat improved, but the big break-through is in air mattresses. The Air Lift combines 10 individual 3 mil plastic tubes, each filled with a single breath, in a light nylon zipper-closed cover. A puncture in the night affects only 10% of your bed and a spare tube can be substituted in the morning if patching isn't convenient. Weight is greatly reduced (the 42-inch model weighs 10 oz.) and cold convective air currents are somewhat lessened. Prices range $20-40 for 42 and 72-inch models of this low bulk mattress. A more sophisticated entry in the new wave of air mattresses is Stephenson's DAM, mentioned earlier, in which down effectively prevents ground cold from reaching the sleeper. Custom made for Warmlite bags, it costs $75 and weighs 20 oz.

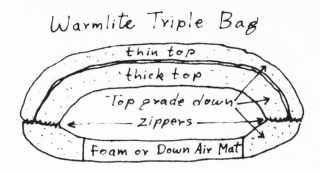

Warmlite Triple Bag

thin top
thick top
Top grade down
Zippers
Foam or Down Air Mat

But the most exciting, comfortable, inexpensive and versatile development is the Therm-a-Rest Mattress. It's simply a nylon air mattress built around open celled foam. The foam makes it self-inflating, prevents convection currents and increases cushioning. The foam squashes flat when you open the valve and roll it tightly into a four inch diameter cylinder (the ¾ length Backpacker). To inflate, simply open the valve and toss it where it can expand. By the time the tent is up it's fully inflated; in fact you'll have to squeeze out a little air for maximum comfort.

The Therm-a-rest rarely leaks, doesn't leave you flat (thanks to the foam) if it does, and is easily patched. Like any air mattress, it requires a bedsite free of sharp objects and protection from a ground cloth or tent floor—or an EVA pad in winter. The mattress is so tough, effective and foolproof that it survives rental well—the ultimate test of gear durability. The Backpacker weighs 24 oz., and costs about $35. Its 6-foot long big brother weighs 2¼ lbs. and costs about $45. The weight is substantial but the comfort may be worth it. As one of my friends put it, "It's the next best thing to a waterbed." It's gear like this that makes sleeping in the wilds more comfortable in the eighties than ever before.

6 FOOD

John Muir, we are told, regularly set forth into the high Sierra provisioned solely with bread stuffed in the pockets of his greatcoat. Tibetan monks sustain themselves with little more than nettle soup. An Indian cowboy with whom I traveled in the Mexican desert subsisted on tea made from herbs he picked along the way and a scrap of meat slapped on the coals of our evening campfire.

These gentlemen's somewhat extreme approach to eating have one thing in common: simplicity. And it's a message worth heeding. Most of us would benefit by simplifying our grub lists. The efforts I've made in that direction in recent years have substantially reduced my cooking chores and made my trips more carefree. Life in the wilds should be simpler, not more complex. After all, it's supposed to be a vacation!

That doesn't mean I skimp on planning. Just the opposite. I'm willing to put a little more effort into planning and preparing at home in order to be more carefree in camp. I've learned the hard way that food can make or break a trip. Backpackers, like armies, travel on their stomachs. The scenery will pale if the food doesn't satisfy. And the pitfalls of poor planning are many. You can carry far too much, bringing half of it home. Or you can run out and go hungry. Excess weight becomes a burden, and so does excessive preparation. Balance may be bad, power insufficient, or the taste so dreary that eating becomes a chore. I therefore urge you to take food planning seriously, even if it bores you, and to put your emphasis on simple as well as succulent meals. The rewards can be great—and the alternatives grim.

My chief strategy for reducing the burden of meal planning is taking notes. By writing down briefly what I'm taking before I leave (items, quantities), then making notes as soon as I return on how things turned out (surpluses, insufficiencies, failures, unfulfilled cravings, ideas), I produce a record that makes planning food for the next trip twice as easy. Why start from scratch every time? By making notes—and keeping them—food lists are continually refined, the planning ordeal is greatly reduced and you eat better each trip.

A principal pitfall in food planning is the instinctive urge to produce city-type meals in the wilds. One must set aside the rigid and ritualized habits of urban eating. Forget the three square meal structure of city life, which frowns on between-meal snacks. One eats in the wilds to keep the body continuously fueled, happy and capable of sustained effort. The easiest way to stay continuously fueled is to eat small quantities continuously. Small meals and frequent snacks provide easier digestion during activity and better energy production. The food planner should concern himself with weight, ease of preparation, calorie production, balance between fat, protein and carbohydrates, bulk, resistance to spoilage, palatibility and cost—not necessarily in that order.

There is no such thing as the perfect menu. On an easy summer overnight or weekend trip with my wife and daughter I use one criteria. If I am planning a long and strenuous cross-country trip my priorities are much different and so is my food list. Weather and climate have strong effects on food selection. Snow, jungle and desert require different menus. I know backpackers who happily go heavily laden to the wilderness to sit around camp and practice their gourmet cooking. I know others who think nothing of eating the same thing every day for a week to cut weight and preparation to the bone. I put myself somewhere in between. What I carry depends on trip length, terrain, weather and whim.

I'm not fanatic about lightness—providing my pack isn't heavy—but when it comes to preparation in camp I'm very finicky. I've spent too many hungry, miserable hours struggling to put meals together under adverse conditions. In my view the importance of easy preparation can scarcely by over-emphasized. After a long hard day on the trail in bad weather, the weary, starving backpacker, crouched in the dirt over an open fire in the cold, wind and dark needs all the help he can get. At such times boiling a pot of water and dumping in the food can be heavy, demanding, exasperating work.

Preparation that would be trivial in the city becomes somewhere between difficult and impossible. In the wind, cooked food may be five times as hard to prepare as cold food. A recipe that calls for milk may be twice the work of one that merely requires water. At high altitude, raw dry food may take ten times as long to cook as a pre-cooked freeze-dried dish. And there's nothing more frustrating after an exhausting day than trying to read complicated recipes by flashlight while nursing a smoky fire. Even walking gourmets will therefore be well advised to include a supply of zero preparation meals.

Foods designed specifically for backpacking are improving every year in terms of both appeal and simplified preparation. The same is true of lightweight dishes packaged for the housewife in super-markets, health food stores and delis. But there are still a great many foods that will make the backpacker salivate that are basically city meals and require a real kitchen for "easy" preparation. If the direc-

simple directions on the package mean easy preparation in camp.

tions run more than a sentence, or if more than one pot is required, I quickly lose interest.

Two dishes designed to be eaten at the same time I pass over quickly. Dinners with low caloric yield are swiftly rejected. Packages containing three or four separate packets make me suspicious. Freeze-dried foods form the nucleus of my menu, but I manage to buy the majority of my provisions from sources other than mountain shops. I'm always on the lookout for suitable backpacking foods when cruising places that sell food. And I do my experimenting at home. The trail is not the place to gamble. It's also not the time to diet.

A backpacker's tastes usually change in the wilds. The body's needs are altered by heavy outdoor exertion, and these needs frequently are reflected in cravings for carbohydrates, (liquids, salty foods and sweets) and a corresponding disinterest in other foods (like fats, meat and vegetables). Individual meals lose much of their significance. To keep the body continuously fueled, the backpacker should eat or nibble almost constantly. Many snacks and small meals provide better food digestion, which means better energy production.

As *Freedom of the Hills* puts it, "As soon as breakfast is completed the climber commences lunch, which he continues to eat as long as he is awake, stopping briefly for supper." I generally start nibbling an hour or two after breakfast if I am hiking, and I eat two lunches instead of one, the first in late morning and another in mid-afternoon. I know hikers who go a step further to escape food preparation altogether: they abolish distinct meals, eating every hour and fixing a larger or hot snack when they feel the need.

A hiker living outdoors should drink at least as often as he eats. If he is shirtless or the weather is warm his body may easily lose a gallon of water in a day! Since dehydrated food absorbs water from the body after it is eaten, still more water is needed. A backpacker can scarcely drink too much—provided he takes only a little at a time. Severe dehydration results if most of the fluids lost during the day are not replaced before bedtime.

Since water loss means salt loss, salty foods are unusually welcome. Although the body replaces salt lost normally, continuous, excessive sweating may justify taking salt tablets. A salt deficiency (from extreme water loss) can result in nausea, aches or cramps. But overdosing on salt is dangerous too. To protect yourself, take no more than two salt tablets with every quart of water you drink. To purify suspect water, boil it or add a trace of iodine. Halazone will not kill the bugs found in really bad water such as that found in the jungle, in primitive countries and downstream of any habitation.

Since heating food greatly increases preparation, requires weighty equipment (pots, stove) and provides only psychological benefit—cooking only reduces nutritive value—more than a few backpackers avoid cooking in the wilds altogether. They find the saving in time, labor and weight more than offsets the lack of comforting warmth. Denton W. Crocker (Wilderness Camping, Vol 6, No. 2) after careful experimentation devised a menu of precooked meatless foods that kept him looking forward to mealtime even after eating the same thing every day for nearly two weeks on the trail. Cost and bulk of his provisions are low, food weight is less than two pounds daily, and leaving home pots and stove reduced pack weight by another two pounds. The menu produces a balanced 3000 plus calories/day, and meal preparation is almost zero.

For breakfast Crocker eats a prepackaged ⅔ cup of home roasted potent granola that contains oats, wheat germ, brown sugar, salt, oil, corn syrup, vanilla, sunflower seeds and raisins. He also drinks a cup of Tang. For lunch there's a mix of equal portions of peanut butter, honey and milk powder, plus chocolate, crackers, dried fruit and a quart of Kool-Aid. Dinner consists of a home-baked trail bar composed of whole wheat and soy flour, wheat germ, skim milk powder, salt, currants, raisins, chopped dates, eggs, oil, molasses and vanilla. In addition there is a drink made of skim milk and malted milk powder. Needing only a spoon and a one-pint plastic bottle, Crocker found "there is something remarkably peaceful about an evening meal where I can just reach into the pack, pull out two small packages and, with a cup of water, have my supper ready."

Another approach to simplicity in the outdoor kitchen relies on the creative addition of spices and condiments to simple dishes to produce variety without complicating food preparation. For instance, on a relatively short easy trip, I might increase both the power and the flavor of a packaged stew by adding several of the following: freeze-dried sliced mushrooms, a pinch of Fines Herbs (spice mix), a gob of butter or margarine, parsley flakes, onion or garlic powder, a lump of cheese, crumpled bacon bar or vegetable bacon bits, tabasco sauce, and so forth. I could eat the same basic stew for a week but enjoy a different flavor every night by the restrained use of these and other

seasonings. Or take another of my staple foods, applesauce. I keep it exciting day after day by the judicious use of: cinnamon, raisins, lemon powder, vanilla, chopped dates, nutmeg, ginger, nuts, honey and coconut in varying combinations.

On a long hard trip, seasonings and spices become even more vital in the battle against boring, bland meals. A dash or two of chili powder and a shake of onion flakes will turn a dreary pot of beans into spicy chili. A little curry powder will liven up the rice. Jazz up a dreary casserole with dry mustard and Worcestershire sauce. If trout are on the menu, I briefly shake the dampened fish in a plastic bag containing a few ounces of my cornstarch, cornmeal, salt, pepper, onion and garlic powder mix before frying. Trout are also good baked in a butter sauce with sage and basil.

Other versatile ingredients include: sunflower and sesame seeds, slivered almonds, fruit crystals, wheat germ, coriander, bouillon cubes, tomato, beef and chicken base, peanuts, banana flakes, various freeze-dried fruits and vegetables, bay leaves, and oregano. For packaging seasonings for the trail, waterproof plastic medicine and cosmetic bottles and vials are best for the vanilla, Worcestershire and tabasco sauces.

Film cans and snap lid plastic containers are far better than plastic bags for dry spices. If you're going to be out for more than a weekend you'll find your condiments will be easier to find and use when kept together as a spice kit in their own drawstring bag. Don't turn your back on seasonings because you're not a cook. Neither am I, but I've learned that, with a little practice, anyone can turn dreary food into exciting fare with a little magic from the spice kit.

Sometimes flavor isn't the only reason for embellishment. If a stew or casserole is suspect in the realm of caloric punch, the deficiency can be corrected by fortifying it with TVP, freeze-dry meat, margarine, bacon bar, instant potato, wheat germ, cooking oil or other items of known caloric clout. In this manner a mere soup can be transformed into a high potency stew.

In case you wondered why white sugar wasn't listed, it's because I became convinced some years ago that refined sugar is distinctly unhealthy. I do not wish to preach, only to explain why I avoid sugar and sugar-rich foods like candy, jello and fudge. They no longer agree with me and since my sugar addiction has disappeared I no longer have the craving for sweets. While I substitute honey, molasses, and such sweet fruits as pineapple, dates, and bananas for most sugars, I recognize that many people will continue to rely (as I did for years) on the quick energy conveniently and appealingly provided by candy and sugar in various forms.

Talk about cravings, an old friend and hiking partner of mine used to begin losing sleep after 4-5 days on the trail for lack of a beloved milkshake. He talked quietly but often of his hunger. One night after dinner, feeling critically deprived, he could stand it no longer and headed for the trailhead. He was back in camp the next day—in time for lunch of course—having walked through the night in order to gorge himself on a huge breakfast and chocolate malt. For the rest of the trip he was either content—or too tired to complain.

Since backpacking is decidedly strenuous, it is hardly surprising that the body's fuel intake must increase significantly in order to keep up with demand. The body's energy requirements and the energy production of food are both measured in calories. It takes twice as many calories to walk at 3 mph as it does to walk at 2 mph. Walking at 4 mph doubles the calorie requirements again, and it take 2½ times as many calories to gain a 1000 feet of elevation as it does to walk at 2 mph. A variety of studies have shown that—depending on innumerable factors (like body and pack weight, distance covered, terrain, etc)—it takes 3000-4500 calories a day to keep a backpacker fueled. Easy family trips might require 2000-2500 while climbers may need 5000.

Backpackers who take in fewer calories than their systems need will find the body compensates by burning fat to produce energy. Stored fat is efficiently converted to fuel at the rate of 4100 calories per pound. The backpacker who burns 4000 calories, but takes in only 3590 (410 fewer), will theoretically make up the difference by burning a tenth of a pound of body fat, although individuals vary widely where fat conversion is concerned.

Backpackers unused to strenuous exercise will usually lose weight, but probably not from lack of caloric energy. Exposure to the elements results in water loss, and the change from the high bulk diet of civilization to low bulk dehydrated foods tends to shrink the stomach. For most people, a little hunger and a loss of weight is beneficial to health and need not be construed as the first signs of malnutrition—as long as energy levels remain ample.

The wanderer who carries concentrated, low bulk dehydrated food on his back needs to know something about the calorie power it will deliver—if only to prevent overeating. If the food is well chosen, about two pounds of it (before rehydration) will provide the approximately four thousand calories necessary to keep the body well stoked under load at high altitude.

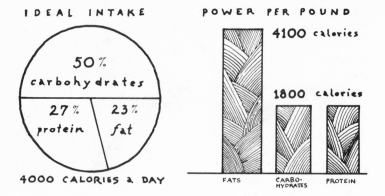

IDEAL INTAKE

50%
carbohydrates

27%
protein

23%
fat

4000 CALORIES a DAY

POWER PER POUND

4100 calories

1800 calories

FATS   CARBO-   PROTEIN
            HYDRATES

In the city we customarily eat till we are full. In the wilds, where energy expenditure is far greater, we tend to be anxious about keeping the body fueled; consequently there is a powerful instinct to stuff ourselves with food until we feel comfortably full. In the process it is easy to eat two days' ration at one sitting and get up feeling slightly sick and bloated. The extra power is wasted since the body will not accept any more than it can use. It requires some knowledge of the caloric output of foods and the body's likely needs, but if the traveler can muster the necessary self discipline and restraint, he will discover he can eat less with no loss of energy.

This tendency to overeat, in my experience, is as little recognized as it is fundamentally important. Think back to those trips on which you ran out of food. Instead of trusting the menu you originally devised, you probably decided—on the basis of bulk alone—that you weren't getting enough to eat, so you increased the rations. You damned the company that labeled your dinner "serves four," because it barely filled up two of you. It probably didn't occur to you that there might have been enough calories for four and that you didn't have to eat till you were stuffed. With a little knowledge of caloric production, the veteran traveler realizes that the slightly empty feeling in his stomach —and even loss of weight—reflects a healthy lack of bulk, not a dangerous shortage of nourishment.

Because freeze-dry foods cost 2-3 times as much as comparable dehydrated dishes, many hikers (and writers) dismiss them as too expensive. But cost per ounce can be a poor measure of value. A menu liberally supplied with freeze-dried foods will still cost less than $10 per day per person. Where can you vacation and eat in modest restaurants that cheaply? Considering the shortness (four days) of most backpacking vacations and the necessity of carrying everything on one's back, skimping on prime quality seems foolish. After a hard day in the wilds the best is sometimes barely good enough!

Freeze-dried food is often best for wilderness travel because of its ease of preparation, low bulk, rapid rehydration, nutritional values, superior taste, texture, form, color and long shelf life. Air or vacuum dehydrating loses some proteins and vitamins. Weight is usually about the same for both dehydrated and freeze-dried foods, since both processes leave about 5% water and 25% of original weight, but dehydrated foods take 2-3 times as long to rehydrate (soak), a severe drawback when you're ravenous even before you stop to camp for the night. Air dried food contains as much as 25% water. I'm willing to simmer my pre-cooked, fresh-tasting freeze-dried stew for 20 minutes at high altitude, but an hour (and sometimes two!) is too long to wait for a less appetizing air-dried dinner to cook. At such a time, cost is meaningless. The weight of cooking gear can often be shaved because pre-cooked freeze-dried foods need only the addition of hot water to the package. I'm not a spendthrift, but when it comes to food I'm going to carry on my back, I want the best I can buy.

When it comes to shelf life, it's the packaging that counts. Food in polyethelene bags is always good for a year, but the safe maximum is two years. Vacuum packed foods in foil are good indefinitely—as long as the seal isn't broken. When the vacuum goes (easily determined visually) shelf life drops to the polyethelene level. Food vacuum packed in nitrogen in cans has no known shelf life limit, except for high fat foods (butter, buttermilk, peanut butter powders) which have a five year life expectancy.

Food is divided into three major components: fats, proteins and carbohydrates, all of which are essential to the backpacker's diet. The ideal proportions are essentially unknown and vary according to the temperature, individual, environment and type of activity—but a rule of thumb suggests that caloric intake be roughly 50% carbohydrates, 25-30% protein and 20-25% fats. There is a myth that the more strenuous the activity the greater the protein need, and many backpackers go to great lengths to load their diets with the common proteins: meat, cheese, milk and eggs.

Actually, protein requirements are unaffected by activity. Excess protein can be a liability in that it is comparatively difficult and slow to digest. Large intakes are poorly assimilated and provide no immediate energy. Furthermore, protein at 1800 calories per pound provides less than half the energy per pound of fat (4100). Most protein-happy hikers would do better to switch their enthusiasm to fat, in which they probably are deficient.

The National Academy of Sciences says we eat 50% more protein than we can utilize. Protein serves only to maintain existing muscle. On a rigorous trip, all that's needed is .015 ounces per pound of body weight per day. That means a 100 pound woman needs only an ounce and a half, while her 200 pound boyfriend needs a mere three ounces. More than that is wasted!

Fats are no easier to digest than proteins, but they supply more than twice the energy and release it gradually over a long period of time. The principal fat sources for backpackers are oil, butter, margarine, nuts, meat fat and cheese. The digestion of protein and fat demands the full attention of the body's resources for a considerable period of time. Consumption should be spread through breakfast, lunch and snacks rather than being concentrated in a heavy dinner. Even relatively small amounts should not be eaten before or during strenuous exercise. The blood cannot be expected to circulate rapidly through exercising muscles and digest complex food in the stomach at the same time without failing at one function or the other—usually both.

When heavy demands are made on both the digestion system and the muscles, the body is likely to rebel with shortness of breath, cramps, nausea and dizziness. The first signs are low energy and fatigue. Carbohydrates may conveniently be thought of as pure energy. Digestion is rapid, undemanding and efficient and the energy is released within minutes of consumption. But fast energy release means that carbohydrates are completely exhausted of their power in as little as an hour, and more must be ingested if the energy level is to be maintained. The backpacker who lives on carbohydrates must eat almost continuously to avoid running out of fuel. The common sources of carbohydrate are fruits, cereals, vegetables, starches, honey and sugars.

An example may clarify what I think of as "selective eating." One January day in the high Sierra I set out on snowshoes to climb the steep mountain that rises behind my cabin. In my day pack I carried a banana, chicken leg, cookies, a chunk of cheese and raisins. The going was strenuous and hot and despite a good breakfast I began to grow faint and tired around ten, well below the summit. I found a shady flat rock thrusting up through the snow, and I sat down to eat the carbohydrate portion of my larder: the banana, raisins and cookies. After resting for fifteen minutes flat on my back, I started off again feeling noticeably stronger and without any discomfort.

An hour and a half later when I reached the top I polished off the fat-rich chicken leg, the cheese and the last of the cookies. After a nap and a relatively easy hour exploring the summit ridge I made the quick trip down feeling comfortable and strong. If I had eaten the fat and protein components of my lunch instead of the carbohydrates before reaching the top I know from experience that I would have been very uncomfortable when I resumed the climb. I would also have been further slowed by the lack of quick energy which the carbohydrate provided me. Since fat digestion yields the most heat, it makes sense in cold country to partake just before retiring on a cold night for leisurely digestion while you sleep. There is no more potent source of fat calories than cooking oil, so I take a pull on the bottle or pour a dash in the stew when calories are needed and there's time for digestion.

With the exception of vitamin C (which is a natural antibiotic and prevents infection and is best taken in pill form), vitamins and minerals can usually be forgotten since they are provided in adequate quantity by any reasonably balanced diet. Even though storage is comparatively small, there is virtually no effect on the body for at least a month if vitamins and minerals are absent under normal conditions.

Severe conditions are different. For instance, on a month long mountaineering trip above 14,000 feet in the Bolivian Andes I daily took Stress Potency Vitamin C and B Complex for better body performance. A climber friend takes along Vitamin E because it aids oxygenating his blood at high altitude. And people who are going to feel weak or uneasy without their vitamin pills should certainly take them along.

In recent years, there has been considerable study and experimentation in an effort to produce maximum work capacity in climbers, backpackers and cross-country skiiers. Dr. Per-Olaf Astrand (*Nutrition Today*, June 1968) suggests that work capacity can be increased as much as 300% by careful dietary preparation. His studies show that a carbohydrate-rich diet several days in advance of heavy prolonged exercise greatly improves the body's respiratory quotient (oxygen supply) and thereby improves capacity for prolonged hard work. (Utilization of carbohydrate depends on the rate at which oxygen is supplied to working muscles.)

The most startling increase in work capacity comes from emptying the body's store of glycogen about a week in advance, then building up a fresh store just a few days before the trip. Glycogen is a starch normally stored in the body in small quantities. It can be quickly converted into glucose to answer sudden energy demands upon the body. The higher the body's glycogen content, the greater its work capacity.

Dr. Astrand found that a man who could do one hour of heavy work on a fat-protein diet could do two and a half hours of the same work after that diet had been heavily supplemented with carbohydrates for three days. When the man flushed the glycogen from his system a week in advance and followed the same diet, he was able to produce up to four hours of work.

So the backpacker who wishes to start a trip on Sunday with the greatest possible capacity for prolonged exertion should, the Sunday before, load up a pack and take a practice hike that thoroughly tires him out. Then on Sunday, Monday and Tuesday he should eat fat and protein exclusively to keep his glycogen down—avoiding carbohydrates—get plenty of sleep and limit his exercise to a walk around the block. On Wednesday, Thursday, Friday and Saturday he should gorge on carbohydrates while continuing to consume ample protein and fat. On Sunday he should be admirably prepared for the most strenuous hike.

To prepare balanced, potent menus the backpacker obviously needs to be able to evaluate any given food. The best source of information I know is Agriculture Handbook No. 8, entitled *Composition of Foods* (available from the U.S. Government Printing Office, Washington, D.C. 20402).

For each of the thousands of foods listed the number of calories per

lunch time..

pound or per 100 grams (equal to 3½ ounces) is given, as well as a percentage breakdown into water, protein, fat, carbohydrates vitamins and minerals. Food combinations like granola are not listed and cannot be computed accurately, and brand names have been excluded, but it is possible to estimate the quantity and types of fuel contained in most backpacking foods with reasonable accuracy.

Before considering individual foods, it might be worthwhile to take a look at what I eat on a typical summer day at, say, 8,000 feet in the California Sierra.

DINNER: Invariably I begin with a Maggi, Knorr or Lipton Soup Mix that yields 1½-2 cups of thick, hot soup per man, the first step in replacing liquid lost during the day. For maximum potency I fortify the soup with a gob of butter or a slosh of cooking oil and perhaps some bacon bar or TVP. Any leftover jerky or milk powder may also get dumped in the soup. We cook it in our one big pot and drink it out of our oversized plastic cups, accompanied with a few crackers from the lunch supply.

When there is still half an inch of soup in the pot (for flavor) I empty in the contents of one of my favorite Oregon Freeze Dry dinners and stir in the required amount of cold water. This is contrary to the directions on the package which call for adding boiling water, but by mixing ingredients before heating I maximize valuable soaking time. At 8,000 feet the time needed to rehydrate the casserole may be twice the five minutes advertised, and twenty minutes is better than ten if you don't like your meat hard and rubbery. When the meal, say Beef Almondine, is half cooked (i.e. the meat portion is no longer rock hard) I add my salt and pepper mix (to taste), mushroom slices, fine herbs mix (with restraint) and whatever other flavors or fortifications that seem appropriate on that particular evening.

With the aid of big spoons we eat the resulting stew in our unwashed soup cups. The moment the pot is empty and scraped, I fill it with water to simplify future cleaning because experience has taught me that stew allowed to dry will set up like concrete! Once the stew is off the stove a small pot or teakettle containing about three cups of water goes on—saving stove fuel. When the water is half heated we use a little in our empty cups to clean out the grease, polishing with a piece of paper towel. Into the hot water goes applesauce, probably pre-mixed with cinnamon and nutmeg. By the time a few raisins and a dash of honey have been stirred in, this pre-cooked dish is ready for consumption in the cleaned soup-stew cups. The final course is hot tea, along with snack foods, and it continues until bedtime.

BREAKFAST: I'm rarely hungry in the morning and therefore eat more from necessity (to fuel the furnace) than desire. I have no interest in eating bacon and eggs, and still less in the arduous preparation involved. But I get off to a good start nevertheless, with a cup of granola or Birchermuseli, which has been pre-mixed with Milkman milk powder, raisins, dates and nuts. In mild weather I add cold water and perhaps a topping of crunchy freeze-dry Mountain House strawberries.

If it's cold or the morning will be strenuous, I transform my mixture into hot cereal by adding boiling water and a dollop of honey. I'll also drink a cup or two of Sherpa tea (a tablespoon of butter, margarine or cooking oil and Milkman in strong brewed tea), with honey and maybe a squirt of lemon juice. Sherpa tea, a sort of hot buttered rum—with tea instead of rum—is all that sustains the Sherpa porters who carry enormous loads at extremely high elevation in the Himalayas. Taken with plenty of carbohydrates, its fat content poses no digestive problems, even for early starts on the trail.

LUNCH: As soon as I feel the first faint pangs of hunger or fatigue I begin to eat lunch. What I eat depends a lot on whether I'm climbing, hiking under load or just sitting in camp watching the squirrels play. In the morning I favor pure carbohydrates: periodic sucks on the honey bottle, dried fruit and crackers. At a "sit down" lunch we customarily break out the thin-sliced, compressed Pumpernickle and make sand-wiches with butter, cheese, salami, peanut butter and jam, and make up a quart of Wyler's lemonade. If the morning has been strenuous we may substitute Gookinaid ERG, a sugarless electrolyte that's less tasty but more thirst-quenching. We may also dip into the dates or banana flakes to satisfy a sweet tooth, or break open the bag of gorp. Tradi-tional gorp is equal parts raisins, peanuts and M & M chocolate drops. I substitute carob drops for difficult-to-digest chocolate and salted al-monds or cashews for peanuts, and I use honey-dipped raisins. My gorp may also include banana flakes, sunflower seeds, date nuggets, and so forth. I like my gorp salty and will shake in salt if needed. Gorp is concentrated and potent and should be eaten in small quantities, along with plenty of liquid to avoid a stomach ache. Together with dried fruit it keeps me going until dinner is ready. I try to remind myself that what I'm eating is low on bulk but dehydrated and concentrated: so I must drink lots of liquids and restrain myself from the urge to eat until full.

making dinner — the hard way

There are too many potentially good backpacking foods for anyone to list, much less try, them all. Over the years I've developed a list of foodstuffs that meet my criteria and continue to satisfy. Listings are alphabetical.

APPLESAUCE, apple slices, etc. The apple is the most widely available, generally most pleasing of dehydrated or dried fruits, and it has the highest calorie count (353 per 3½ oz.) of the common fruits. As indicated earlier, applesauce lends itself to a variety of spices and additives. There are myriad brands to choose from, some raw, some instant, some with sugar, some without. I buy mine freeze-dried in bulk from Mountain House and prepackage it by the meal with cinnamon, etc.

BACON, raw. While delicious and a great source of fat calories, bacon is heavy, prone to spoil, messy, difficult to prepare, and 80% of its calories end up in the grease which is difficult to handle and generally thrown away. Furthermore it requires carrying a skillet. I love crisp bacon but I wouldn't think of taking the raw stuff backpacking.

BACON BAR, made by Wilsons, Richmoor and Mountain House, on the other hand, is a nearly perfect product. It's three ounces of precooked, lean bacon offers a compressed, well packaged, zero preparation, succulent source of fat and protein that's equivalent to three times as much raw bacon. It's high calories and strong flavor make it useful as spice and fortification as well as a snack and emergency ration. I think of it as the modern day equivalent of the fabled and invaluable pemmican.

BAKING: A great many people enjoy baking biscuits, cornbread, gingerbread, bannock, coffee cake and the like, and fresh baked breads are extremely welcome, even craved, after a number of days on the trail. Bakery products can provide considerable power, especially the sweet ones that are cooked with (or eaten with) butter or margarine. However, pre-baked products (bread, cake, doughnuts) are seldom practical for backpacking trips, being usually mangled and squashed into an unrecognizable paste.

BEANS: A staple for travelers since the beginning of time, beans provide a fair source of carbohydrate and bulk and a popular starch base for many one-pot dinners. The raw bean is virtually uncookable at high altitude. Only precooked dehydrated or freeze-dry beans should be carried.

BOOZE (serious): Except for beer in warm weather I'm not a drinking man, but I've learned that a small belt of something potent can be marvelously beneficial under certain circumstances. Spirits are low at the end of a hard day when you ease the pack off weary shoulders and grimly contemplate setting up camp and cooking dinner in the wind and dark. At such a time, nothing restores cheer by blotting out discomfort like a shot of painkiller, even if you don't drink. Some like the shot of the legendary 200 (actually 190) proof rum in a cup of snow; others prefer a tall one to help relieve thirst. I nearly always carry a few ounces of something potent in a sturdy plastic bottle for those tired times at the end of some days. My surprised companions, even the non-drinkers, are delighted!

BREAD: The problem with breads is bulk, spoilage, ease of crushing and drying out. Generally speaking, the harder and darker the better. Pumpernickle, Rye, Oatmeal and German Black are all good, yielding about 250 calories per 3½ ounces. A variety of small unsliced exotic loaves are now available at organic and health stores, but one must beware of labels that brag of absence of preservatives, for mold will quickly grow. My favorite bread in recent years has been either of two brands by Orowheat: Westphalian Pumpernickle squares and Oro d'Oeuvre. A one pound "loaf" of either contains two packets, each with a dozen compressed, cracker-thin slices of strong delicious dark rye. Amazingly enough it keeps for more than a year, spreads easily and resists mangling and crumbling.

BOUILLON: Virtually weightless, ageless, foil-wrapped cubes are ideal for flavoring soups and casseroles and for impromptu broth when the body is too tired for food or a sudden storm makes a hot drink at lunchtime desirable.

BUTTER (MARGARINE): Only oils and animal fats surpass butter and margarine (about 720 calories per 3½ ounces) as a source of fat. Served in Sherpa tea at breakfast, on bread or crackers at lunch, and in soup or stew at dinner, butter palatably provides an ideal source of high yield, long-lasting energy. Parkay offers margarine in a lock-top plastic squeeze bottle designed for camping.

CANDY: Because candy is mostly sugar, which I believe harms the body, I no longer carry it, substituting honey and such sweet fruits as dates, raisins, pineapple and bananas. But candy provides quick carbohydrate energy and is often craved in the wilds. Favorites are lemon drops, toffee, caramels, hard candies, sour balls, butterscotch and bitter orange.

CANNED GOODS: Many a backpacker still carries canned tuna, corned beef, Spam, sardines, Vienna sausage, etc. for lunch or to bulwark a starchy dinner. Not only is such food unjustifiably heavy, the cans, when empty, are often left in the wilds. With all the good inexpensive dehydrated food available in the markets nowadays, there's no excuse for carrying canned foods into the wilderness. And in some areas glass and cans are now banned.

CASSEROLES made from scratch allow experienced trail cooks to concoct their favorite one pot dinners for any number of people with some cost savings over pre-packaged freeze-dried dinners. See the end of the chapter for recipe sources.

CEREALS, COLD: Birchermuesli, with an energy yield of about 350 calories per 3½ ounce serving, is a long-time favorite backpacking dry cereal, but the profusion of packaged and homemade granolas are just as powerful, especially when fortified with wheat germ, nuts, fruit, milk powder. etc. A pre-mixed, sackful that allows close to a cup per person per morning conveniently solves the breakfast problem for many, especially those of us who don't care much for breakfast, especially if we have to cook it.

CEREAL, HOT: Cold cereal, of course, can provide additional comfort if made with boiling water, but in heavy weather with a strenuous morning ahead nothing provides long lasting power better than fresh cooked oatmeal or other high potency hot cereal, especially if fortified with butter, milk, honey, raisins, etc. Single serving packets of pre-cooked instant oatmeal with fruit or spice and sugar (called "minute mush" at our house) are wonderfully convenient but carry considerably less punch than uncooked oats.

CHEESE: Deservedly a mountaineering staple because of its high energy output (almost 400 calories per 3½ ounces for Cheddar— divided about equally between protein and fat), cheese, nevertheless, produces little more than half the energy per ounce of margarine. And even relatively dry Cheddar and Swiss have a very considerable (34-40%) water content. Soft cheese like Jack, Edam and Blue are often more than 50% water. The driest cheeses are Italian Romano, Parmesan, Provoloni, Kasseri, etc. I love cheese but carry it mainly on day hikes or short trips because it's heavy and doesn't travel well.

CHOCOLATE: is one of the most difficult-to-digest foods known to man, partly because it's more than half fat and protein. It's a grave mistake to think of it as candy. Eaten during strenuous exercise it's more likely to provide a queasy stomach than a burst of energy. In addition it contains more caffein than coffee, and eaten before bed it may easily inhibit sleep. I mention it only because its sweetness has made it popular with trail travelers, not because I ever carry it. Be warned! Cocoa mix is likewise popular because of its sweetness, but I avoid it because of its chocolate content. Carob (bars, drink, chips, etc.) is a delicious high potency carbohydrate substitute for chocolate. It is available wherever natural or health foods are sold.

COOKIES and bars are always popular in the wilds because sweets and bakery goods enjoy enhanced appeal. The fignewton is the classic backpacking cookie but oatmeal cookies have always been my favorites. An increasing number of fruit and granola bars on the market are augmented by numerous recipes for homemade creations. Basically these are compounded of the ingredients of granolas, gorps and fruits, mixed together with eggs, water, shortening and salt and baked in the oven. At some point cookies merge with...

CRACKERS: Hard biscuits and crackers, hard-pan, pilot biscuit, Triscuit and the like, though subject to breakage, are preferred by many to bread, because of the reduced bulk and water content and freedom from slicing and spoilage. Wheat thins, rye saltines, Rye-crisp, Melba toast and Zweibach all have their fans. The chief drawback to crackers is their tendency to shatter and crumble, but I like them well enough to carry a lightweight plastic box that keeps them intact for lunch, soup-dipping and snacks.

DRINKS, FRUIT: Wyler's lemonade and other flavors, and similar drinks by a number of imitators, come in foil envelopes weighing 3½ ounces, including sugar, that make a quart of imitation, but refreshing lemonade with a few shakes of the poly bottle. Also popular are fruit juices made from citric powders, orange and grapefruit crystals, Tang, Kool Aid and Fizzies. Artificially sweetened drinks are lighter and less bulky. Tea and coffee, though easy to make with bags and freeze-dried powders, offer zero food value unless fortified with butter (Sherpa Tea), milk powder, honey or sugar. The stimulation they provide comes from caffein. Herb teas won't keep you awake.

ERG, as previously noted, is superior to lemonade and similar drinks in that it is formulated as an electrolyte to replace nutrients lost in sweating and therefore quench thirst; it is also free of sugar. Long distance runners rely on it. Canned fruit juices are popular on deserts or climbs where water is absent and must be carried, but should not be considered for ordinary backpacking.

EGGS, OMELETES: Powdered eggs have come a long way since they gagged the foot soldier in World War II; they now are available from every food manufacturer in a variety of highly edible forms. Omelet fanciers and those for whom breakfast is not breakfast without eggs, can easily find a different featherweight dish for every morning of the week packed in foil or plastic, usually with ham or bacon bits. Calorie content is very substantial (usually upwards of 600 calories per 3½ ounces). I don't carry eggs because I'm not fond of them, dislike the preparation and cleanup entailed and rarely carry the necessary frying pan or skillet.

FREEZE-DRY FOODS: Makers of pre-cooked, heat-in-the-package, freeze-dry dishes and meals for backpackers have continually improved and refined their products. The leader, Oregon Freeze-Dry, offers more than 100 different entrees, fruits, soups, snacks, desserts and drinks under its Mountain House label, found in mountaineering stores, and still others under its pan-packed Teakettle brand, found in markets. Developed for Apollo and Sky Lab Astronauts, these foods are now compressed for lowest bulk, and a breakdown of nutritional values aids menu planning. Richmoor, with its Cook-in-the-bag entrees, leads a number of other freeze-dry food processors.

FRUIT, DRIED: Sun or sulphur dried apricots, peaches, dates, figs, prunes, bananas, etc. contain 25% water and are consequently heavy, but their chewiness make them delightful as snacks on trips where weight is not critical. Whereas sun-dried apricots yield 260 calories per 3½ oz. serving, the dehydrated version, with only 3.5% water, provides 332 calories. Fruit is excellent stewed, with cereal and baked in breads or cake. When I go day hiking I nearly always carry sweet, sticky dried bananas from Ecuador, honey-dipped pineapple from Taiwan or Greek figs. On longer trips I lean toward lighter banana chips, date nuggets and freeze-dried peaches and strawberries.

molasses – a natural laxative

GORP recipes are legion. While the traditional mix is salted peanuts, M & M chocolates and raisins, gorp can be broadly defined as a sack full of mixed dry high-potency savory snack foods. Extremists live on it. Others dislike it. I eat it at any time of the day if I'm hungry. It flavors and fortifies breakfast oatmeal mush, keeps my energy up on the trail during the day and serves as dessert after lunch and dinner. My basic ingredients are carob chips, salted cashews or almonds and honey dipped raisins.

HONEY is indispensible for those of us who don't carry sugar. Although sticky, heavy and liquid, honey behaves well enough in a sturdy screw-capped squeeze bottle or Gerry tube. There is no quicker source of potent carbohydrate energy (300 calories per 3½ oz.), and honey is only 17.2% water. It's sweet delicate flavor makes it valuable as a spread, dessert, syrup, frosting and sweetener for drinks.

making lemonade

INSTANT BREAKFAST: On the face of it, Instant breakfast and its relatives like Tiger's Milk should be ideal for backpacking, but my friends and I have reluctantly abandoned them because they dependably produce diarrhea within an hour if we are hiking. I have not tried them on inactive layover days, but I suffer no ill effects in the city where fresh, rather than powdered milk is used.

JAM: Like honey, jam and jelly tend to be messy and should be packed in reusable Gerry tubes. They offer slightly fewer calories and nearly 30% water, but are extremely welcome in the wilds.

JELLO has its fans as a drink, hot or cold, and as a chilled and set dessert, often with fruits or vegetables mixed in. I no longer carry it because it's mostly sugar and because preparation and cleanup efforts do not seem justified.

MEAT, FRESH: For years I carried a fresh, juicy steak to broil the first night out. Gradually I discovered that it was my city oriented association with steak, not the steak itself, that seemed appetizing. On that first night in the wilds, steak usually has less appeal for the weary hiker than soup, starchy stew and cold lemonade.

MEAT, DRIED: Freeze-dried chicken, beef and meatballs are invaluable when making stews from scratch, but ham and corned beef offer more flavor. Allow maximum time for rehydration, preferably in hot bouillon, if you don't want it rubbery because water penetrates meat cells slowly. Beef jerky is a tasty trail food, but cannot be re-constituted and is therefore unavailable for cooking (it will flavor soup, but bouillon is better and cheaper). Dry salami, though 30% water, yields 450 calories of fat and protein per 3½ ounces and keeps very well unsliced inside its skin.

MILK, ETC.: Like dried eggs, dehydrated milk has gradually come to taste almost like the real thing—especially when allowed to stand fifteen minutes, and served cold. Most convenient are 4 ounce foil packages of Milkman instant low-fat dry milk product, which make a quart with a few shakes of the poly bottle. The flavor is better than that of whole, skim or non-fat milk products. A few drops of vanilla or a little coffee or cocoa mix help mask the slightly artificial flavor. Malted milk powder and milkshake mixes are favored by some, but the latter, including sugar, seems excessively heavy. Milkman probably yields over 400 calories per 3½ ounces.

MOLASSES: This raw, crude liquid cane sugar, though nearly 25% water, quickly converts to energy and is used like honey or jam by those who like the strong sweet flavor. And a teaspoon or two works beautifully as a gentle natural food laxative—often necessary after a change from city fare to a steady diet of low bulk, dehydrated food.

NUTS: Dried, roasted, salted nuts (almonds, walnuts, pecans, peanuts, etc.) contain very little water and yield 525-700 calories per 3½ ounces, divided roughly into two parts fat and one part each of protein and carbohydrate. Nuts are an ideal snack and a perfect complement to high carbohydrate candy, fruit and bread. Peanut butter, though sticky, is a fine source of protein and fat when carried in a Gerry squeeze tube or a can. Sunflower, sesame and other seeds are equally potent and popular as snack food and in gorp or granola.

OIL, carried mainly for frying pancakes or fish, is the unexcelled source of pure fat calories, producing 884 per 3½ oz. Ultra weight conscious extremists have tried to subsist on periodically ingested oil capsules, severely taxing their digestive systems and inviting difficulty during strenuous activity. Vegaline is easier to use than butter or margarine for greasing the skillet. I generally carry a small plastic bottle of cooking oil, even though I am not equipped to fry, and use it to fortify stews and other dishes when there is leisure for fat digestion. And I sometimes take a pull on the bottle before retiring on especially cold nights.

PANCAKES: I shudder when I think how many hours I have spent cooking pancakes in the hot morning sun and then cleaning out the gluey batter pot. Pancakes, in my view, belong to the dark ages of backpacking on the basis of preparation alone.

PEMMICAN: The legendary wonder food on which the mountain

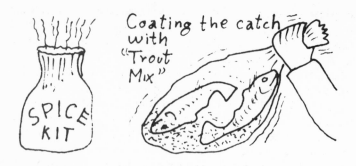

Coating the catch with "Trout Mix"

SPICE KIT

men of the early west lived almost exclusively, takes some getting used to and is therefore not ideal as a steady diet for recreational backpackers on comparatively short trips. A balanced diet, strong on carbohydrates, will produce more energy and contentment. True pemmican is half lean dried meat, half cooked animal fat, with the two mashed together into a paste. Recipes for pemmican and jerky are widely available. See Bacon Bar.

POTATOES: Like beans, potatoes are a favorite base and source of bulk in one-pot dinners. Instant potato powders easily produce genuine-tasting mashed potatoes, and the leftovers can be fried for breakfast. Potato cubes are great in stews, hash and french-fried.

PUDDINGS: Satisfying desserts that contrast well with sweet trail snacks can be a problem in the wilds where sweets are craved. Puddings (like Jello Instant) can be bought cheaply in the markets and shaken with milk powder in a plastic bag (later burned); since they set promptly without regard to temperature, they are a boon to backpackers. Mountaineering shops offer a number of excellent puddings, as well as strudels, cobblers, pies and cheesecakes, many of which (ideally) require neither cooking nor containers.

SPICES, as earlier detailed, are the essential ingredients I rely on to transform comparatively simple fare into exciting eating. A word of warning: use restraint. Too much of the wrong spice can impair edibility. On overnight or weekend trips I rely solely on my salt mixture and Spice Islands' "Fines Herbes," a mixture of thyme, oregano, sage, rosemary, marjoram and basil. A half teaspoon of this safe, all-purpose seasoning will perk up any one-pot dinner.

SALTS: Individual shakers for various salts and peppers are a nuisance to open and close in the dark. After struggling with various clever designs, I have returned to a single shaker loaded with two parts salt to one each of pepper and onion, garlic and celery salt. This all-purpose seasoning is just as good on eggs or stew as on trout; my companions have yet to complain. With my salt mix in one shaker and Spice Islands Fines Herbes in another, I am well equipped with flavor for short trips.

STARCHES, OTHER: Like beans, potatoes and pancakes, spaghetti, noodles, rice and macaroni form the heart (and provide the bulk) of a backpacker's casserole. Kraft Dinner, which served me in Boy Scout days, is still a good bet, especially when cooked with a packet of freeze-dried chicken, slivered almonds, sliced mushrooms and the above mentioned herb mix.

Pre-cooked Minute rice is the quickest of starches to prepare, but pasta has more protein and a shade more calories. The most convenient starch I know is Top Ramen, now widely available in markets. Three ounce packets of pre-cooked, dry Chinese noodles are packaged with pork, chicken, beef, oriental or onion bouillon mix. With three cups of boiling water, Top Ramen is noodle soup for two in three minutes. With only one cup, you have the starchy base on which to build a satisfying noodle dinner.

TVP stands for "textured vegetable protein." Made from de-fatted soybean flour, this widely available product contains more than 50% protein and 10% fat. Far superior to "hamburger helpers," it comes flavored to taste like ham, beef, chicken, bacon, hamburger—especially if simmered in the appropriate bouillon base. Although soy protein lacks some of the amino acids found in meat, milk, cheese, or eggs, it has been a boon to the backpacker as a potent, fast-cooking meat substitute additive, economically stretching expensive freeze-dried meat. In fact, TVP has revolutionized backpack cooking.

VEGETABLES are despised by many (at home as well as on the trail), but they are indispensible as components of balanced, interesting one pot dinners. I depend on mushrooms, onions, peas, carrots, celery and tomato flakes to add bulk, flavor and calories to an over-concentrated, low-bulk diet. The longer I am out, the better vegetables taste.

With my emphasis on simplicity and my insistence on ease of preparation, I am doubtless missing out on some marvelous dishes. Readers seeking inspiration, or recipes, are urged to obtain THE WELL-FED BACKPACKER by June Fleming and/or BACKPACKER'S COOKBOOK by Margaret Cross and Jean Fiske. These ladies know their way around in both the wilds and the kitchen.

7 COOKING

For most backpackers, unfortunately, cooking in the wilds is a necessary evil. So anything that promotes greater comfort in the kitchen will surely enhance the pleasure of a trip. As with most aspects of backpacking, the simpler and easier the arrangements, the smoother things go. Unless you're a gourmet, cooking will be easier if you carry a stove.

A decade ago the backpacking stove was a mysterious contrivance carried by climbers traveling on snow or well above treeline, or a luxury for the fussy or mechanically minded. Today it is regarded as essential equipment by a majority of backpackers. The biggest reason for the change is the growing scarcity of firewood in the high country. Wilderness managers have encouraged the use of stoves in heavily traveled areas or where fire danger is high, and in a few places wood fires have been banned altogether, making a stove a necessity. Lesser contributing factors include the improvement and refinement of the stoves themselves, leading to an increase in their popularity. Then there is the growing disinclination to deal with sooty pots and smoky fires, and the trend toward simple one-pot dinners—aided considerably by the proliferation of good freeze-dried and dehydrated meals in local markets.

In summary, people nowadays want cooking to be as easy as possible. They carry a stove to avoid mess, uncertainty and extra hours in the kitchen—as well as to conserve firewood. They have learned that a stove means even, dependable, controllable heat, without the need to build a rock fireplace, hunt for wood, nurse a fire, fight smoke and falling ashes, and deal with wildly varying heat output that often means scorched or uncooked food. Backpacking stoves have not only gained acceptance, they have become a badge of outdoor know-how and ecological awareness—heavily used areas are beginning to benefit.

Stoves, of course, have drawbacks, too. The small single burner means only one dish at a time can be cooked, and the first course will not stay warm while the next is cooking. The small concentrated circle of heat makes cooking on large surfaces (frying pancakes or trout) difficult. No stove works well, if at all, if not well-sheltered from wind. A shelter must be built if none can be found. Then there is the fiddling with fuel, the assembling, priming and preheating, and, of course, the weight of the stove and fuel. But I view the lack of a second burner as a blessing rather than a limitation; it forces me to employ one-dish dinners or eat in courses, which enormously simplifies meal planning and automatically rules out fussy, difficult-to-prepare city-type meals.

A good many backpackers have never purchased a stove because they look so intricate, because they are rumored to explode, or simply because the catalogs and shops offer such a bewildering assortment. With as many as three dozen models to choose from, how does one know which is best? The guidelines that follow should reassure the buyer as to intricacy and safety and help him narrow the field to not more than two or three models.

The majority of stoves can be eliminated, for instance, if your stove must work in the snow. Conversely, if temperatures will always be above freezing, you can afford to carry lighter, cheaper stoves. But even if you're a summer camper, high altitude use means your stove must have cold weather capability. Will your stove have to cook for only one or two, or will you require a stove able to handle big pots. If your family or group usually numbers four, will you prefer two small ones or a big one? Do you need a torch for melting snow, or a stove that will simmer a delicate dish?

Once you've answered these questions you can consider weight. Stoves come in a wide range of weights, from 1-3½ lbs., without fuel. Obviously the big winter stoves will weigh the most—as much as three times the weight of a summer stove. Most backpackers feel strongly about weight. Many will say, "I'm willing to carry X pounds, but no more." Stoves tend to bring forth emotions. People often discover they have strong—and sometimes contradictory— feelings about one or more aspects of stove ownership and operation, and these feelings usually have a strong influence on choice.

Stove weight cannot be considered arbitrarily. Heavy stoves offer more power and sometimes other advantages, such as simmering ability, stability, durability, etc. And stove weight cannot be considered without regard to the fuel weight needed to do the necessary cooking. Light stoves tend to cook more slowly and use more fuel to accomplish their work. Over a period of a week, a light but inefficient stove might use so much more fuel that its weight advantage completely disappears when compared to a heavier but more efficient stove. So the lightest stove is not always best, or even the lightest source of the needed heat. Don't choose your stove on weight alone.

Ease of operation can also be a snare. While operating instructions are often mind boggling the first time you read them, be assured that they become routine and automatic once learned—and the learning can and should be done at home. Don't reject a stove on the basis of what look like complicated instructions. After fiddling at home for an hour or two you'll be able to forget the directions and set forth confidently, knowing you'll be able to run the stove without inordinate thought—except for safety procedures. Nevertheless, some stoves are far easier to operate than others, and since simplicity is the watchword I would urge you to pick the simplest stove that meets all other criteria.

Cost will be a big factor for some people. Again it will be necessary to consider the cost of fuel, which has been steadily rising since the oil shortage began. Fuel cost was negligible when kerosene and white gas both cost less than a dollar a gallon. But fuel for a long trip can now cost almost as much as the stove. Stoves now cost $12-70, but Chevron Blazo (white gas) now costs $3 a gallon and kerosene, once the cheap fuel, is close to $5. But the comparable cost of butane or propane may be 3-800% higher. Butane stoves cost $12-30; kerosene models run $35-65 and gas stoves range $25-75.

Heat output or stove power is usually measured (for purposes of comparison only) in the time required to boil a quart of water. It is vital to evaluate stove performance under the worst conditions you expect to face. Remember that heat output can be sharply reduced by cold and virtually destroyed if the stove is not protected from wind. Kept above freezing and sheltered from the breeze, most stoves to be considered here will perform adequately, and boiling time will not be an important factor—unless conditions are always cold, the cook is impatient or the trip is unusually long. As with other criteria, you'll be happier in the kitchen if you do not skimp on stove capability.

Fuel capacities of backpacking stoves vary greatly, but with few exceptions frequent refueling is part of the price you pay for small weight and bulk in a backpacking stove. The essential thing is to avoid refueling while dinner is cooking, which is accomplished by planning ahead more than buying a stove with a large fuel tank. Few stoves will go without refueling for even a short weekend trip, much as we wish they would. People can get quite emotional about refueling and carrying extra fuel, with all the risks of spilling, puncture, explosion, etc. Some travelers carry butane stoves solely to avoid the necessity of ever having to worry about a bottle of gasoline or kerosene in their pack. Be sure to carefully consider burning time before you purchase a stove. With any stove you're going to have to compute before each trip just how much fuel you'll have to take along. You'll feel sorry for yourself if you bring home too much, or if you run out ahead of time.

Some stoves offer very little flame adjustment. They're either on or they're off and difficult or impossible to adjust. About the only use for such a stove, to my way of thinking, is melting great quantities of snow efficiently—providing you've another stove for simmering the stew. While a good many of the best backpacking meals only require adding the contents of the package to boiling water (turn off stove, stir, wait five minutes, then eat) I insist on good flame adjustability, and the best new stoves provide it. It's exasperating to try to cook on a

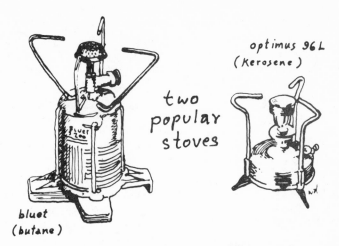

optimus 96 L
(Kerosene)

two
popular
stoves

bluet
(butane)

stove that burns whatever is on the bottom of the pot and goes out when you try to turn it down. To me, simmering (low flame) ability is important for even primitive cooking. Gourmets feel even more strongly on this point.

Easy starting is another endearing attribute in a stove. The procedure, as will be seen, is quite different for each class of stove and type of fuel. A great many people will choose a butane stove solely because it starts just like the gas stove at home, whereas liquid fuel stoves require a more involved and often alarming procedure. Lighting a pool of gasoline and watching the stove enveloped in a flaring flame can produce great anxiety, especially inside a tent. Still, the anxiety disappears in most people once proficiency is attained and the process becomes automatic.

Stove stability may not seem important until you've had a stove fall over and the dinner you've been hungrily awaiting ends up in the dirt. Stove makers have put insufficient thought into stability design and a good many of their creations are still dangerously wobbly. Beware a stove that has skimpy pot supports, tips easily, has a small base or stands inordinately tall. Poor stability in the kitchen will produce anxiety in the cook.

Wind resistance is of prime importance. It is placed near the end of the list because comparatively few stoves offer adequate wind protection. It isn't so much a matter of choice as it is of placing the stove thoughtfully out of the wind. Wind protection is something you arrange or construct in the field, rather than something you buy in the store. The only stove that's well protected against wind is the MSR, and unfortunately the same principle cannot be transferred to other stoves. Because the lightest zephyr strongly affects stove performance —especially on simmer—wind protection remains the largest unsolved problem in the operation of most backpacking stoves.

Safety is the other great concern. The subject is complex because it's part psychological. All stoves, by their very nature, are potential bombs. Caution is always required. There are no foolproof stoves, but the dangers differ greatly in different kinds of stoves. Fuel connections, starting procedures, fuel volatility and the refueling process produce the greatest potential dangers. Experience, patience, common sense and caution, however, reduce the hazards for most people to acceptable levels. Specific danger areas will be discussed for each fuel and stove type.

The final considerations are durability, dependability and cleaning. Stoves that have been on the market for many years have proved durable and dependable. The bugs have been worked out, design has been refined and safety levels are usually good. Beware a brand new stove. Very few come to the marketplace without some flaw—and in some cases the flaws have been extremely dangerous. It's better to stick to the tried and true stoves described below rather than hope for miracles in an untried offering.

All liquid fuel stoves need to be cleaned, some more than others. Cleaning is either manual (with a fine wire that you run through the burner orifice) or built-in (the cleaning needle is integral, operated by a lever or valve). When impurities in liquid fuel cause inevitable clogging, the stove stops or runs poorly until the orifice is reamed out. The recent change in small Optimus gas stoves (Svea 123, 8R and 99) from manual to built-in cleaning has produced some problems. When the valve-activated cleaning needle sticks or runs off the track the flame is diminished or the stove is reluctant to shut off. The solution is to remove the burner with the wrench provided, turn the stove over so the needle assembly falls out, replace the burner and rely in the future on manual cleaning.

Fuel: White Gas, Kerosene, Butane, Propane

White gasoline (or the cleaner commercial versions: Coleman Fuel and Chevron Blazo) is highly potent, extremely volatile and quite capable of exploding. Unlike kerosene, spilled gasoline lights readily on clothes, hands or tent. Its cost is reasonable ($3/gallon and increasing), it is generally available in this country and it tends to be clean smelling, oil-free and produces less soot than kerosene. There are two classes of white gas stoves: the majority that require priming to heat the generator, and the Coleman Peak 1 and Optimus 323 which do not. On the one hand the volatility of white gas permits it to be used as its own priming fuel, so no separate priming fuel is needed. On the other hand this is a distinctly hazardous procedure—probably the greatest source of gas stove accidents—and ought to be avoided at all costs in tents. A variety of safe and convenient priming fuels (solid or paste) are available as an alternative, and I strongly urge readers to use them.

Kerosene, once the favored small stove fuel, is making a comeback —despite the fact that very few stoves are made for it and the once negligible price has now soared past that of white gas to nearly $5/gallon. Kerosene is slightly heavier than white gas but it is also

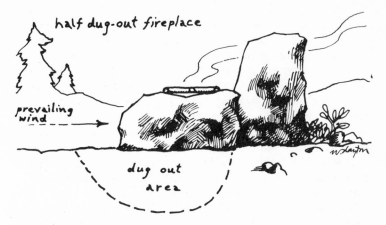

half dug-out fireplace

prevailing wind

dug out area

somewhat hotter. It produces more odor and soot, and since it does not light readily a separate priming fuel (again solid or paste primers are far safer than gasoline) is generally prescribed.

Kerosene is far more likely to be available in the distant corners of the world favored by expeditions and trekkers than is white gas, but the biggest reason for its recent gain in popularity is its safety. It will not explode under ordinary circumstances and spilled fuel will not turn into an instant fireball if accidentally ignited. If the winter camping trend continues (often requiring cooking in tents) more kerosene stoves will probably become available.

Butane and propane are compressed gasses sold in pressurized metal cartridges. The liability of explosion is low providing used cartridges are not thrown in the fire. Both fuels are considerably less potent than kerosene or gasoline, comparatively expensive and the least readily available. But both are clean and soot free. Since butane and propane stoves require no filling, priming or pre-heating, they are unquestionably the easiest and most convenient of backpacking stoves.

Butane comes in a low-pressure steel canister which is comparatively light, but the low pressure means that the gas will not vaporize when the temperature is below the freezing point of water (32°F) at sea level. And when butane is cold or the canister is near empty the flow is very poor. So butane is inefficient below 40°F and fails entirely when colder—except at altitude. The higher you go the better butane performs. It is important to remember when shopping for stoves that butane is basically a warm weather fuel.

Propane is stored under great pressure, which means that flow is excellent in cold weather or when the canister is nearly empty, but canisters must be thick walled to withstand the pressure. Although burning time is an impressive six hours, they are too heavy (two pounds, full) to be carried by most recreational backpackers. Propane stoves are used chiefly by large groups which have porters (or boy scouts) to carry the fuel. The greatest advantage of butane and propane is that lighting the stove is no more difficult than lighting a kitchen stove that has no pilot. Simply hold a lighted match to the burner an instant *before* turning on the gas.

Since all stoves are designed for maximum heat output, there are a number of operating hazards that the user should be aware of. In gas stoves the principal dangers occur during refueling. Funnels overflow, fuel bottles get knocked over, gas gets spilled on a hot stove, fuel tanks get too hot, campfires ignite nearby gasoline supplies, the cook panics during a flareup and knocks over the stove, burning himself and catching the tent on fire, a fuel check while cooking causes burnt fingers, a spill or a flare-up. Never forget that gas stoves can explode and spilled fuel can ignite in a flash. Because kerosene is far less volatile, all or most of these hazards are much reduced or nonexistent in kerosene stoves. But since the stove is red hot you can still get burned if you are less than cautious, and spilled kerosene can still burn up your tent.

Butane and propane stoves, because they're simple, are considered safe by many campers—and this is a dangerous assumption. Cartridge type stoves are just as dangerous as gas stoves, but the dangers are different, often unpredictable and less dramatically evident. Punctured canisters can turn into torches if ignited or foul your pack if undetected on the trail. And removing a canister that's defective or not yet empty, I can say from personal experience, can freeze your skin painfully. On rare occasions defective or poorly connected canisters spout fire like a torch without warning. Empty canisters thrown in the fire can explode, and butane stoves can erupt in tent-burning flareups when the canisters have been shaken vigorously or the temperature is too low.

Any kind of stove will produce dangerous levels of carbon monoxide if run in an enclosed space (tent). Carbon monoxide is sneaky stuff, invisible, almost odorless. The product of inevitable incomplete fuel combustion, it reduces the blood's ability to transport oxygen. Since high altitude has the same effect, it can be seen that the two are additive: the higher you are the more lethal carbon monoxide poisoning will be.

If tent ventilation isn't vigorous—as when buttoned up tightly against wind or storm—a burning stove consumes all the oxygen, causing the occupants of the tent to sweat, gasp and complain of headache and nausea. The danger is greatest in tube, Goretex or sealed fabric tents without vents. It is likewise greatest with the larger stoves, owing to their greater energy output and greater oxygen consumption. Pans so close to the burner that they deform the flame also contribute to incomplete combustion and therefore carbon monoxide production. If you cook in the tent, what you imagine to be high altitude sickness may, at least in part, be carbon monoxide poisoning. Beware!

Kerosene stoves can be lighted without a priming fuel by creating a wick. A twisted square of toilet paper tucked into a circle in the kerosene-filled spirit cup will light easily enough. But solid or paste

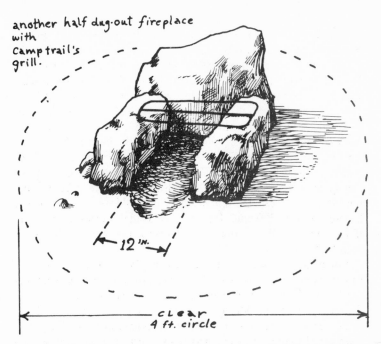

another half dug-out fireplace with Camptrail's grill.

←— 12 IN. —→

←————————— CLeaR —————————→
4 ft. circle

primers are safer, cleaner and much easier to use. And their value goes up if you must cook in a tent. Dependable primers include ESBIT fuel pellets, Optimus priming paste, Heat Tabs, Fire Ribbon and Hexamine. There are doubtless other good ones. Avoid lighter fluid, which is just as dangerouss as white gas.

With this background, the reader, it is hoped, will be able to more effectively consider the relative merits of the thirteen popular stoves I feel should be discussed.

ALPINMATIC is a butane stove with electronic ignition that makes it perhaps the easiest stove to use. Though new in this country, the stove has been made for 15 years and comes from Alladin Industries, long a fine maker of stoves. The cartridge which burns 2½-5 hours also fits the Bleuet and some Optimus stoves. Since the cartridge is the base, stability is only fair. Without cartridge the well-made but wind-vulnerable stove weighs only 10 oz. and costs $25.

BLEUET S200S is probably the most popular and most reliable butane stove ever made. Nevertheless, it has several drawbacks: even with the optional steel windscreen (4 oz.), the stove is highly wind vulnerable. The collapsable plastic base and the stove's considerable height make it distinctly rickety and unstable unless handled with great care. Like the Alpinmatic, and most butane stoves, the canister cannot be removed until empty and it takes experience to estimate gas remaining by weight. Finally, butane is a warm weather fuel unless the altitude is considerable. The Bleuet weighs 15 oz. without cartridge and sells for as little as $12. Cartridges last 2-3 hours, weigh 10 oz. and cost about $1.50 each, so fuel cost is high compared to liquid fuels.

GAZ GLOBETROTTER is the Bleuet's slicked up little brother. It comes neatly packed in a pair of aluminum cups which can be used for cooking. Using a half-sized cartridge, it sits closer to the ground and is therefore more stable, but fuel weight and cost are nearly doubled. The stove is also heavier (1 lb.) and more expensive ($22) than its brother. It is hard to see any net advantage in this easily packed, stable stove unless you have only one meal to prepare.

COLEMAN PEAK 1 may well be the best all around choice for a backpacking stove. Folding legs and low profile provide good stability. Its integral windscreen divides the flame into four segments, only one of which will blow out in moderate breezes. This is the first gas stove that requires no priming, so starting is quick and safe, and the integral pump provides high heat output even at high altitude or in cold weather. The flame is easily adjustable for excellent simmering control and the burner diameter is twice that of most stoves spreading the heat. Coleman has refined this stove considerably since it first came on the market, and now it's hard to beat. Weight is a hefty 1¾ pounds, empty, and a one pound filling of gas lasts almost 2½ hours at full throttle. Cost for the stove is a modest $30.

MSR (MOUNTAIN SAFETY RESEARCH) makes two models: the G burns white gas and the GK burns white gas plus kerosene, auto gas, diesel fuel, solvent, and stove oil, although most of the latter clog the orifice and require periodic cleanings. This unique and controversial stove substitutes a pump screwed into a Sigg pint or quart fuel bottle for the conventional fuel tank, cutting refueling chores considerably, providing fine stability and permitting the highly effective use of the MSR windscreen without overheating the remote fuel tank. There is a handy flint sparker for easy lighting, power output is unexcelled and performance is virtually unaffected by altitude, wind or cold. No stove offers better wind protection or more heat.

Now for the drawbacks. At $65-70 the stove is expensive—and that doesn't include the fuel bottle. Simmering control is very poor and the stove is fussy at less than full throttle. In fact this stove is a tinkerer's delight, a complex mechanism that requires considerable experience and mechanical ability before it is as "field maintainable" as advertised. Flare-up is common during priming and the design makes use of solid primers awkward. This is a fine stove for serious long distance trekkers, especially for melting great quantities of snow, but not for the casual summer weekend backpacker. Weight is 1¼ pounds for the stove alone and 2¾ pounds when a full quart Sigg bottle is added (for which burning time is an impressive 6½ hours, wide open).

OPTIMUS 8R is a small white gas stove which swings out of the compact blue box in which it is mounted. Unlike the Peak 1, it has no pump and requires priming to start. Consequently performance drops in the cold and high altitude when pressure inside the fuel tank may be difficult to maintain. To provide room for pressure buildup, the tank must never be filled more than three quarters full, and it must never be

sigg pot lids lift off easily when fitted with homemade knobs.

burned when empty or the wick will char and refuse to draw enough (or any) gas to the burner.

The 8R, believe it or not, is a modernized version (the case and low profile) of the sort of white gas stoves we used to use cheerfully because they were the best available. They still work well if conditions are right and you don't mind the fiddling or the hazards of priming. But at $35, the cost is $5 more than the superior Peak 1, and the weight saving is only 4 ounces.

OPTIMUS 99 is the 8R in an aluminum case, the top of which becomes a pot—if you don't mind a gasoline taste. There is also a convenient folding aluminum windscreen. The 99 costs about $4 more but weighs 2 oz. less. Otherwise, everything said about the 8R applies.

SVEA 123 works exactly the same as the 99 and 8R, but the configuration is completely different. The burner is mounted directly over the tank rather than beside it, and this means faster starting and less vulnerability to cold. This tiny round brass stove comes with a separate combination pot and top and a ventilated circular windscreen that is moderately effective in a small breeze. Though difficult to prime and only moderately stable, the Svea is an extremely popular small stove. Since it burns at full flame for little more than one hour, extra fuel must be carried for even a weekend trip. Like the 99 and 8R it has a built-in cleaning needle that sometimes gives trouble. Though designed to be primed with their own fuel, all three stoves are more safely and easily primed with the aforementioned solid or paste primers. Weight is just over a pound and cost is about $30.

The OPTIMUS PUMP was developed in the late seventies as an accessory to aid in starting the 8R, 99 and Svea in cold or high altitude conditions. It screws into the gas tank to provide instant pressure. Contrary to the hope of some, it does not alter priming requirements in the slightest. You still have to vaporize the gas before the stove will work. While the extra pressure produced by the pump yields a bigger, hotter flame that will cook faster, the increased heating capacity is more than offset by greater fuel consumption. Because the pump gets hot in the Svea's flame, all pumping must be completed before lighting the stove. The pump, which weighs 2 oz. and costs about $6, is a gadget to leave home unless you will be depending on one of these stoves in below freezing weather.

OPTIMUS 323 is clearly a copy of the wildly successful Peak 1. It is three ounces lighter, but in every other respect it is inferior to the original. Controls are badly placed, power, wind resistance, burning time and stability are all inferior and the price, at $45, is 50% higher.

OPTIMUS 111B is the big brother of the 8R, a gas stove with built-in pump that earned the accolade "a veritable blowtorch." Unfortunately, it is one of the heaviest (4 lbs.) and most expensive ($65-75) of all stoves. Like the MSR it is a powerful snow melter and nothing can excel it for cooking a two-gallon pot of stew (except perhaps its kerosene-fueled twin). For casual or small party summer backpacking, it's something of a dinosaur.

OPTIMUS 111 is a 3-oz. heavier model that runs on kerosene and costs about the same. Unlike most other kerosene stoves, which have no fuel valves, simmering control is quite good. Kerosene, remember, has the hottest flame, is easily obtainable and will not flash or explode under most circumstances. Jack Stephenson solves the weight problem by leaving the 34-oz. steel case home and replacing it with the Optimus 124 6-piece cook set and windscreen (12 oz., $19) to produce a safe, potent 4-season cooker for a sizeable party, easily lighted with ⅓ ESBIT fuel pellet.

OPTIMUS 45 is a handsome, all brass expedition-size kerosene stove with large fuel capacity for large groups. Stability is great, even with the largest kettles. Like other kerosene stoves it is unaffected by cold and can also burn stove oil and diesel fuel. Weight is a hefty 2½ lbs. and cost is $40 plus.

OPTIMUS 00(formerly OOL) is a scaled down model of the 45, an excellent, safe stove for a party of two. Since there is no fuel valve, flame height must be controlled solely by pressure maintained by the pump, which takes some practice and still does not yield a simmer flame to compete with the Peak 1. Kerosene provides some soot and has a distinctive odor. This little brass classic weights 1 lb., 11 oz. and costs $37. Neither of these stoves comes equipped with any sort of windscreen.

Wind is the number one nemesis of outdoor cooks, and veteran backpackers have learned that sheltering the stove from all but the faintest zephyr is an art that must be mastered if cooking is to be quick and efficient. Except for the MSR's effective circle of protection, windscreens that come with stoves are undependable at best. The burden is on the cook to build a wall or screen of rock or wood, get behind a downed tree, find a hollow, use a cooker or, as a last resort, retreat to the tent to find the still air essential to carefree cooking. If a part of the stove's burner will not stay lit or the flame blows out from under the pot, there is a serious loss of efficiency that should be corrected. Otherwise, fuel is wasted, cooking time is prolonged or food may never completely cook.

my best knife

The first step is to take pains to find a sheltered place to cook. Don't just set up the stove in the middle of camp. Number two, if shelter isn't sufficient, take the trouble to build an effective windbreak. Third (and easiest), don't set forth into the wilds without lids that fit snugly on every pot—and use them! Four, for windy conditions, pick a stove with good protection, use windscreens provided (as with the Bleuet, Svea, etc.) and reduce the space between pot and burner to about a quarter inch (if possible) by bending or modifying pot supports. You might also consider windscreens sold by Antelope and Trailwise.

Whatever stove you choose, you'll have to carry extra fuel. For gasoline or kerosene stoves that means tinned steel German fuel flasks with pouring spouts that pack conveniently because they're flat, or sleek, beautiful Sigg bottles. Both come in three sizes from ½ pint to quart. Bottles run 2-5 oz. and cost $4-5 while flasks are heavier (4-6 oz.) and cost $7.50-8. Plastic bottles are not suitable for fuel. Heavy cloth and plastic bags are useful for packing stoves, especially where a box is not included (or has been discarded). Also needed is a rag for cleaning both stove and cook, and the proper stove cleaning needle.

One of the prime disadvantages of stoves—keeping the first course warm while the second is cooking can be somewhat overcome by using a cooker, like the Sigg Tourist, made for the Svea 123. This 5-piece combination provides wind shelter for the stove, cooks one course while keeping another fairly warm and can function as a double boiler. It weighs a hefty 2¼ pounds and costs $28.

an eye-dropper fills the spirit cup.

The alternative to carrying a stove, of course, is to build one out of native material and gather native fuel to fire it. Ease, efficiency, and effectiveness are generally doubled by carrying a small grill. The smallest and lightest measures five by fifteen inches, is made of welded tubular steel, weighs only four ounces, cleans easily, comes in a fabric case and costs $8. It is easily mounted on a modest rock fireplace and will accommodate two carefully placed pots. There are many others variously available. The cheapest grills are oven and refrigerator shelves and broiler racks from used appliance and second-hand stores.

My favorite cooking fireplace design is the half-dugout. There are two advantages: smaller, flatter rocks can be used to insure a more stable structure, and the fire is easier to light and easier to protect from wind. If I were faced with rebuilding a heap of blackened rocks into an efficient cookstove—assuming the location is appropriate and safe—I would first clear a circle about four feet across and sort through the rocks in hopes of finding a matched pair about the size and shape of bricks. Such rocks are never to be found, of course, so I settle for the best I can find (concave upper surfaces are better than convex).

Using the direction of the breeze, the lay of the land and the pattern of branches on nearby trees to determine the path of the prevailing wind, I place my rocks parallel to that path and also to each other—about a foot apart. On the downwind end, I place a larger rock (or rocks) to form a chimney, so the resulting structure forms a squat 'U.' Then, using a sharp rock fragment as a trowel, I excavate about four inches of earth and charcoal from inside the pit. Now I am ready to place my lightweight grill across the opening, supporting it on the two 'bricks' as close as possible to the chimney. Care must be taken to see that it is solid and will not slide or wobble—or the dinner may end up in the fire!

I like to set my grill about two inches above ground level and six inches above the bottom of the firepit, but the proportions must sometimes be altered. On a windy day, I dig deeper and sometimes have to block the windward end with rocks to control the draft. Where there are no rocks at all and the grill sits directly on the ground, the firepit must be deeper still. Inexperienced stove builders invariably build too large a firebox and set the grill much too high. Increasing grill height from six to ten inches probably triples the volume of wood needed to cook dinner. Small fires are easier on the cook, easier on the wood supply and heat is more easily regulated. Expert backpackers emulate the Indian and try to cook their food with the smallest fire possible.

The traditional structures for kindling a camp fire are the lean-to (match-sized twigs leaned against a larger piece) or the tepee (a cone of twigs). The most common mistake among fire builders is not having good quantities of dry twigs, tinder, toilet paper and burnables of all sizes within easy reach before the first match is struck. I usually start with three squares of toilet paper loosely crumpled, cover that with a handful of dry pine needles, then build a tepee of the smallest, lightest twigs by tilting them against the paper from all sides.

After carefully leaning half a dozen finger sized sticks against the pile, I crouch low to block the prevailing breze (if it is strong, I block the entrance to the fire pit temporarily with rocks) and thrust a lighted kitchen match beneath the paper with one hand while I shelter the match from stray zephyrs with the other. Once the paper is lighted, I add the match to the tepee and use both hands to shelter the embryo blaze until all the wood has caught. Care must be taken not to put the fire out by knocking down the tepee with fresh wood, by skipping the intermediate-sized sticks and adding heavy branches, or by letting the tepee burn up before adding fresh wood.

There are differences of opinion, not surprisingly, about matches and lighting fires. Some people carry only paper book matches, others (like myself) take only wooden kitchen matches; wooden safety matches that can only be lighted on the box are a bother in the summer but indispensable in the winter when snow covers the rocks. I have used commercially waterproofed and windproofed matches and found them excellent, though expensive, for difficult conditions and emergency kits. Some people dip their matches in paraffin or candle wax.

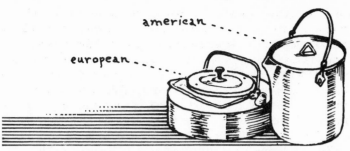

a tea or coffee pot is the ideal 'second pot'.

Still others carry all their matches in waterproof matchboxes. My simpler, but probably less secure strategy is to stuff lots of matches in all the waterproof outside pockets of my pack. Another dozen are inside my watertight first aid kit. The climate of the California summer Sierra does not seem to me to demand a waterproof matchbox. A handful in a securely closed plastic bag makes a decent enough emergency supply. In wet country or for winter mountaineering, fire starters are valuable both for open fires and for stoves.

Today there are a number of good cook kits on the market for small groups and a variety of good pots, pans and kettles. But thoughtful backpackers will still be well advised to devise combinations suited to the particular requirements of their menus. And the Goodwill stores and supermarkets still offer bargains and a variety not to be found in mountaineering shops.

Ideal pot design depends somewhat on whether a stove or open fire is to be used. For stoves, pots need small, perfectly flat bottoms of small diameter for maximum stability. The thicker the bottom the less likely that the small concentration of heat will cause scorching or burning. Heat is not a problem at the handle, bail or lid. Pots for an open fire can be any shape and uneven on the bottom, but lids should be easily removed and handles or bails must be usable when flames envelop them. All pots should have rounded edges and no grooves or seams or cracks to trap food and dirt.

Tin cans, or billycans, for this reason, are poor except for making tea. For many years the standard by which other pots were judged was the Sigg kettle of grooveless spun aluminum. Nowadays a wide selection of cookware and kits can be found in mountain shops, especially the large ones like REI and EMS that also issue catalogs. The trend is toward teflon (even more valuable in the wilds than at home) and rounded, easily cleaned shapes. Sigg pots come in 2½, 3½, 5¼, 7 and 8¾ pint sizes (which nest) and are widely available at prices ranging from $7-10 each.

Since I rarely use the lids for cooking, but find them impossible to lift with any gripper, I fit mine with a knob by drilling a hole and running a half inch long bolt from the inside to a pair of easily gripped nuts on the outside.

Frying pans or griddles are a nuisance for the backpacker because they require a wood fire which blackens them and thus require a heavy cloth or plastic case. Decent frying pans and griddles are not light because heavy gauge metal is needed to evenly spread the heat and prevent burning. The best compromise for the backpacker is a shallow eight or nine inch pan of thin steel or thicker aluminum, with either a ridged or waffled interior to spread heat, or a teflon coating to prevent sticking. Or cook your trout in the ashes—after first wrapping it in foil.

After making coffee or tea for many years in whatever pot was available, it dawned on me that I could do a far better job and leave one pot at home (not to mention avoiding a scum of grease from the soup) by carrying a real teapot.

People who are deeply attached to certain dishes, or who genuinely like to prepare fancy meals, are often obliged to carry additional equipment, like ovens, toasters and pressure cookers. Fresh bread, biscuits, gingerbread and cake are extremely welcome in the wilds, more so after a week of dried foods. The Optimus Mini-oven makes baking relatively simple. Built like a sponge cake pan, it cleverly provides heat on top as well as the bottom and is designed to work on most stoves. It weighs just under a pound and costs $15-17. And Solar Southwest makes a solar oven that will even work on sub-zero days. It generates up to 375° heat, weighs 1½ lbs., costs $14 and folds flat for easy carrying.

Though its use requires more experimentation and fiddling, an oven made from two aluminum pie pans fastened together with two spring stationary clamps and suspended over a bed of coals is far lighter and cheaper and nearly as effective. Coals must also be spread on the top pan and covered with a piece of aluminum foil.

Eating and cooking utensil requirements range all the way from the couple who carry a single large spoon and jackknife between them, to parties in which each person has his own knife, fork and spoon, wears a sheathknife, and carries additional utensils for the cook. Obviously, the larger the party, the more cooking gear required. Most experienced backpackers using easily prepared dishes forget about table knives and forks and carry only a soup spoon apiece and a good-sized simple pocketknife.

A knife is an absolute necessity in the wilds, but knives have become so fashionable that some people carry far more knife than they need. Buck and other expensive heavy knives are status symbols for some, and many rationalize a need to carry (preferably in a leather holster) Swiss army knives (or imitations) that offer a bewildering assortment of heavy, bulky rarely-used gadgets. The knife I like best has a big, bread blade suitable for spreading crackers and cutting salami—and a shorter, slimmer sharply pointed blade for cleaning trout. Brightly colored handles help prevent loss. If I am traveling alone, I put a tiny single-bladed spare jackknife in the outside pack pocket containing the first aid or fishing kit.

tube
&
clip
for
carrying
jam
or
honey

Pot grippers or tongs or pliers may be needed to lift lids and serve as pot handles. Aluminum pot grippers weigh little more than an ounce and are fine for stoves, but the handle is too short for an open fire and the lack of a spring makes operation awkward. Longer, stronger spring-loaded steel grippers of similar design weigh a quarter of a pound. Neither fits all pots. I prefer cast aluminum hot pot tongs which, being a large pair of pliers, is a more versatile tool. Many of us find an old padded cloth pot holder indispensable.

Can openers will not be needed if canned food is left at home, but a good many of us, after many weight-saving economies, like to take along some canned luxury like sliced apricots in heavy syrup. Besides, copies of the army can opener weigh only and eighth of an ounce. Other sometimes useful kitchen tools are spatulas, forks, mixing and stirring spoons, and water dippers. Nylon spatulas though subject to fire damage are light, cheap and needed for teflon pans.

Every backpacker needs a cup, and the more experienced choose large ones and dispense with plates. In the west, where the influence of the Sierra Club is strongest, the Sierra (or Sierra Club) cup has become an object of worship to some, and consequently an object of scorn to others. This wide-mouthed, nesting, stainless steel cup holds 12 ounces and weighs 3 ounces. The wire handle which hooks to the belt, stays cool enough to hold when the cup is filled with boiling tea. Cost is $2. But I much prefer a 12-ounce plastic cup which costs 40¢, weighs only 1½ ounces, retains food heat better, cleans more easily and, when the bottom of the handle is cut, snaps more securely to a belt or nylon line.

For backpackers not yet ready to eat from their cups—or who cannot abide an oily film from the stew in their tea—a small, deep, unbreakable, boilable polyethelene bowl, (50¢, 1½ ounces) is a greatly superior alternative to metal or paper plates.

When it comes to food storage, plastic bottles, bags, boxes, canisters and jars have all but replaced containers of all other materials. Many containers are so commonly available in markets that

foil ..... pie pan oven ..... hot coals

office clamps ..... pie pans

some mountaineering shops no longer bother to stock them. I make a habit of cruising the kitchenware sections of supermarkets to hunt for merchandise adaptable to backpacking.

In choosing plastic containers, I shun all but screw-on caps likely to form a watertight seal and avoid corners and recessed seams that will trap food and be hard to clean. And I buy wide-mouthed containers whenever there is a choice. Some of my best containers are recycled. When I spot an unusual bottle around the house, I wait until it is empty and then boil it out and add it to my collection.

Refillable squeeze tubes are invaluable for leakproof, easy dispensing of jam, jelly, catsup, butter, honey, peanut butter—anything of similar consistency. They boil out easily between trips and have yet to leak when properly assembled. Powdered milk presents a more difficult problem. When the wind is blowing the only way to avoid considerable spillage is to squirt the powder from a plastic catsup squirter bottle (available at large supermarkets) directly into the cup.

Salt and pepper shakers come in half a dozen clever designs that weigh ½ to 1½ ounces and cost 50¢ to $3 at mountain shops. Unfortunately, they hold enough for only 2-3 days for 2-3 persons. Salt companies now offer a variety of pre-filled plastic and cardboard shakers which are handy and safe if carried in plastic bags. For many years, I carried an old tin spice can filled with a mixture of three parts salt and one each of pepper, onion, garlic and celery salts. It is still one of my favorite shakers.

For larger parties or where water is scarce, collapsable jugs and bags are extremely convenient. They range in capacity from 1-5 gallons and weigh as little as 7 ounces for a 2½ gallon bag. Five quart jugs weigh 4 ounces and cost about $2.50. They roll up or press flat, and eventually they spring leaks, but if I am planning a dry camp on a ridge I carry a collapsable jug to fill at the highest water.

Though the quart poly bottle I carry for making lemonade doubles as a canteen in wet country, where water is scarce and must continually be carried, the one quart, rigid plastic Oasis canteen with belt clip and attached metal cap may be preferable although the $4 price is more than double that of my poly bottle. Flat plastic flasks for 'sportsmen' come in various sizes, but I often use a reclaimed vitamin pill bottle to carry 4 ounces of brandy.

To keep containerless stoves and fire blackened pots from spreading soot in one's pack means storing them in bags. Even heavy plastic does not do nearly as well as cloth. All kitchenware must be washed daily to prevent the formation of bacteria that can cause debilitating stomach illness. A few people scrupulously boil everything in soapy water after every meal; many only scrape out pots and pans and rinse in cold water—and cross their fingers. My procedure lies somewhere in between. For a short 2-3 man trip, I carry a 4-inch square abrasive scouring cloth and a 3-inch square sponge backed with emery cloth. Both are soapless. For burned pot bottoms I take a "chore girl" and I always take a dish cloth. Completing my kit are a vial of liquid bio-degradable soap—which is very effective at cleaning skin as well as pots—and a clean diaper or small absorbent hand towel. Old threadbare towels are inefficient. Fire blackened pots are best wiped with wet paper towels, rinsed and allowed to dry before being packed away in plastic or cloth bags. And if you rub a pot with soap before putting it on the fire, the soot will come off with comparative ease.

Cooking, for most of us, will never rival good eating, but if you keep it simple—a good stove, simple menus and ample advance planning—your time in the kitchen will be surprisingly pleasant and rewarding.

8 SHELTER

Tent making took a giant leap forward in the 1970s. If you thought a tent was too heavy or too expensive for the kind of trips you take, think again. If you think of tents as confining, claustrophobic, cramped closets in which to crouch, you're in for a surprise. Thanks to new designs, new materials and improved production techniques, shelter in the wilds is getting better, lighter and more easily affordable.

Back in the early seventies, probably ninety percent of backpacking tents were A-frames, improved versions of the old army pup tent. A-frames are still the best sellers for 2-man, 3-season tents, but they've been constantly refined and modified to the point where they are highly functional, roomier, lighter and better buys than ever before. But much as A-frames have improved, two new designs are gaining on them. Domes and tunnels are not new but they're just now coming into their own. Thanks to new pole materials and clever pole configurations, all three basic types can now be made ''free-standing,'' escaping the nuisance of guy lines. Each has certain strengths and weaknesses.

The A-frame is probably the leader when it comes to shedding rain. Thanks to refinements in production, it is also clearly the least expensive, pound for pound. When well pitched it is extremely secure in high winds, and its rectangular shape makes it efficient as a bedroom. Poles, fabrics and designs are improved, interior space is increased and the configuration lends itself to chimney ventilation, which is essential, as will be seen, in minimizing condensation. A-frames, being familiar, are easily pitched in minimal space in the dark and wind without much thought. Though most A-frames must be guyed and staked, a small but rapidly increasing number come equipped with ridge poles that join the two A-frames under tension and make the tent rigid and essentially free-standing. Good, up-to-date 2-man A-frames, with flies and ridgepoles, can be purchased for as little as $100 at total weights of about seven pounds. Except for those employing Goretex, few cost as much as $200.

The typical tunnel tent has basically the same rectangular pup tent shape, but it uses curved hoops instead of straight poles. It looks a little like the canopy on a covered wagon. Where most A-frames are rectangular, tunnel tents often taper to points. Most of them are narrower or lower at the foot than at the head; consequently they usually have only one door. Domes look like igloos, but they too are modified in various ways. Though they are vaguely dome shaped, dome tents are rarely if ever perfect hemispheres. Some are flattened, others elongated. There are all kinds of other shapes among the new tents and fresh ones appear continually, especially in tents for three or more persons, but A-frames, tunnels and domes probably account for 95% of tent sales, and their characteristics have been proven by considerable experience.

Back-packing tent

The greatest advantage of the billowy domes and tunnels over flat-walled A-frames is useable space, specifically headroom. Because the walls rise more or less vertically on all sides, domes and tunnels have almost half again as much volume as an A-frame with the same floor area. You don't have to wriggle on your belly or sit in the middle to avoid rubbing against the wall. In stormy weather, when you must live in your tent around the clock, not just sleep in it, and when condensation and frost make touching the walls uncomfortable or worse, this extra living space is valuable—both physically and psychologically.

Domes are warmer when it's cold because the minimum possible fabric area is exposed to the weather for the cubic foot volume enclosed. And warmth is important because tent wall temperature is critical when there's a threat of condensation. The minimal surface is further reflected in lighter weight and lower cost. In theory, domes and tunnels are especially good in the wind because the smooth rounded surfaces offer nothing to grip on, but in fact domes are notorious for their "bowl of jelly" softness, because their poles are flexible instead of rigid. Because most domes are self-supporting, they can be easily moved and positioned, and there are fewer stakes to set and no guylines to trip over. For many, the freedom from guylines is what sells the tent. As one tent maker puts it, "People will pay for something that's easier."

cay camp tent

But domes and tunnels, not surprisingly, have other drawbacks. Pitching can be complicated, at least at first, because they need up to four times as many feet of tent pole as A-frames require. If you've never pitched a dome you had better memorize or bring along the instruction sheet. All those miles of tent poles, however, cause other problems: they make a bundle in your pack that can be awkward and vulnerable. And because the poles are bent and under tension when the tent is pitched, they are considerably more vulnerable to stress and strain.

Just bending them into shape can use as much as 80% of their strength! Since each pole is made up of many short shockcorded sections, there are a great many joints under tension, and all are vulnerable to failure. Tunnels—and especially domes—are hard to ventilate because there are no vertical walls near the top. When flysheets are pitched the problem is compounded. Finally, these roomy new designs tend to be expensive.

Tunnel tents come in a much greater range of sizes, shapes and configurations than do predictable A-frames. They range in weight from 2½ to 6 pounds, are usually rated to sleep two and generally cost $2-300. Domes, being round or oval, make bed arrangement more puzzling and use space less efficiently. They are vaguely rated to sleep 2, 2-3, 3 or 3-4, depending on sleeping space required. They generally weigh 6½-9 pounds and cost $2-400.

The tent that will suit you, if you're shopping for shelter, depends less on shape than it does on the use to which you will put it, the emphasis you give weight and your willingness to spend money. There's no such thing as the ideal tent. If there was it would have to weigh 17 pounds—and that would hardly be ideal. Lightweight tents are designed for certain combinations of conditions. A snow tent would be useless in the jungle. A desert tent would leak in heavy rains. So the first thing to decide is the sort of conditions you'll generally encounter and the kind(s) of protection you'll most often need.

You can eliminate vast numbers of tents by setting priorities on sleeping capacity, weight and price. Let's say you've decided on a tent for the summer high Sierra, which means you need protection against occasional wind, rain, cold and bugs. You don't expect prolonged extreme conditions so most of the time you'll only sleep in your tent during nights that are close to freezing. The next thing to decide is how many people the tent must sleep. The vast majority of tents sleep two. One-man tents are virtually non-existent, but elaborate bivouac sacks that protect the solo sleeper have been flourishing since Goretex became popular. Three and four-man tents were rather scarce until domes became popular. Most tents for more than four are made either for expeditions or Boy Scouts and probably would be less satisfactory for most families than taking two tents.

Cost and weight limitations are largely arbitrary decisions. While some people are willing to pay more than they expected to get the tent that seems right for them, others will be unable to come up with extra money under any circumstances. If you can budget $200 you should be able to buy almost any 2-man, 3-season tent to meet almost any needs. If you're limited to $100 the selection will be much smaller. Still, there are I-pole nylon tents for as little as $30, pitching tarps for $35, Goretex bivy sacks for $50 and plastic tube tents for as little as $6.50.

Weight considerations are more personal. At one extreme is the often inexperienced buyer who falls in love with a piece of gear and doesn't stop to consider the weight. At the other extreme is the veteran who's allergic to an extra ounce. He cuts the handle from his tooth-brush, tears the paper tabs from teabags, and he often goes tentless in the summer to save weight. He wants comfort on the trail, even at the

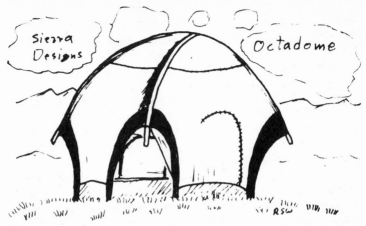

expense of some comfort in camp. If he carries a tent it's got to be light enough to justify itself.

Before looking at features to be assessed while shopping for tents, it is important to consider the problems presented by living in small portable spaces and the strategies tent makers have devised for solving them. The number one problem in tents—as in clothing—is condensation. Ironically, it's a problem that many have never encountered if their tenting experience is limited to dry, breezy conditions in moderate temperatures. But when condensation strikes, the experience is likely to be intensely unpleasant, even dangerous in extreme conditions.

When water vapor in the tent turns to water on the walls that wets everything it touches and runs down to form puddles on the floor and soaks your sleeping bag, that's extreme condensation. If the temperature is below freezing, the walls turn frosty instead of wet and the frost falls on your bed instead of making puddles under it. Since humans, as we have seen, are constantly producing moisture as they breathe and perspire, the concentration of water vapor in the small volume of a backpacking tent is unavoidably high. If the tent is closed tight against rain, cold or wind, this concentration is likely to increase.

Condensation occurs when the tent wall is colder than the surrounding air—or the air on one side of it. There are three ways this can happen: (1) From cold radiation on still, clear cold nights. (Condensation is rare when the wind is blowing.) (2) When cold rain falls on the tent, and (3) When there is excess heat and moisture within the tent so that the interior air is warmer than the tent wall. The last of these conditions almost always exists in occupied tents.

You typically lose about 8 cups of water during the night from perspiration and breathing. That vapor is confined in perhaps 70 cubic feet in the average 2-man, A-frame. That much extra water (16 cups if there are 2 of you) is bound to overload the small volume of air unless it's somehow vented from the tent. If it isn't removed it is bound to condense on tent walls whenever they are substantially colder (highly likely) than the air inside.

There isn't much you can do about water loss from breathing—although one man rigged a breathing tube that ran outside the tent so he was breathing fresh air and not exhaling in the tent—except perhaps to acclimate yourself if the altitude is high, which will substantially decrease the volume of air you breathe and the water vapor you exhale.

Fortunately, air has a considerable capacity for holding moisture suspended as water vapor. The warmer the air, the more it can hold. It is only when the air reaches saturation ("dewpoint") that condensation must occur. So there are a combination of factors that lead to condensation and their interaction is subtle.

Knowledgeable designers of sophisticated tents know that small changes in the balance can make an enormous difference in the condensation level. Improve venting slightly or raise wall temperature a few degrees and you may manage to keep below the condensation level. Unfortunately, a good many tent makers either do not understand anti-condensation design, give it a low priority or ignore it altogether. The subject is complex, beliefs have changed in recent years and there are several points of view. The first backpacking tents were made of heavy cotton. They leaked a little but condensation was no problem because the thick cotton fabric absorbed it and hid it. Of course, drying time was extremely long. When condensation was extreme inside the first coated nylon tents (coated because uncoated nylon passes water like a sieve) the coated nylon was blamed. It wasn't realized until recently that the coated nylon did not cause, or even increase, the condensation level. It merely failed to conceal it because it was non-absorbent.

The mistaken belief that coated nylon caused condensation gave rise to the double-walled tent with a space in-between. The inner wall was "breathable" uncoated nylon fabric. This was the tent itself. The outer wall was a separate rain fly or flysheet of coated (waterproof) nylon. In theory the breathable tent wall would allow the warmth and water vapor generated by breathing, sweating occupants and their cookpots, to pass through into the space beneath the fly where air flow would dissipate it. Meanwhile the fly would protect the tent from wetting in case it rained. This arrangement worked moderately well: rain was kept out and condensation was distinctly less troublesome than it had been with a single wall of coated nylon. But at times condensation was still appallingly severe.

In the last ten years it has been discovered that the major assumptions were false. Breathability, as was shown in chapters 1 and 2, deserves little credit because the volume of vapor passed is so negligible. The apparent improvement in condensation levels was (again) partly illusion: the porous nylon inner wall sponged up a good deal of condensation, just as the old cotton tents had done. The actual reduction in condensation was due to the fact that two walls kept the inner wall warmer, thus raising its dewpoint.

Unfortunately, a great many tent makers have made no use of these

Stephenson's
Warmlite tent

discoveries. They still believe in breathability so they build their tents with porous walls and design their flies for maximum airflow underneath. And when conditions are bad enough their customers are still deluged with condensed water and ice. Another group of tent makers, likewise ignoring the facts, has gone to single wall tents of Goretex. Naively believing its unwarranted claims of breathability, they assert that double-walled tents are no longer needed to prevent condensation. Unfortunately, single-walled Goretex tents quickly proved themselves significantly more subject to condensation than old-style double walled tents. Most of them are also heavier and prices are nearly double that of conventional tent fabrics.

But a few tent makers took advantage of what had been learned about fabrics and condensation, and they set out to make adjustments in design. The leader among these was Jack Stephenson, a former aerospace engineer. Because breathability had failed, he saw that some driving force would be needed to rid the tent of excess humid air. Wind could not be depended upon because it often was absent under conditions that caused humidity; besides, wind would chill the occupants and was difficult to control. Instead he took advantage of the fact that both warm air and water vapor are light and therefore rise.

Vents had been used before with only partial success, but Jack reasoned that, since venting had to work in still air, it could be greatly improved by imitating the chimney. Plugging holes in a chimney improves the draft. When he covered is tent with a plastic sheet to seal it, he found venting was improved and the tent stayed drier. Finally, to maximize the draft he repositioned vents so that cool air could enter only at floor level and warm humid air could escape only at a vent in the tent's peak. Strong convection currents were generated that continually forced out warm humid air and replaced it with drier, cooler outside air. He also employed sealed double walls instead of a separate fly, and sought minimum air circulation between them to maximize insulation and therefore wall temperature.

There are a number of things you can do to keep down the moisture level, and they may easily determine whether or not you stay comfortable during conditions ripe for condensation. (1) Be careful not to spill drinking water. (2) If you must cook inside the tent, keep a tight lid on the cook pot and run the stove for a few minutes after dinner to warm up the tent interior so excessive moisture can easily escape from the vent you should have at the peak of the roof. A great many problems and dangers can be avoided by cooking outside. Do so if you possibly can. (3) Use a vapor barrier liner in your sleeping bag and wear vapor barrier clothing to keep you warmer, reduce sweating and dehydration, and avoid sweating up your clothes.

(4) Don't dry those rain or sweat clothes in the tent. If you can't leave sweaty clothes outside, keep them in a closed plastic bag so they don't contribute dampness to the atmosphere. (5) If it's raining or snowing when you enter the tent, take the trouble to shake off excess moisture outside, remove wet outer clothing as you enter and fold it inward on itself to minimize exposure to the air inside. Best of all, use an umbrella! (6) If the tent leaks rain, try to find the trouble spot. Patch holes with tape and seal leaky seams with sealant right away if possible; otherwise mark leaks for between-trip repairs at home. Leaks generally are small and water often flows unnoticed down walls or seams to form a puddle that may convince you it's the floor that's leaking. Don't be fooled.

(7) Pitch your tent or trench around it so that water cannot run beneath it. The best tub floor should not be mistaken for a boat. Water under a tent is almost certain to enter. (8) Even in dry weather ground dampness has a tendency to rise through waterproof tent floors and condense inside. To protect against this phenomena on damp ground or snow, place an unpunctured polyethelene sheet beneath the tent before you pitch it. (9) Nylon expands when wet, so rain or dew can make your tightly pitched tent sag and flap, which disturbs the insulating air gap between walls and thus cools the inner wall, inviting condensation.

If you do what you can to reduce moisture and pitch and vent your tent properly, you should rarely encounter significant condensation. But when you do, wipe it off with a small sponge periodically so it won't collect and drip or run down the wall to puddle beneath your bed.

In summary, tent design can minimize condensation partly by (1) providing effective vertical chimney venting and partly (2) by shielding the sealed inner wall from the cold outer wall. The object in both cases is to minimize contact of humid interior air with cold tent surfaces. Don't be alarmed by this long dissertation on condensation and its control. Most of the time conditions are such that condensation is no threat, even without chimney venting and scrupulous attention to the water vapor level. Nevertheless, since heavy condensation can be brutally uncomfortable, it makes sense to understand its causes and cures and to buy a tent designed to resist it.

When Goretex appeared in the mid-seventies, ballyhooed by heavy advertising, it was hoped by many that a solution to the tent problem

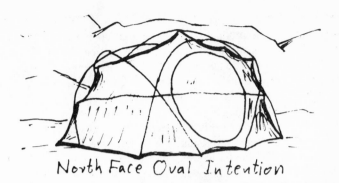

North Face Oval Intention

was at hand. A few tent makers offer single wall Goretex laminates that are claimed to both shed rain and permit water vapor generated inside to escape. To a certain extent Goretex can do both—but unfortunately not very well at the same time!

As I tried to show in chapters 1 and 2, the breathability of porous nylon really isn't great enough to pass much body-generated water vapor, and Goretex coating cuts that capacity in half. The notion that vapor pressure has sufficient driving force to help the process along just isn't accurate. And when it rains on your Goretex tent the wetness seals the pores and prevents the escape of water vapor from inside. The only time Goretex "breathes" is when conditions are good and "breathability" is of no help. Although many a Goretex tent owner will rave about performance, conditions probably were such that any material would have performed well. Or perhaps ventilation was good.

Goretex is poor for tents because its porosity interferes with the chimney venting that actually beats condensation. Tent makers who believe in Gore's claim of a partial-pressure driving force provide no vents to sabotage it. The results can be horrible condensation where conditions are ripe for it. Cooking in such a tent risks dangerous, even fatal, carbon monoxide poisoning. Goretex has proven to produce more frost condensation, whatever the venting, than conventional nylon canopies, coated or uncoated. Finally, as in other applications, Goretex commonly adds to the weight, nearly doubles the cost, is stiff and often noisy.

Next in importance is tent poles. I neglected to mention that the original pup tent design came with I-poles, vertical front and aft shafts that neatly bisect and block the triangular tent entrance. Quite a number of inexpensive tents and pitched tarps still come equipped with I-poles. Eureka offers half a dozen models. This is shelter at its crudest, commonly costing under $50. In high quality tents the I-pole was long ago superseded by A-poles, usually made in small diameter and relatively thick-walled 6000 series aircraft aluminum. Stronger, lighter, and more rigid poles, however, can be made by using thinwalled poles of lighter high strength 7000 series aluminum.

The development of domes and tunnels, with their curves and arcs, presented a need to produce poles that would curve. Most tent makers gave little thought to making curved poles. Instead they developed small diameter poles that would bend, first of aluminum, then of solid fiberglass and now of hollow fiberglass. Unfortunately, poles that bend when the tent is pitched, will bend further when the wind blows, distorting the tent, making it flap and function poorly. Because all these poles are made up of short sections, enormous strain is placed on the many joints. Not surprisingly, joint failure is common in even moderate winds. The basic weakness is inherent in the fact that the poles are made to flex, and when flexed they are under tension and stress that weaken the entire system.

The problem is worst in domes because a considerable number of very long poles are required for pitching this shape, and there is no way to escape the need for all poles to bend. Domes are often soft and vulnerable and there is continuous strain on every single pole and joint every minute the tent is pitched, even if there isn't a breath of wind. As a consequence, while the dome in theory is a good wind shape, in practice it is highly vulnerable to deformation and pole failure. One possible solution (which as far as I know hasn't been tried) is detach-able clamps. When domes are pitched there is considerable criss-crossing of poles. At present this provides little structural benefit. But if miniature clamps could be tightened to lock the joint at each intersection, the pole system would achieve enormously improved rigidity and double the strength. Inherent strain in the joints of bent poles would, of course, still be a problem, but the "bowl of jello" shakiness of domes would disappear.

Most tunnels use flexible aluminum or fiberglass poles, but in this design the vulnerability is sometimes slightly reduced because the configuration is different. Stephenson's tent escapes the strained pole problem by producing curved, rigid sections that form the necessary arcs without any more tension than is found in the equally troublefree A-frame. In flexing poles, generally speaking, solid fiberglass is heavy, vulnerable, cheap, and cannot be shockcorded. Aluminum makes for a more rigid tent but is expensive, prone to "set" (stay bent) and split. Hollow fiberglass is lighter, also expensive, less rigid, and more breakable. Even more important than the material is the joint where sections meet, and there are many different kinds to ponder and test. Try the fit, bend it and take your pick. Shockcording is even more helpful on the maze of poles required to pitch domes than it is on A-frames. Good tent makers always provide it unless they use solid fiberglass.

Many of the features that were rare or optional in the tents of the early seventies have become standard in quality shelter offered in the eighties. The best tent makers work hard to avoid seams in the floor. Unfortunately, floor fabrics do not come wider than 45 and 54 inches, and seams are inevitable. North Face and other top tent makers

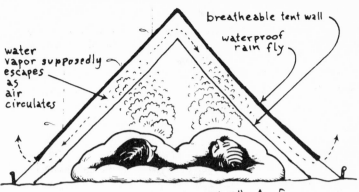

water
vapor supposedly
escapes
as
air
circulates

breatheable tent wall

waterproof
rain fly

Conventional "breatheable?" A-frame

construct "tub floors" which run floor fabric part way up the sidewall. This eliminates vulnerable perimeter seams at ground level but increases the need for pieced floors. Equally prestigious Sierra Designs takes a different approach. It employs perimeter seams which pitch an inch or two above the ground and thus minimize the need for pieced floors. And when the floor must be replaced the cost is less than half that of replacing a tub floor.

The once sophisticated catenary cut of a tent ridgeline that builds A-frame sag into the pattern to prevent flapping and insure taut pitch is now standard. Treatment of tent fabric with fire-retardent chemicals is now required by law in most states, but don't get careless. Treated tents will still burn. Goretex, incidentally, fails to meet fire retardant standards in five states, including California. Cookholes, popular in the early seventies, have largely been forgotten because drawbacks offset advantages. Good tents now offer one or more inside pockets per occupant, ideally made of netting with elasticized tops. And there are d-rings or loops in the roof for hanging clotheslines, lights, etc.

All reputable tent makers use overlapping flat felled seams with double rows of lockstitching with 6-10 stitches per inch; at least they should. The best acknowledge that needle holes will leak and provide seam sealant (if they don't do the job themselves), with instructions for using it. The protective reinforcement of seams, stake loops, pole tubes, corners, guy line tabs and all other stress points still separates tents in terms of construction quality. Shoppers should look closely and critically at seams, loops, stitching, reinforcement and finishing before buying any tent.

The next area of concern is entrances and zippers. The best doors are large and zip up from the bottom with YKK zippers and are backed by independently opened nylon mosquito netting. On A-frames and where zippers are straight and the fabric is not under great tension, toothed zippers with brass sliders are best. On tunnels, domes and where zippers must curve, they are continuous coil with soft aluminum sliders that often spread until they fail. When that happens run them back to square one and squeeze the slider back together with pliers to effect a repair. This will work 4-5 times before the zipper must be replaced. The secret in avoiding zipper failure is simply to hold the two edges together before you zip.

Beware mosquito netting that doesn't zip completley shut on all sides. One mosquito is all it takes on a sultry night, and dozens will discover a dime-sized gap. Jammed zippers indoors are such a threat to safety in snow that some winter campers insist on a tunnel entrance in addition. Secured by ties, tunnel entrances are not only independent of zippers, they provide a convenient passageway for knocking off snow or joining two tents together. Vestibules do the same thing and sometimes provide cooking and storage space as well. Like tunnels they are chiefly found on A-frames.

When considering how much capacity will be needed in the tent you seek, don't limit yourself to sleeping area. Be sure you'll have the needed shelter for all the gear you must keep dry. A tent you have to live and maybe cook in should be substantially larger than one you only sleep in. Finally, give a thought to ease of pitching. It can be important if you move every day and may have to set up and take down the tent on the run or in the dark and rain.

Having dealt with all the major considerations in tent selection, it's time to take a look at individual tents. No single person can claim to have tested all the hundreds of tents available, so I will limit my remarks to the good tents I know first hand or have examined. It will come as no surprise that the tent I know best and like most is made by Stephenson. In the early 1960s Jack discovered that a half-cylinder with pointed ends had the best stability in wind from any direction and also provided minimum surface area. Stephenson tents have a long-established reputation for peak performance in severe weather. But what lifts them above every other tent on the market is that in addition to their stormproofness and condensation resistance, they offer unexcelled lightness. For instance, the 2-man model is nine feet long, five feet wide at the front and weighs less than three pounds!

Though Stephenson's is a small company, with no retail stores and only mail order sales from a rarely advertised catalog, its unique gear has long been the choice of experienced, veteran wilderness travelers. For instance, one night by a glacier in southern Patagonia a group of us were huddled over a windy fire when a young American couple pedaled up on battered, overloaded bikes and gratefully joined us. They had been on the road for more than a year having started in Fairbanks, Alaska. They had ridden every foot of the Pan American highway and were now near its end at Tierra del Fuego. After sharing our dinner they unpacked the battered, faded, patched Stephenson tent they had carried all the way. Though it seemed to be in tatters it still pitched tight in the wind. The aluminized coating was gone and it was no longer waterproof (necessitating the use of a plastic sheet when it rained) but otherwise this lightest of tents was intact and fully func-

tarp tents:

tional. More than half of us at the fire, we discovered, were Stephenson tent owners. It was like a reunion, and into the night we traded "There I was..." stories about the little tent's heroics.

Stephenson's makes just one tent shape, but it comes in different models with a wide variety of options so that it can be made to suit almost any use: from Arctic to Sahara. A number of its features are unique—or were until tent makers by the score began making copies. The tent has a double roof (not a separate fly) and both are feather-weight coated nylon. The inner walls have an aluminized coating to reduce radiant heat loss by reducing emissivity of the fabric. This makes tents warmer in the cold and cooler when it's hot. The double wall is constructed to provide an insulating layer of still air in-between. By blocking the passage of water vapor, total condensation on both walls is reduced.

There are sheltered, zippered ground level vents on both ends of the tent and a larger stormproof chimney vent in the roof peak. When the tent is inhabited (generating heat and humidity) and the doors are closed tight (essential for good draft), the sealed fabric enables the tent to draw strongly, like a good fireplace. Warm moist air rises directly to the chimney vent and the convection current produced provides suction to draw cool, dry outside air in to replace it. A marvelous feature for mild evenings is the "drop front," which enables the wakeful occupant to reach out of his sleeping bag and unzip and drop the end of the tent for an unobstructed view of the stars. For people who find tents claustrophobic or confining, this option is a boon. When weather is foul and persistent wind has stretched the tent walls, internally adjust-able guy lines make it possible to tighten the tent's pitch without leaving the warmth of your bed.

Most tent makers feel that durability and wind stability require comparatively heavy fabrics, then they try to save weight and space by using flexible poles. Jack achieves far lighter, more stable tents by using the lightest possible fabrics (1.6 oz. walls, 2 oz. nylon floors) in his aerodynamic-thermodynamic design, but controls tent shape by the use of rigid, thin-walled, large diameter, shockcorded, pre-curved pole sections. Because the two poles form rigid unstressed arcs they are immensely stronger than tensioned flexible poles used by most other tent makers, and Jack's tents hold their shape and tautness in winds that deform or flatten tents equipped with flimsy, flexing fiberglass or small diameter aluminum poles. The curved pole sections easily plug into one another as you slide them into the pole sleeves—after you've done it once or twice. Other options include stake out side windows, end liners, and middle poles on larger tents.

The Stephenson 2-man (2RS) sells for $250, the 3-man (3RS) for $310 and the 5-man (5RS) goes for $390, with side windows but no drop front. Weights are 3¼, 4⅓ and 5.9 pounds respectively. If these unexcelled weights are too heavy for you, Stephenson's offers 2 and 3-man single wall tents made of a tough aluminized nylon-mylar laminate that is stronger and lighter but not quite as warm and condensation resistant as the RS series. The 2XS and 3XS sell for the same prices as their urethane-coated brothers, but the weights are an astounding 1¾ and 2¼ pounds, including poles, making them by far the lightest tents made anywhere in the world. Jack does not recommend them for winter because they are slightly more vulnerable to frosting due to the colder single wall.

In fairness I must report that Stephenson tents are fragile. Some customers complain that floors loose waterproofing too quickly, pole sockets can rip out if the tent is allowed to flap and the tent as a whole is distinctly delicate. The tent must be handled with consideration and respect. Jack doesn't pretend otherwise, in fact his instructions read, "the tent...is light enough to be rapidly destroyed by unnecessary rough abuse." People who are hard on their equipment should not consider it. But a distinction must be made between fragile and flimsy. While the tent is fragile it will stand up far better than most to whatever abuse *nature* can muster—provided it is carefully pitched. And when it comes to saving weight here's a chance to save pounds, not ounces. It seems to me false economy to make sacrifices that shave an ounce or two, then choose a seven pound A-frame instead of a three pound Stephenson tent!

tent pegs

Because I live part-time in Berkeley, home of the "big three" (Trailwise, North Face and Sierra Designs), I know their tents better than most. And the quality and workmanship of all three are dependably high. Trailwise, the eldest of the tribe, specializes mostly in tried and true designs and superb quality control. Its Fitzroy III and Two Man Mountain Tent, both A-frames, are dependable, durable, traditional shelters with adequate but unsophisticated ventilation. The Fitzroy's A-frames angle outward, making it self-supporting without guy lines, while the 2-Man offers a tunnel entrance in addition to the standard zippered door. With coated separate flies over porous tent walls, both weigh about 7 pounds and cost about $225. Of newer and more radical design is the Trailwise Great Arc Dome, an elongated, six sided flattened dome supported by six stressed shockcord loaded aluminum poles. It sleeps 2-3, weighs 8½ lbs. and costs $275. This tunnel-dome quickly became a favorite for seasoned travelers.

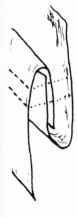

Lap felled double-stitched seam

Like Trailwise, North Face offers two superior, conventional 2-man A-frames with separate coated flies over porous walls. Design, workmanship and durability are excellent in these refined 3-season tents. The Sierra is easy to pitch and extremely stable in wind while the Mountain Tent offers a tunnel entrance on the rear end. Both weigh close to seven pounds and cost around $200. The North Face introduced the second (after Jansport) production dome tent when the Oval Intention was unveiled in 1972. I have spent a good deal of time in this shelter and am pleased to recommend it. While at first the pitching with a maze of long springy poles seemed beyond my capabilities, I quickly learned to erect the tent or take it down in the dark and rain with a flashlight in my mouth.

The flysheet clips onto pole sockets, the tent is tautly free-standing and very pleasant to live inside during protracted storms. Venting is conventional with no chimney at the peak, and the tent door is somewhat vulnerable when opened in a storm, but these are problems common to most domes. The Oval Intention rides well in moderate wind inside its network of tensioned aluminum poles, and sheds snow nicely. It weighs just under 10 pounds and costs $335.

The Northstar is a somewhat larger model that features an impressive through-the-fly chimney vent in the peak, and a sheltered entryway beneath the fly. It sleeps four, weighs 15 pounds and costs $500. I also have fond memories of good times in The North Face Morning Glory, a unique 4-man tent of highly convenient floor plan. From a 6-foot high A-frame in the middle it tapers in both directions to ends supported by 3½ foot I-poles. Because of its tall door and central headroom, this tent is ideal for expedition or family outing. It weighs 13½ pounds and costs $410.

corner seams need sealing

Sierra Design, long one of the country's leading tent makers offers top quality conventional A-frames (Wilderness at under 7 pounds and $200, and Glacier which offers a tunnel rear door in the vestibule for winter camping at 7 lbs., 11 oz. and $250). One of my favorite tents is the Three-Man, a six foot high tepee hung from a dependable rigid tripod. Refined over many years, it weighs 8 pounds and costs $250. The Sierra Design Aireflex represents a tunnel-A-frame hybrid that combines three sets of bowed aluminum A-frames, an integral fly and a flexed ridgeline pole that holds the whole thing together. It has clean lines, good space, pitches taut with just six stakes, resists moderate wind, sheds snow and has two end windows which must supply all ventilation. Weight is an excellent 6 lbs., price $240.

The Octadome 5 × 7 (five feet tall, seven feet wide) was inspired by a drying umbrella. Having an integral fly, it can safely provide four netting-covered vents high in the roof, but no venting is provided in the fly. Four arched vertical short walls, each with a window, support the back comfortably for sitting, and a carefully reasoned color scheme make this tent one of the most civilized and liveable of portable dwellings. Because of its considerable size and flexible poles the Octadome is unavoidably soft and floppy in more than moderate wind, but its weight is an impressive 8¼ pounds and cost is $325. One of Sierra Design's most successful small tents is the Starflight which offers exceptional headroom, under the single A-frame, easy pitching, great stability and snug room for two at a light 4 lbs. 11 oz., for only $145. For the weight, price and functional efficiency, this is a fine small, 3-season tent.

Because of its claims of waterproofness while permitting the passage of water vapor, Goretex was eagerly tried or considered by all major tent makers in the hope that significant weight could be saved by building a single wall tent, instead of using a waterproof fly over a breathable tent. Most makers were disappointed. The North Face, for instance, constructed an Oval Intention in single wall Goretex and set it up alongside the conventional model with fly pitched. Two children slept in each tent on a clear, cold night in Washington. In the middle of the night the kids in the Goretex tent abandoned it because they couldn't stand it any longer. The walls were streaming with condensation and their beds were soaked. Condensation in the other tent was only moderate.

Nevertheless, a few makers offer Goretex tents, and some of them bear and uncanny resemblance (in shape, at least) to Stephenson's 2R. Marmot Mountain Works makes the Taku, which at just under 5 pounds and $340 is 40% heavier and $90 more expensive than the 2R though it has only one wall. And instead of Jack's curved, no-load, rigid aluminum poles, the Taku comes with hollow fiberglass poles which flex and are under stress when pitched. A more compact version, the Featherlight, weighs 3 lbs. 11 oz. and costs $299. Stephenson-style chimney ventilation has proved quite effective at reducing condensation potential. As usual Marmot workmanship is excellent.

The largest selection of Goretex tents comes from Early Winters. Both the Light Dimension and its bigger brother the Winterlight employ the same basic design as the Stephenson tunnel but like the Marmot tents they use hollow, flexing fiberglass poles that are under tension and make the tents vulnerable to wind deformation. The Light Dimension utilizes a single wall of three-layer Goretex, shockcorded poles, weighs 3¾ pounds and costs $254. The Winterlight has three sets of poles instead of two, weighs 4½ pounds and sells for $295. The Early Winters Omnipotent, a tunnel with four hoops of fiberglass, has an integral double wall of coated nylon (not Goretexed) like the Stephenson tents. Early Winters also offers two single walled Goretex domes: the Starship for two people and Earth Station for 3-4. Neither provides minimally adequate ventilation.

Jansport pioneered the production dome tents and still offers a selection of innovative, free-standing, decently-made models supported by fiberglass poles and roofed for rain with detachable coated flysheets. Eureka is the largest tent maker in the world, offering the

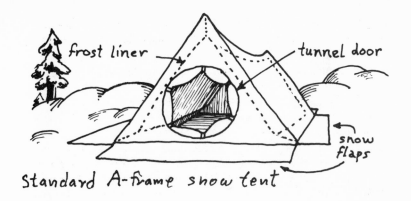

frost liner — tunnel door

snow flaps

Standard A-frame snow tent

greatest assortment of highly conventional tents, ranging from walk-in campground models to primitive I-pole pup tents that are little more than pitched tarps with doors. In between are a sprinkling of tunnels, domes and Draw-Tite designs with external frames and A-frames with ridgepoles. Quality workmanship, niceties and taut pitching are sometimes missing, but selection is large, prices are unexcelled and value per dollar spent is often good.

Moss Tent Works, maker of the first domes, offers several highly individual and beautifully scuptural tents that are appropriate for backpacking. particularly the magnificently vented Stargazer at 6 lbs. and $230, and the two and three-man Eave tents at the same weight and prices of $210 and $230 respectively. Shapes are difficult to describe. Holubar makes several high quality tents, including an impressively ventilated A-frame tunnel hybrid that sleeps three, weighs 10¼ lbs. and sells for $235, or "Sew-it-Yourself" from their kit for $145. Frostline likewise offers two and three-man tents with flies in kit form for $107 to $150 for those with sewing experience and a heavy duty machine.

Other noteworthy makers of tents are L.L. Bean, Bishop, Cannondale, Caribou, Gerry, Lowe and Recreational Equipment. More complete listings and evaluations can be found from time to time in Backpacker Magazine and its periodically published Backpacking Equipment Buyer's Guide.

For people who find tents claustrophobic, or are enterprising enough to improvise their own shelter, pitching tarps have some appeal, especially for group sleeping where bugs and wind are not a problem and the only need is to keep off the sun or dew. Tarps also appeal to those who are unwilling to pay for a lightweight tent or carry a heavy cheaper one. Mostly, however, they are for the rugged individualist who wants both minimal shelter and the feeling of being out in the open. Their numbers are dwindling in a day when convenience seems to hold top priority.

Tarp tents offer adaptability to the terrain. Tarps designed expressly for pitching can be difficult to find, but each of the biggest companies still offers one or two. Styles, prices, weights and rigging points vary almost as widely as the ways in which they can be pitched. The best tarps have the fewest seams and the greatest number of fastening points.

Tube tents are not as popular as they were during the seventies because too many people have discovered that what sounds and looks like a good idea has definite limitations. Because a tube of plastic is completely sealed, it won't leak a drop as long as it's intact, but it may get you and your bed wetter from the oceans of condensation produced than the rain would. Tube tents need both ends wide open to allow sufficient venting to hold down condensation. So for protracted rain they simply aren't practical. As lightweight emergency-backup protection against possible brief thundershowers (such as those that last only an hour or two on summer Sierra afternoons) or in dry climates when storms are not expected, however, they can be well worth carrying.

Before I discovered the three pound Stephenson tent, I carried a 3½ pound tube tent for several hundred miles in the summer Sierra without ever unfolding it. Although I never quite needed it, it provided a sense of security because I knew I could keep myself and my bed dry during the fiercest brief deluge. Tube tents, like pitching tarps, can be hard to find outside the big companies. Many firms discontinued them solely because so many thoughtless people abandoned them in the wilds. Fortunately, this negligent practice has been greatly reduced in recent years. While a tube tent costs only $5-10, many people opt instead for longer lasting primitive I-pole coated tents that are easier to pitch, offer more comfort and cost only $25-50.

Ground sheet and poncho shelters are essentially emergency versions of the tarp tent. Though comparatively inflexible and inefficient, they yield short notice shelter that often makes the difference between misery and comparative comfort. Sometimes their convertibility to shelter hinges on the presence of a few strategically located grommets or the possession of fifty feet of nylon line. More often it depends on the backpacker's foresight.

For several years I carried a 7 × 9 foot coated fabric poncho. When combined with the 6 × 8 foot plastic ground sheet carried by my partner, it provided us considerable shelter. After carefully preparing the bedsite to reduce the chance of puncture, I used it as a ground sheet, covering my bag on cold or dewy nights. Two corners on one side were fitted with permanent peg loops while the other two were fitted with 20-foot nylon cords.

When it threatened to rain, we tied off the hood, drove pegs to windward, tied the cords to trees to make a lean-to (or used pack frames for poles and pegged them down if it were treeless); we did what we could about controlling the drainage and wrapped our bags in the ground cloth. Many a short thunderstorm was weathered in this manner, and we once endured two days of solid rain on the shores of Lake Shasta without wetting our bags.

Shock cord-loaded poles spring into shape.

hollows can turn into puddles.

There has been a revival of interest in recent years in bivy sacks, thanks to the emergence of Goretex. Although Goretex will not simultaneously breathe and shed water in bivy sacks any better than it will in clothes, tents or sleeping bags, it is definitely superior to coated fabrics in this application. For years when I carried no tent in the benign summer Sierra (tents in those days were crude, heavy, confining and beyond my means) I relied on some sort of sleeping bag cover. Various companies made (and still make) flat envelopes with coated fabric on the bottom and porous nylon on the top. For instance the North Face Super Bivouac Cover is 8 feet long, weighs one pound and costs $30. It isn't waterproof on top, has no hood and isn't made of Goretex.

My cover had much more appeal than a mere ground cloth because it kept my bag and pad clean and provided a place to stuff clothes away from the dew. It was a dresser drawer during the day, and on cold nights it gave my bag extra warmth. On sweltering evenings I could lay beneath its cover on top of my bag without exposing myself to swarms of mosquitos. But most of all I liked the snug, cozy feeling of security the cover provided—without the confinement of a tent. The sleeping bag cover functioned for me well as a one-man tent, largely, I'm sure, because I rarely got rained on.

The Goretex bivy sack (bivouac sacks are coated fabric bags carried by climbers for emergency protection when they must unexpectedly spend the night without a sleeping bag) is a big step up from the humble envelopes I once carried, but they are still a poor substitute for a tent if it rains. And remember as you read on that all the advantages of a spacious two-man tent (Stephenson's, of course) can be yours for under three pounds and $250. As Jack bluntly asks, ''Why add the weight of a tent to avoid the tent, and how do you expect to get in and out of your bag in the rain?'' Also remember that once your Goretex bivy sack gets wet, even from heavy dew, breathability is further reduced.

Nevertheless, the Goretex bivy sack is well worth considering as a cheaper, lighter alternative—if you're going alone—to carrying a two-man tent. In many situations (like cold, bugs, wind-driven rain) it also makes more sense than a pitching tarp, ground cloth, poncho or Goretex-covered sleeping bag, but only if you're alone. The condensation problem inside the bivy sack, since it's too small and snug to ventilate, has only one solution: a vapor barrier liner inside your sleeping bag. That will take care of your sweat if not the condensate from your breath. Some people find bivy sacks more claustrophobic by far than tents, and they certainly are confining. But with me it's the other way around. If I can open my eyes and see the stars, I don't feel confined. But if the forecast is for other than clear weather, I'll take a tent.

Bivy sacks are conventionally designed as cocoons that conform to mummy bag shape, with Goretex on all or most of the top and coated nylon on the bottom. Some have Goretex bottoms but that makes no sense to me since it adds weight, cost and the certainty of soiling—and soiling can cause Goretex to leak. The biggest design change from the old sleeping bag cover is the inventive attempt to protect the head from bugs and rain while providing badly needed ventilation. Bivy sacks range $50-100 and weigh 1¼ to almost two pounds. All those I tried, when closed around the head, were wetted with condensation from my breath by morning. But that's almost inevitable.

Marmot's Burrow features a four piece fiberglass pole that forms an arch at the head to support the hood, which is faced with netting. Headroom is good. Pak Foam's Bivy Sack has an even larger canopy, easy access and good ventilation. The only trouble with these designs comes if you thrash in your sleep and upset the supports that provide your headroom. Both these models cost close to $100 and weigh more than 1½ lbs.

Taking a different approach are Arcata Transit Authority, Banana Equipment, Down Home and Early Winters. Their bivy sacks make no effort to recreate a tent effect by using poles, guy lines and stakes to procure headroom, but all have fold-over hoods designed to protect the head. These simpler sacks tend to be a little lighter and less expensive. Most have netting and all are secured with well-placed zippers, snaps and velcro.

So there you have it: a hundred different ways to find shelter in the wilds. Whether you choose a bivy sack, tube tent, flapping tarp, or sophisticated backpacking tent, you'll find the pleasure of any trip will be substantially increased by the security of having dependable shelter from the ravages of wilderness weather.

9 GETTING READY

Nothing dooms a trip like slipshod preparation. It only takes one or two little mistakes. Many a veteran backpacker has seen a trip ruined for lack of a map, knife, salt or match. Still more common is the beginner who, determined to camp in comfort, can barely stagger up the trail under a gargantuan load. The line between comfort and misery is far too thin for any backpacker to take getting ready lightly.

But preparing to go backpacking need not be drudgery. There is keen pleasure in working out a route for a fine summer trip on a dark and drizzly January night. And there is satisfaction in planning a trip into wild and distant country that delicately balances the weight of food and gear against the necessity of traveling light. The more that is accomplished beforehand at home—getting in shape, experimenting with foods, memorizing maps, breaking in boots—the smoother and more carefree the trip will be.

By systemitizing the job to reduce the work, one can make getting ready a pleasant prologue to the trip. The subject divides itself conveniently into four distinct phases: (1) Trip Planning: where, when and how to go, (2) Preparation: deciding exactly what to take, then getting it together, (3) Physical Conditioning: getting in shape before the trip, and (4) Packing up: getting to the trailhead and making up packs.

Trip Planning

As backpacking becomes more popular, it becomes easier and easier for the beginner to get started. Probably the best sources of help are the big organizations like the Sierra Club, Mazamas and Mountaineers in the west, and the Adirondack, Appalachian and Green Mountain Clubs in the east. Not only are they unexcelled sources of information about their respective territories, they offer organized outings of all types on which the beginner can safely become acquainted with the country and acquire experience with equipment and technique. You may also want to become part of the backpackers' lobby by joining The American Hiking Society, 317 Pennsylvania Ave., Washington, DC 20003.

Trip planning, like wilderness travel, requires the ability to read and use maps. Probably no other skill is more important to all aspects of backpacking. No one should enter wild country unsupervised without appropriate maps and the ability to use them. Of course a map is useless if directions are unknown, so a compass becomes a necessity. There is a tendency among amateurs and strangers to the outdoors to regard the compass as a toy for Boy Scouts. But in strange country where landmarks are unfamiliar, a compass is no less than indispensable. Many times I have worked out my true location or avoided a wrong turn by referring to a dollar-sized compass that weighs a fraction of an ounce and cost less than a dollar.

Navigation in the wilderness is a book-length subject in itself, and I urge all backpackers to become familiar with the rudiments. Proficiency could save your life, and it will certainly increase your confidence and security when entering new country. While a cheap floating-dial compass, used with understanding, will be adequate for trail-travel in familiar country, an "orienteering" compass will be needed for genuine navigation. These instruments can be recognized by their movable dials and transparent bases. Prime examples are the Suunto Wayfinder and the Silva Ranger, which will cost $20-35 and weigh 2-3 oz. The built-in protractor and locking device make it possible to quickly and easily determine bearings with a map.

With the aid of instructions, it is possible to teach yourself navigation in half an hour. Precision compasses rarely are needed in wild country simply because it's impossible for the hiker to measure distance accurately and maintain precise bearings. One degree of error in a mile amounts to only 92 feet, so compasses that can be read to the nearest five degrees will be accurate enough for most purposes. For more critical route-finding, the Suunto KB-20 can provide 0.2 degree accuracy, but it is far less suitable for general backpacking conditions. The sport of orienteering, long popular in Europe and gaining ground in this country, provides valuable and stimulating practice for outdoor navigators.

Another useful (but rarely essential) aid to routefinding is the altimeter barometer. Besides measuring elevation gain, it can be used to compute progress, determine location, plan rest stops, and forecast the weather—especially in combination with a thermometer. Altimeters are also fun to play with if you like gadgets. To be useful they need to "compensate for temperature," and even then their readings will be far from precise. My favorite compromise between quality, price and weight is the Gischard, temperature compensated, which also functions as a barometer. Resembling a pocket watch, it weights 3½ oz. and costs $45-50. I use it with a half ounce bi-metallic dial thermometer that costs $4 (from REI). Conventional glass, liquid-filled thermometers are vulnerable to breakage, undependable, heavier and more expensive.

Since there is no substitute for proficiency with map and compass, the inexperienced backpacker is well advised to invest his spare time

an oriented map:

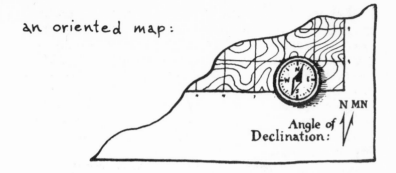

N MN

Angle of
Declination:

in mastering both. The book *Be Expert with Map and Compass,* by Bjorn Kjellstrom, available from most mountaineering shops that handle books, covers the subject and offers instruction, quizzes, drills, field problems, games, sample topographic maps and related tools. Even more valuable is the chapter on navigation in The Mountaineers' *Mountaineering: The Freedom of the Hills.*

The single best map for the backpacker's purpose is the topographic (topo) map published by the U.S. Geological Survey in a variety of scales. Topo maps dependably offer more information per square mile than any other kind of map. It may be useful, however, to transfer to the topo map from more up-to-date local and Forest Service maps such useful data on 'improvements' as trails, roads, campgrounds and the like. While the very large scale 7½-minute topos provide marvelous detail, smaller scale maps that show distant landmarks will also be needed for orientation.

Though a first glance at a topo map is liable to be confusing, they are really not difficult to understand. Winter is an excellent time to study maps, plan trips and become familiar with topography. The first principle of map use is orientation—lining up the map with the country. The traveler simply spreads out his map with the compass on top so that north points directly to the top of the sheet. The map and compass are then turned as a unit until the north needle points directly to north. When the magnetic declination (difference between true and magnetic north) is set off (it is shown on all topo maps) the map will be oriented.

When one's position is known and the map is oriented, it becomes easy to identify visible features of the countryside by transferring line-of-sight bearings to the map by means of a straight edge. When only one's general location is known, but several landmarks have been positively identified, it is possible to discover one's precise location by transferring line-of-sight bearings to two known landmarks onto the map. The intersecting lines reveal the compassman's exact location. This won't work, of course, where convenient landmarks can't be seen.

The competent woodsman or mountaineer always tries to develop some inner orientation to make him independent of his compass. To this end, my friends and I play a game on the trail—while taking a rest—that has proven both amusing and instructive. Each of us draws a line in the dirt toward what he believes is true north. Then the compass is brought out, the declination marked off, and the winner declared. The next time the game is played the previous session's winner must draw first. It is surprising how quickly this game develops a sharp sense of direction

Reading the rise and fall of the land on a topo map is more a matter of practice than talent. The best place to begin is with solitary peaks or hills where the contour lines form concentric circles that get smaller as they go higher toward the summit circle in the center. Widely spaced lines indicate a gentle slope while lines bunched together describe a cliff. Contour lines form arrows that point upstream as they cross water courses and downhill as they descend a ridge or bluff. As one becomes adept at reading topo maps, the actual shapes of landforms begin to materialize on the map so that maps become pictures of the country.

When this happens, topo maps take on a singular fascination. They also become incredibly useful. For instance, by measuring the ups and downs of a trail one can estimate with fair accuracy the time that will be required to traverse a given section of country. This, in turn, allows the trip planner to work out logical camping spots and estimate the time needed for any itinerary. Superior map reading ability is a prime prerequisite for safely visiting the wildest of trailless country. Proficiency with map and compass has saved a great many lives.

There are various ways to plan routes. Newcomers to the outdoors may want to car camp at the trailhead for a day or two and make exploratory day trips into the wilds until they become acclimated and find an appealing campsite that seems within their reach. Families and other groups with limited range often set up a base camp within an easy walk of the car and then make daily side trips into surrounding country.

Groups with greater mobility or the urge to move may decide to shift their base camp one or more times; others make a practice of packing up and moving every other day. Inexperienced or cautious backpackers often take the shortest route to their goal, then retrace their steps going home. More practiced and imaginative hikers go to some pains to plot a route that makes some kind of circle or loop in order to see more country and avoid treading the same ground twice.

Another popular plan is the shuttle trip. Two cars drive the party to the exit trailhead, where one car is left. Sandwiched into the second car, the party then drives to the entrance trailhead to begin a backpacking traverse between the two. There is also the exotic 'double shuttle' in which two traversing parties start at opposite ends of the same route and trade car keys when they pass on the trail, perhaps sharing a meal or camping a night together.

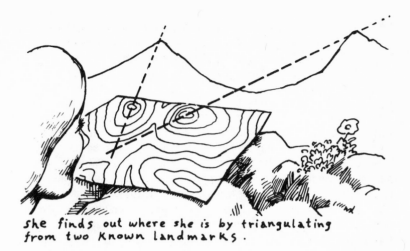

she finds out where she is by triangulating
from two known landmarks.

Some backpackers find a greater sense of adventure in deliberately planning no itinerary, going where and when the spirit moves them. Others, similarly motivated, spurn trails altogether in favor of cross-country travel, finding pleasure in avoiding people and the beaten path. Since true wilderness does not begin until the trail has been left behind, it should probably be the goal of most backpackers to travel cross-country, even if only for an hour's day hike from base camp. Wilderness travel means getting off the trail.

I like to start thinking about future trips while I am still in the mountains. I find myself wondering, for instance, whether the rocky, trailess canyon I am passing could be ascended, under pack, to the lake that lies above. As I move along, I try to estimate the difficulty of reaching passes, following ridges and crossing slopes, with an eye toward future trips. I study the topo map to learn what lies on the other side of the mountain and to compare the bunching of contour lines with those on slopes I can see or have already climbed. And I often take pictures of country that interests me for reference in planning future trips.

This type of on-the-spot research becomes invaluable for plotting feasible cross-country routes in trailess country. A glance up a canyon on this year's trip may warn me against including it in the next year's itinerary because the gentle slope suggested by the topo map turns out to be a series of ledges and cliffs. Or I confidently plan a route down a forbiddingly steep slope because I know it to be an easy sand and scree slide.

The question inevitably asked by strangers to the wilderness is how fast will I travel? Or, how far should I plan to go in a day? There are no answers, only generalities. On relatively level trails at moderate elevations, a lightly burdened, long legged well-conditioned man may manage 4 m.p.h. At elevations over 6000 feet in rolling country, a well-acclimated backpacker is moving extremely well if he can cover

3 m.p.h. The average backpacker, fresh from the city, with a full pack, heading up into the moutains will be lucky to average 2 m.p.h. These speeds are for hikers who keep moving and should probably be cut in half for those who want to poke along, smell the flowers, take pictures and enjoy the view.

People who are overburdened or climbing steeply or moving cross country may average only 1 m.p.h. Children, the elderly and hikers strongly affected by the altitude may manage as little as half a mile an hour. A friend of mine has devised a useful formula for predicting his speed. He plans every hour to cover two miles if the trail is flat or mildly descending. For each thousand feet of rise he adds another hour. For steeply descending trail he adds a half hour per thousand feet, increasing that to a full hour for extremely steep downhill. By plotting a rough profile of the trail from the topo map and applying his formula, he can estimate quite accurately the time needed to walk it with a moderate—under 30 pound—load.

How far one should attempt to go in a given day is equally hard to answer. The first day out is always the hardest, especially if the hiker has gained a mile or two of altitude between home and the trailhead, carries a healthy pack and is in less than top physical conditon. In these circumstances, five miles may be a full day's work. Well-conditioned backpackers who know their capabilities may cover ten or more miles the first day and not suffer unduly, but most people will be happier if they schedule considerably less. On succeeding days it becomes possible to cover more ground with less discomfort. I have covered 15 or 20 miles on the third or fourth day with greater comfort than I felt after eight miles the first day.

There is no particular virtue in covering great distances. I have received more pleasure, solitude and a sense of wilderness from backpacking less than two miles cross-country into a neglected corner than I have from following sixty miles of well-traveled trail and camping in battered, over-used campsites. I customarily spend the summer on the edge of California's Desolation Wilderness, a place of extremely heavy use, but I know any number of charming, well-watered off-trail spots within an hour or two of the trailheads where I can camp in peace on virgin ground. As backcountry use continues to increase, backpackers determined to find solitude and unspoiled country will have to invest more time dreaming over their maps to find the less obvious routes that lie between the trails.

When to go is often determined by school and business vacation schedules. In California's high Sierra, spring, summer and fall are compressed into three or four months and consequently it makes a great deal of difference whether a trip is scheduled for June or August. Often it will snow every day for a week in early June, yet the country is dusty and parched by August. The beginner should gather all the information he can about likely conditons in his area for various reasons. If there is one season to avoid, it is probably spring. Even if the weather is miraculously fair, the ground is almost certain to be wet. Indians generally avoided spring travel, preferring the middle of winter. Spring is a good time to car camp in comfort and settle for day hikes into the wilderness.

Preparation

Once the route has been determined, the length of the trip decided and the starting date set, it becomes possible to determine what must be taken along. Actually, I like to begin my preparations before the end of the previous trip. In camp on the last leg of a trip, or perhaps at the trailhead—after exchanging my pack for an ice cold drink—I sit down with my notebook while memories are fresh, and make pertinent notes about the trip. I criticize the food, recording both the noteworthy successes and the dishes that need never be carried again. I might write down, for instance, that breakfasts were a little skimpy so the cereal allotment should be increased from three ounces per meal to four.

By making notes before the memory fades, I accomplish three things: (1) I give myself the best possible chance to increase my enjoyment of future trips, (2) I avoid repeating mistakes for failure to remember them, and (3) by putting it all in writing, I avoid the mental drudgery of having to start planning each trip from scratch. Fifteen minutes spent making notes at the end of a trip will save two hours of preparation a month later; I cannot recommend this procedure too highly.

the trip-planner's friends:

The checklist takes the place of a perfect memory, and the longer it runs the more security it provides. Every time I buy a new piece of gear, I add it to my checklist, but I rarely can bring myself to cross anything off, even the items I have not dreamed of carrying in years. Like other backpackers interested in comfort, I enjoy reading other people's lists. The abridged checklist that follows may serve as a starter for newcomers to backpacking—but only as a starter. A checklist is a highly personal thing and the beginner must eventually construct his own, updating it after every trip to make sure it contains every scrap of gear he owns.

A few of the entries on my list need further explanation. I have included gear I take most frequently on 3-season trips in the California Sierra, because that's my home turf. Other areas will require vastly different choices. The lithium battery is another space age development that enormously benefits the backpacker. Although initial cost ($14) is great, lithium has twenty times the life of alkaline batteries and is therefore far cheaper by the hour. Lithium offers twice the voltage as the number of batteries required is cut in half, saving 50% of battery weight.

For back packers, this means few if any spare batteries will be needed (providing 40-45 hours service will suffice) and bulbs last longer. Seasoned travelers carry bulbs of different wattage, changing

My BASIC CHECKLIST

PACKS	Pounds-Ounces
Frame and packbag	3-12
Back Magic	5-2
Orange daypack	9
Fanny pack	5½
Belt pack(s)	2

CLOTHING - FOOTWEAR

Green wind anorak	7½
Straw hat	3
Tennis hat	2
VB shirt	4
VB gloves	
VB socks (Baggies)	
VB Zip Rain Pants	10
String shirt	7
Hickory shirt	10
Moleskin shirt	14
VB-rain storm suit	1-5
Zip-arm pile sweater	1-5
Denim shirt	8
Down sweater	1-1
Hiking shorts	10
Running shorts	2
Bathing suit	5
Stretch rag socks	4
Liner socks	1
Wick Dry socks	3½
Double-zip trousers	1-1
Bandana	¾
Watch cap	2
Balaclava	3
Ben Davis pullover shirt	6
Boxer shorts	3
Odlo long johns	3
Wool mittens	3
Leather gloves	3
Short gaiters	4
DMC GT boots	2-4
Vasque boots	3-4
Go-aheads (sandals)	2
Zip-arm rain parka	1-0

SHELTER

Space rescue blanket	2
Stephenson tent	2-15
GT bivy sack	1-2
Ground cloth (nylon)	12
2-Man tube tent	2-4
Ground cloth (plastic)	12

BEDS

Stephenson bag (thin)	4-2
Zip-lock (foam) bag	5-0
NF superlight bag	3-1
72-In. foam pad	2-0
72-In. Therm-a-Rest	2-8
72-In. Airlift	1-3
72-In. ½'' EVA foam	12

KITCHEN GEAR

Pocketknife (big)	2½
2-Blade Swiss army	1
Bleuet with cartridge	1-13
Extra cartridge	10
Peak 1 stove	2-0
Sigg pint bottle	4
Sigg quart bottle	5
Sigg pot, lid	9
Pot tongs	1½
Chore Girl	½
Salt mix shaker	2
Wooden matches	1
Emery cloth-backed sponge	½
Paper towels and TP	2
Plastic cup	1½
Aluminum measuring cup	¾
1-Quart bottle	5
1-Quart Oasis canteen	5
Tea kettle	3
Gallon jug (plastic)	4
Tubular grill	4
Gerry plastic tube	¾
Fork-spoon	1½
Bio-suds	2

MISCELLANEOUS

Dark glasses	1½
Glacier glasses w/band	2
Lip salve	½
Thermometer	½
Compass	2
Altimeter	3½
Maps	1?
50' 550 lb. test cord	3
Cutters snakebite kit	1
Jungle (bug) Juice	3
Notebook, pencil	2
Creel (loaded)	9
Mallory flashlight	3
Lithium headlamp	1-8

First aid kit (large)	9	Fly rod, reel, line	7½
First aid kit (small)	6	Paperback book	7
Personal kit	3	Sea & Ski tubelet	1
Konica (35mm camera)	13	Plastic garbage bags	1
Extra film	2	Candle	1

when a different level of brightness is needed. Another useful product is the Justrite headlamp (10 oz., $10 without batteries), a tough functional light source that leaves your hands free when hiking, cooking, etc. It's heavy but worthwhile if you have to accomplish a lot in the dark. Climbers and cavers have used it for years.

When I bought my Konica 35 mm camera it was the lightest full frame 35 made at 12 oz., and it cost $75. Now the Minox 35GL, scarcely larger than a pack of cigarettes, weighs less than 7 ounces, with a fully automatic exposure system, and the lens retracts and is fully protected when the case folds closed. Though cost is $200-250, this is the ultimate in a top quality lightweight camera. It's half the weight and twice as easy to use as the more expensive Rollei 35.

Lightness comes from substituting high impact plastic for metal. That's also the secret in the Vivitar 35EM which weighs 9½ ounces, costs about $160 and also has a retractable lens, though it is not protected by a folding case. Budget backpackers should look for reconditioned used folding 35s like the old Kodak Retina, which will fit in a hip pocket. Though they weigh two pounds, you should get a good one for $25-50. I wore out several before the Konica came along.

It isn't widely known that sunglasses often do more harm than good. They trick the eyes into staying open wider than they should in bright conditions, resulting in eyestrain. And the darkened lenses block out healthful rays which are essential to the body. A wide-brimmed hat or sunshade is always preferable. "Dark glasses are a crutch," said the old prospector with whom I used to travel on the desert. "Put them on when it's bright and you'll never take them off." He taught me to squint and wear my hat low for a couple of days to acclimate my eyes, rather then develop a dependency on shades. And it works. I only wear sunglasses now under extreme conditions.

Murl also taught me to use "Indian sunglasses" when vision was vital under extra bright conditions. Put the tips of your middle fingers together, end to end, then tuck the tips of your index fingers together tight against them, just beneath. Hold your four fingertips against your nose in the hollow beneath your brow and look through the easily adjustable slits between your fingers. Now your shaded eyes can stop squinting and open wide for maximum vision, even when looking almost into the sun.

When it comes to buying insect repellent, all that counts is how much you're getting of the active ingredient, N. N-Diethyl meta-toluamide. The heavily advertised Cutters preparation is only 28% active, but one ounce costs $260, so the price per ounce of the active ingredient is a whopping $10, a ripoff I'm happy to expose. By comparison the 4 ounce pump bottle of Repel is 52% active and sells for $3.95, or less than $2 per active ounce.

By far the best commercial buy is Jungle Juice, made for the Army's use in Vietnam and sold by REI among others. It's over 71% active and a two ounce bottle sells for 95¢, for an active ingredient cost of only 66¢/oz. If you need bug repellant in quantity it makes sense to buy the diethyl metatoluamide at the drugstore and make your own dilution. A dosage of 200 milligrams/day of vitamin B-1 taken orally will make your perspiration repellent to mosquitos and thus keep them away. So will the heavy cosumption of garlic.

Many writers insist rather rigidly that no traveler should ever set forth into the wilderness without the security of certain (usually 10) essentials. I disagree, in the interests of simplicity. Most people take too much, too many gadgets. I would urge people to take only what they really need, develop more self-reliance and not try to protect themselves against every possible hazard.

The properly equipped backpacker should already be carrying everything essential. He doesn't need an additional security blanket. It's a different story for the dayhiker. He needs to be prepared for getting hurt, caught in a storm or delayed past sunset, but what he actually should carry will vary too widely to be codified into a list of "essentials."

Once a new trip has been planned, I can turn to the preparation stage with much of the work already done. Having determined where, when and for how long I am going, I get myself a pair of empty cartons, assemble my notebooks and spread out my checklist. I read my notes from the previous trip, then I make my way down the list, considering each entry in terms of my needs for the trip in question. Each item selected is fished out of its storage box and put in the appropriate trip box. One box is for community gear (food, cooking paraphernalia, first aid kit, etc.), the other is for my personal gear (sleeping bag, clothing, etc.).

With the equipment all assembled (or at least planned and noted) I consult old menus and the comments made at the end of previous trips. After figuring the required number of breakfasts, lunches and dinners, I consider the appetites and preferences of party members, the likelihood of our catching trout and the possibility of our staying out a little longer than planned. Then I compose a tentative menu which will be discussed and probably changed before the actual shopping begins.

Once the menu is set and the food acquired, most of it needs to be repackaged. Some people go so far as to separately package every meal so they need only dig out the appropriately labeled bag. In my view, this sort of packaging is excessive for short or casual trips where measurements need not be precise and where an extra ounce of cereal for breakfast for several days will not result in starvation the last day out.

for getting in shape, nothing beats running up hills.

My repackaging consists of stripping away all cardboard, paper, cellophane and light plastic and replacing it with large, heavy duty polyethylene bags. I like to tie the long neck of the bag into an overhand knot rather than struggle with rubber bands, twisties, paper clips or heat sealing. Bags that will repeatedly be opened (gorp, cereal) and thus subject to more wear are usually doubled. I buy the heaviest bags I can find, rather than risk the puncture and spilling inevitable with flimsy bags that are cheap or free. After repackaging appropriately, I put fresh food (butter, meat, cheese) in the refrigerator. Everything else goes into the food box—including a boldly written reminder to collect the refrigerated food before leaving

On the evening before departure, I assemble the clothes I expect to put on in the morning and set them beside my bed. I also gather the clothes and food and drink that I will look forward to finding in the car at the end of the trip. As a final step, I run quickly down my checklist one last time. Everything should now be ready.

Conditioning

Many a trip has been ruined—and I speak from experience—by the failure to get in halfway reasonable shape beforehand. I can remember trips which seemed to be one long nightmare of aching legs, bursting lungs and a desperate effort to keep up with the party. It is simply impossible to turn from sedentary city life to high altitude wilderness backpacking without a certain amount of physical strain. It is however, possible to leave a lot of the discomfort at home.

At home, the conditioning can be as gradual as the hiker cares to make it, thus spreading and actually reducing the discomfort. It can be performed within easy reach of a hot shower, soft bed and the assurance that today's blisters can be babied tomorrow. On the trip itself, there is more than enough discomfort from hiking under load at high altitude, sleeping on the ground, wind, sweaty clothes, cold water, a noticeable lack of easy chairs and hot showers—without unnecessarily adding a lack of physical preparation.

There is no better investment of time during the several weeks prior to a demanding trip than a program of conditioning that will bridge part of the gap between city living and wilderness travel. It is far better to discover blisters while walking near home than it is at ten thousand feet in a cold, windy camp, with ten miles to cover the following day.

It is perfectly possible for a sedentary city worker in his spare time to significantly improve the capability of his legs, lungs, shoulders, feet and skin, depending on his condition, in anywhere from a week to a month. The program actually required will depend on many factors: age, experience, physical condition, time available, determination, rigorousness of the trip contemplated, etc.

The jogging-running boom of the late seventies made vast numbers of Americans aware for the first time of the pleasures and benefits of running. While there is probably no better activity for getting in shape for backpacking or climbing, certain exercises derived from Yoga can be extremely helpful too. As all who have studied the hosts of running books know, it can be vital to loosen, stretch and warm-up the muscles before actually running. The alternative can be stiffness, soreness, early fatigue and pulled muscles. It is most important to stretch the back of the leg (hamstrings) and the Achilles tendon. The various exercises prescribed can easily be found in running books and exercise courses.

Comparatively few people know the great benefits available from Yoga exercises practiced during and after running, walking and especially arduous backpacking. When I shuck off my pack after a long haul I often feel stiff and weary—until five minutes of Yoga stretching on my foam pad rejuvinates and refreshes me. The transformation must be experienced to be believed. When ligaments and muscles are gently guided back into their natural state after prolonged effort, stiffness and fatigue simply dissolve. The single most rewarding exercise for me after hard hiking involves lying on my stomach, putting my hands in the push-up position, then, keeping my pelvis on the mat, gradually straightening my arms, throwing back my head and bending my spine backward, keeping my knees locked.

After several deep breaths, I turn my head as far as possible (until I can see my feet) on one side then the other. Then I relax my knees, lower my elbows to the pad and lie relaxed, back still bent, breathing deeply for another minute. Other stretches of great benefit after removing a pack include slowly rotating the neck, rotating the shoulders and rotating the ankles. If you find these stretches as invigorating and relaxing as millions of us do and you want to learn more, write *Backpacker* magazine and ask for a reprint of Anne

Richard's "Backpacking Yoga" in issue 35, or buy a paperback book on Yoga.

The following program is suggested for a badly out of shape, no-longer-young backpacker planning an ambitious two week trip at high altitude which will begin on a weekend. About three weeks ahead of time our man should, with the aid of a city map, mark out rather precise one, two and three mile courses that begin and end with his home. Traffic lights, crowded sidewalks, even stop signs should be avoided so there is no necessity to stop.

After work, instead of opening a beer, our man should go walking. Early risers may prefer to get up and walk at dawn; it is a marvelous time to be about. Since our man is in really rotten shape, he may have trouble the first time just getting around a one mile course. Nevertheless, he should time his walk in order to chart his improvement. If he is too sore after that first walk, he can take the next day off. Weight lifters and long distance runners often work out every other day, allowing the body to rest and assimilate the changes on rest days. On the third day, our man should try two miles and try not to stop. A brisk pace is actually more comfortable and less tiring than starting and stopping or an aimless saunter.

At the end of the first week, our man should be able to cover the mile courses in 20-30 minutes and the two miles in less than an hour. By the end of the second week he should be able to do three miles in an hour; the weekend before he leaves he ought to walk the three miles twice in a period of two hours. Walking regularly (at least every other day) and briskly (charting the times and always trying to improve) will strengthen the legs and provide endurance.

To develop the lungs and toughen the knees there is nothing like running. Once the body is used to walking, it is safe to go running. I find shorter distances (50 to 200 yards) of hard running to be more effective than a mile of slow jogging. The high school track is a good place to run. To increase my wind I run until I am gasping, then I run another twenty yards before slowing to a walk. When our man runs out of breath, he should walk slowly but not stop until his breathing returns to normal and then start running again.

By the end of two weeks, he will find his wind greatly improved and he should be able to navigate the one mile course, alternately running and walking. As his lung capacity grows and begins to catch up to his leg development, he will begin to feel fatigue in his knees. The ideally conditioned backpacker on a difficult stretch should feel approximately equal discomfort in his knees and lungs.

To condition the shoulders to the pull of his pack, it is only necessary for our man—probably the second or third week—to start wearing it on his walks. Books make good ballast and ten or fifteen pounds will be enough for the first tour of his routes under load. This can be increased to twenty-five shortly before the trip. Since backpacks are not made for running, our man will want to alternate unladen run-walk tours of his routes with pack carrying tours. So far, all of his work has probably been on flat, paved sidewalk. But backpacking usually means traversing rough, steep country, so our man should hunt out the steepest, roughest terrain in the area and work out a course or two for the final week of conditioning.

Only on steep trails are the conditions in mountain wilderness closely approximated. The knees need the unique strains produced by going up and down hill and the ankles need rough and uneven terrain to develop toughness and resistance to sprain. No amount of walking or running on city sidewalks can accomplish the same thing. I find the bulldozed fire trails in the steep Berkeley hills behind my home to be perfect. When I was working at a desk job and wanted to get ready for a weekend trip, I would drive to the fire trails on the preceeding Sunday, Tuesday and Thursday evenings and spend an hour or two running uphill until either my legs or lungs forced me to stop. Then I would slow to a walk until I was sufficiently recovered to run again. A great amount of conditioning can be compressed into a week in this manner—providing the body is in reasonably good shape beforehand.

In addition to run-walk tours in the hills, our man should carry a loaded pack on perhaps a total of ten miles worth of walking trips through the hills. The weight of the pack will condition the shoulders, knees, ankles and feet to the strain and jarring that rough country provides. Hiking in the hills with a pack and run-walk tours without one—this is the real conditioning. Walking and running on city sidewalks is only 'pre-conditioning' for people unaccustomed to vigorous exercise.

From the beginning of this program, the feet should receive special consideration. On all excursions, our man should be wearing the boots and socks he wll take on his trip. This will break in the boots and mate them to the feet before the trip begins, and it will toughen the feet

Dividing up the community gear.

sufficiently to prevent chafing and blistering in the wilds. Un-doubtedly, the most overlooked and easiest part of foot conditioning is cutting the toenails.

Long toenails will make boots seem too short and can be painfully crippling on downhill stretches. Cutting long toenails the night before a trip will result in pain and inflamation on the trail. Great discomfort (and holes in worn socks) can be prevented by awareness of the problem. I try to keep my toenails reasonably short with frequent cutting, but I also remind myself, sometimes in writing, to cut my toenails four or five days before a trip.

I think the best way to toughen up feet is going barefoot. Before a trip I go barefoot around the house and I like to go for short barefoot walks. Concrete sidewalks are great tougheners and callous builders. Sunlight and fresh air are healthy for feet, cetainly a lot healthier than damp, constricting shoes. I spend enough time barefoot to sport a pretty fair tan on the tops of my feet by the end of the summer. Tanning can be extremely important to the comfort and pleasure of a trip. People who take lily white skin to high altitudes become horribly burned unless they keep themselves carefully and continuously covered.

A tan acquired in the city or at the beach will never fully protect the hiker against fierce high altitude sunlight but it will enable him to travel with only normal discretion without risk of serious burning. Nothing is worse than having to hike in the heat completely shrouded from the sun—unless it is suffering with sunburned shoulders that will have to carry a pack the next day. Trying to safely tan white skin by short periods of exposure to fierce high altitude sun is a bothersome, inconvenient process on a backpacking trip.

Our man will be well advised to start cultivating a tan by getting out in the sun (in a bathing suit if he expects to hike in shorts) on weekends from the begining of his conditioning period—taking care to use discretion and sunburn preventatives. If there is anything more vulnerable to mountain sunshine than city skin it is sunburned city skin that has freshly peeled. Special care should be taken to avoid burning the nose to prevent starting a cycle of peeling, burning and repeeling.

Not many backpackers will need to take the full conditioning course outlined above, but most people will enjoy a more comfortable trip to the extent that they complete their conditioning at home.

Packing Up

With trip planning, preparation and conditioning out of the way, all that remains is to pack up and go. For most people, that means taking a car to the trailhead; and sometimes that journey is the hardest trip their car ever makes. On more than a few trips, the biggest adventure, the greatest challenge and the hardest work is getting the car to the trailhead and back. I have slipped off the road, gotten stuck in the mud and hung up on the rocks. I have run out of water and gas, blown out tires, smashed into rocks and killed the motor fording creeks. Trailheads have a habit of lying deserted at the ends of unmaintained rocky roads, so it behooves the backpacker to take more than a casual interest in the condition of his car.

Backpackers are often so intent on getting their gear into the car and getting away that they forget to carry the extra food, drink, clothing and money that is so welcome at the end of a trip. For purposes of acclimation and an early start, I like to drive from home to the trailhead on the eve of the trip in order to sleep at the highest elevation possible. To simplify matters, I usually take a car camping sleeping bag and mattress to insure a good rest, and no matter how late I arrive I always choose my bedsite carefully and excavate for my hips and shoulders. If I have to cook, I take along a separate stove, food and utensils rather than rummage in my backpacking gear. When possible, it is usually most convenient to eat in a restaurant or brown bag it in the car.

While driving to the trailhead, I try to get a final weather forecast on the car radio. Sometimes at the last available pay phone, I call the nearest Weather Bureau or airport or Highway Patrol office to get an extended forecast. On the basis of this information, together with weather conditons at the trailhead, I make my final selection of protective gear: tents, rain suits, ponchos, ground sheets, tarps, parkas, mittens, caps and sweaters. My usual procedure, after decid-ing what to carry, is to spread out an old tarp, brought along for that purpose, and to empty on to it all the food and community gear.

Then, if there are two of us, one of us divides the pile on the basis of both weight and bulk into two equal stacks; the other man gets first choice. It is probably a good idea to employ a scale to be precise, but we generally just heft comparable items at arms' length and hope that compensating errors will cancel out major differences. Sometimes one man, because of his pack size will be short on space and may request less bulky items, but both hikers still split the weight evenly,

unless there is a marked difference in their size. Carrying ability is proportional to body weight. Your performance will be seriously impaired, say the physiologists, if you try to carry a pack weighing more than 20-25% of your body weight.

After combining my share of the community gear with my personal equipment, I start to make up my pack. First I set aside clothing that may be needed in a hurry, trail food, notebook, pencil, compass, first aid kit, camera, lip salve, sunburn cream, bandana, mosquito dope and anything else I expect to need on the trail. Then, I make a layer of the heaviest, densest items in such a way that the weight will lie as high and as close to my back as possible. From the remaining gear I take those items least likely to be needed and, working my way to the top, fill the remainder of the pack snugly. If I am hiking in shorts, my long trousers are packed on top for easy access, or in the lower compartment of a divided bag.

The gear set aside to be used on the trail is then systematically divided between the pack's outside pockets. To find things fast, it helps to use the same arrangement for every trip. For instance, although I sprinkle wooden kitchen matches in every pocket, the main supply always rides in the upper right hand pocket. With the last of the small items stowed, I stuff my rolled foam mattress into (or onto) the top of the back pack and cinch down the flap over it. My sleeping bag is then strapped or snapped beneath the three quarter pack bag. Last to be attached is my two-piece fly rod, broken down, but with the reel still attached. The butt ends seat in a 35 mm film can taped to the bottom right rail. A thong at the top crossbar lashes the rod to the rail. Finally, I check all zippers, buttons, ties and lashings.

With the pack made up and hoisted onto the hood of the car for easy mounting, I go through my pockets, hide my wallet after extracting two or three dimes for pay phones, and lock the car. Normally I hide the keys nearby, rather than take the chance of losing them. I slip into my pack and adjust the buckles so the weight is bourne equally by my shoulders and hips. With nothing further to detain me, I set forth up the trail.

10 WALKING

There is nothing much to be said about walking . . . on a sidewalk at sea level for short distances, carrying nothing. But walking long distances on rough ground through high altitude wilderness, under sizeable loads, is something else. Luckily there are a few stratagems and techniques that can add considerable pleasure to walking in the wilds.

There is a myth that one should find a comfortable pace and then stick to it. Nothing could be farther from the truth. The most common error among hikers is trying doggedly to maintain a set pace despite changes in the grade. Constant speed is an impossible goal. Comfortable, efficient walking depends on maintaining one's energy output—not one's speed—at a level which will not produce excessive fatigue. This simply means slowing down when the trail climbs, then speeding up when it levels off.

The length of one's stride should also be variable. When the trail suddenly grows steeper, I not only slow down, I take shorter steps. When the trail levels off, my stride gradually lengthens. Walking in this manner, i.e. trying to maintain an even and comfortable output of energy rather than trying to maintain a constant speed, I am never forced to stop from exhaustion, and I log more miles per day in greater comfort.

There's a scientific basis for my "variable speed" philosophy. Specialists have determined that for every individual and set of walking conditions there is an *ideal* pace, an optimal speed which requires minimal energy per step. Our internal computer instinctively tries to conserve energy and it will govern our speed for maximum efficiency—if we let it! Ignoring the clockwork within ourselves—by hurrying and even by moving too slowly—will be far more tiring than the optimal pace because it's using more energy than necessary.

Since every individual will have a different ideal speed, group travel presents certain problems. A 5'2" lady complained, "My 6'3" boyfriend, who is normally very thoughtful, spent a lot of time on our backpacking trip bawling me out for being slow, clumsy and lazy—none of which I am if I'm accepted at my size and weight. It took me three steps for every two of his." Her boyfriend complained about his

40 pound pack, though it was only 20% of his weight, while she struggled to keep up carrying 25 pounds, fully 25% of her hundred pound weight. This couple was trapped into a mutually unhappy situation by his failure to understand their different physical capacities and by the less obvious but more common assumption that they had to travel together—which means at the same speed.

Because of their construction and chemical makeup, women are at a disadvantage carrying a pack in the wilds—quite apart from their lesser size and weight. Couples determined to hike together can best equalize the situation by adjusting their loads. In the case above, I would recommend the lady carry 15 pounds while her boyfriend lugs 50. Where togetherness isn't vital I urge people to travel at their own pace, the tortoises starting earlier and meeting the hares at the halfway point for lunch. I also advise people to savor the joys of solo travel or pick companions with similar capabilities. Increasingly on the trail I meet carefree groups of women happily poking along together, free of the strain of performing or keeping up.

The experts have learned some interesting facts that can help us walk more functionally. Walking involves about a hundred different muscles, but *all* the walker's propulsive thrust is delivered by the terminal bone of the big toe. Our computer propels us by converting potential energy to kinetic energy with almost 50% efficiency. Walking is a state of carefully controlled falling, using the acceleration of gravity for the purpose. There is an advantage, it turns out, to a certain amount of bobbing as we walk. The extra work of raising the body increases the help we get from gravity by permitting us to fall further with each step. Walking downhill is easier because the body can fall further. Freely swinging arms help walking efficiency by stabilizing the shoulders and pelvis with the thrust of their counter rotation.

Hurrying, especially uphill, can be counter productive in another way. Superexertion produces lactic acid in the blood, which hampers muscle performance, causes great discomfort and requires more than an hour for recovery, during which the walker suffers from exhaustion. So the clever backpacker's strategy requires keeping his activity level below the lactic acid formation stage. On difficult grades that means slowing the pace to a comfortable level or stopping frequently to rest and allow oxidation to flush the blood of acid buildup. By experimentation I have discovered that on the steepest trails under heavy load I drop below the level of painful lactic acid buildup by shortening each step from 18 inches to 14. That four inches makes a huge difference in my comfort.

It is important to react immediately to changes in grade. Failure to cut speed instantly when the trail turns abruptly upward places a demand on the body for extra exertion. And extra exertion consumes a disproportionately large part of one's store of energy. For instance, with the energy required to run fifty yards uphill one can easily hike a quarter mile up the same grade—in far greater comfort. Large expenditures of energy—running, lunging, jumping, taking huge steps, even hiking too fast—must be avoided.

On a really steep slope, at high altitude under load, or where the footing is bad (sand, scree or loose snow), I adjust my pace even more precisely by controlling my step-to-breath ratio. I may, for instance, take two steps to the breath, inhaling as I plant my right foot and exhaling as I plant my left. If that proves hard to maintain, I may slow to a breath for every step or even two breaths per step, with a greatly shortened stride. On exceptionally difficult slopes it is better to slow to a crawl, taking six inch steps, then to make the frequent stops a faster pace would require. Starting and stopping consume extra energy. A dependable rule of thumb is that where the going is hard it is better to slow down and keep going than it is to make frequent stops. An unlooked for dividend of step-to-breath counting is the welcome distraction the counting provides.

Every experienced backpacker at some time or other has experienced a sinking feeling when, coming around a bend, he discovers a long, shadeless trail switchbacking endlessly upward toward a high and distant pass. When I find myself faced with a prospect of this sort, I often distract myself from the ordeal with the self-induced euphoria that comes of concentrated daydreaming. In a state of mild self-hypnosis, my daydreams so totally absorb my conscious mind that the discomfort of the grind goes mercifully dim.

As I start upward toward the pass I rummage about in my memory for some event or scene that is so thoroughly pleasant and engrossing that I recall it with consummate relish. Then I unhurriedly embellish my recollection with the endless details that enable it vividly to fill my conscious mind. At first, it may be hard to escape into the past, but as the details pile up my awareness of present time and distance almost ceases. I climb automatically, sufficiently aware of my surroundings to make the necessary adjustments, but too engrossed with my dream to feel the discomfort. In fact, I'm sometimes reluctant, when the pass has been reached, to abandon my dream and shift my attention to the country ahead.

While I find daydreaming dependable and easily sustained, some people prefer the more companionable distraction of conversation. One of my regular walking companions, when we face a demanding stretch of trail, will say "Well, what shall we talk about?" We may very well get rid of a quarter of a mile before we settle on a suitable topic. Often we trade accounts of movies, dreams, books, trout we have caught or mountains we have climbed. Sometimes we may be driven to simple word games (especially useful with children) like Twenty Questions or Animal-Mineral-Vegetable. If we have been out in the country awhile, we may get rid of half an hour concocting menus for fantastic meals. Talking as we move upward tends to slow the pace, but that, in turn, further reduces the discomfort.

Despite my advice "to slow down and keep going," rest stops are a

daydream dis- comfort away.

vital part of walking. Unless the trail is like a sidewalk, one has little opportunity for looking around; the footing requires almost undivided attention. The walking itself is usually the least memorable part of any trip. So rest stops offer a means of savoring the country as well as restoring the body. One school holds that rests ought to be ruled by the clock, i.e. so many minutes of resting followed by so many minutes of hiking. This arbitrary arrangement makes no allowance for the difficulty of the terrain or the allure of the country.

But what's worse is the notion that one needs to be ruled by the clock, even in the wilderness. The tyranny of time, it seems to me, is one of the things that people go to the woods to escape. I am willing to admit the usefulness of a wristwatch in the woods for arranging a rendezvous with other watch-wearing members of the party—but I find clock time as dispensable in the wilds as doorbells, radios, telephones and cars, and I refuse to carry a watch, with only minor inconvenience.

If I really need to know the time my compass will give a rough approximation, provided the sun is shining. I set the compass in the sun, settle the needle on north, then set off the declination (17 degrees east in California). With the compass thus oriented, I stand a straight twig on the compass rim so that its shadow falls across the needle hub to the opposite rim. The position of the shadow on the opposite rim gives me a close approximation of sun time—by thinking of the compass as a watch with north at noon.

To reconcile sun time to daylight saving time, I add an hour. To tell time early or late in the day one only needs to know the hours of sunrise and sunset. Of course, some allowance must be made for mountains that rise high to either the east or west. Time is still important, but it is sun time, not clock time, that counts. How long before sunset, when it starts to grow cool? How long before dark? These are the pertinent questions in the wilds.

Getting back to rest stops, most walkers, provided they have a modicum of self-discipline and know how far they have to go, will find it more satisfactory to rest when they want to or need to. I like to stop, if I can manage it, beside a stream, at the top of a slope, in the first shade after a treeless stretch, where a log or rock forms a natural seat, or at any point where the view is unusually fine. I also favor mossy dells, waterfalls, brilliant patches of wildflowers, and fords where I can wash my feet or set up my rod and take a few casts.

When it comes to a real rest, I like to imagine I have earned it. On a particularly difficult slope, for instance, I might promise myself a rest after another hundred steps. Sometimes a hundred is impossible and I have to settle for fifty or even twenty-five. But if I get to thirty-five and think I can squeeze out another fifteen—I try it. For variety, and to add to the distraction, I sometimes count my steps backwards.

When I am ready to rest I take some pains to enjoy it. I slip out of my pack (leaving it propped against a rock or tree to make it easy to put back on) and sit or lie down. If my boots are the least bit uncomfortable or my feet are damp, I take off both boots and socks and set them to air in the sun or breeze. If there is water running nearby, I give my feet a soapless washing and a rub and let them dry in the sun. If I am feeling faint or tired I lie down with my feet propped high against a tree so the blood can drain from my legs back into my body. Once my fatigue has drained away and my breathing has returned to normal, I usually have something to eat.

Sometimes the greatest benefit of a rest stop—especially if there are children along—is having some fun, doing a little exploring. I like to stroll away from the trail to have a look at country I would otherwise miss. Often enough, I discover something unsuspected—an abandoned prospect hole, a bed of mushrooms, a hidden view, the remains of a lean-to, a tiny spring or a wild sheep horn.

A rest may last anywhere from thirty seconds to overnight! When the time comes to move on, it is vital to start out at a moderate pace. There is a tendency, especially with children, to rocket up the trail after a refreshing rest. I have often seen eager children start off at a run, slow to a walk, then sink into a panting, dispirited trudge—all within sixty seconds.

The single most valuable (and spectacular) walking technique I

rest stops are a vital part of walking.

know of, one which literally flushes away fatigue, is variously called the 'rest step' or 'limp step.' Though little known among backpackers, this mountaineer's trick is based on the simplest of principles. When a hiker climbs steeply or carries great weights, the strain on the muscles around the knee is excessive and these muscles quickly fill with lactic and carbonic acids, the products of fatigue. This buildup of acids in overworked muscles, in turn, produces the painful ache that makes terrific slopes or heavy loads so uncomfortable.

The rest step is designed to flush away the acids of fatigue, thus relieving the ache they create. In the course of normal walking knee muscles never quite relax. But if at some point in the step the leg is allowed to go entirely limp, even for only a fraction of a second, the excess acids are carried away and the pain miraculously disappears.

The necessary relaxation can be managed in either of two ways. The leading leg can be allowed to go limp for an instant just after the foot is placed for a new step and just before the weight is shifted to it. Or the trailing leg can be relaxed just after the weight is transferred to the lead leg and just before the trailing leg is lifted. I have gotten in the habit of relaxing the lead leg, but most people seem to find it easier to let the trailing leg go limp. The trailing leg method is also easier to learn and easier to teach. My daughter learned it when she was eight.

We were day hiking up a relentlessly climbing trail that gains 1200 feet in less than a mile. When she complained that she was tired and her legs hurt, I had her stop and shift all her weight first to one leg then the other, explaining that the pain would go away from a leg allowed to go limp. After she had stopped to flush her legs in this manner several times, I suggested that she take a small step forward with the leg that was relaxed, explaining that it was less tiring to keep going, even very slowly, when you rested your legs. Before we reached the top she was able to flush the fatigue from her legs whenever she needed to, without stopping.

As few as two or three limp steps in succession will usually bring amazing relief. Of course, the acids of fatigue continue to collect as long as the knees continue to work hard, and it soon becomes necessary to flush them again. But I find that after half a dozen limp steps I can return to my normal stride for anywhere from ten to a hundred yards. Besides offering relief from aching muscles, limp-stepping also provides comic relief by causing its practitioners to look a little like staggering drunks.

A technique of somewhat narrower application is the Indian Step, a style of walking long used by cross-country skiers and European gymnasts as well as American Indians. Modern Americans tend to walk without swinging their hips. The Indian travels more efficiently. At the end of each step he swings the hip foreward as well as the leg, pivoting at the waist. And he leans forward slightly as he walks. This forward lean and turing of the hips lengthens the stride, positions the feet directly in front of one another, and minimizes the wasteful up and down movement. The result is a more fluid, floating walk, with less wasted motion. And on easy ground the longer stride produces more speed. The chief disadvantages of the Indian Step are that it is difficult to master, requiring agility and balance; and the advantages are greatest for the unburdened walker.

I occasionally use the Indian Step if I am lightly burdened and wish to travel rapidly across level terrain that offers good footing. I also employ its principles to minimize my up and down motion on a steep climb. The easiest way to get the feel of the step is consciously to stretch the stride, thrusting the hip forwad, aiming the foot for the center of the trail, swinging the shoulders counter to the hip thrust. Once the rhythm is established the shoulder swing can be reduced. Walking on narrow city curbs is a good way to practice.

Having dealt with uphill and level trail hiking, it is time to go down. It is common to feel relief when the trail starts down because it is so much easier on the lungs. But downhill travel is twice as hard on the legs as going up. When descending a steep trail I try to cushion the shock of each downward step by rolling my hip forward (not unlike the Indian Step movement) and placing my foot with the knee slightly bent. As I transfer my weight I allow my knee to flex so that it functions in much the same fashion as an automobile shock absorber, reducing the jarring that downhill travel inevitably produces.

Trails provide a measure of dependability and security. Cross-country walking is altogether different. Instead of relying on an established course, one must find his own way; instead of the improved footing of a prepared trail, there are obstacles to contend with. Carrying a pack cross-country can be serious business and requires much greater experience, balance, strength, adventurousness and caution than does backpacking by trail.

In the California Sierra in the space of a mile, one may have to contend with brush, bog, loose sand, boulder slopes, snow, deadfalls, mud, streams and cliffs. And one of the most treacherous steep slopes I ever descended was covered with innocent-looking tufts of ex-

Limp-stepping brings amazing relief:

tremely slippery grass. Just as slippery are glacially polished slabs that are wet, mossy or invisibly dusted with sand. Footing of this sort demands caution. I often take some trouble to climb around a wet or mossy slab, and when traction is vital I test the slope for sand by listening for the telltale grating sound. When I must cross slippery terrain, I often twist my foot sightly as I put my weight upon it to determine how well my boot soles are gripping.

When climbing a sandy slope it is important to plant the foot as flatly as possible; the greater the surface area of boot on sand the shorter the distance one is likely to slip backward. If there are rocks or patches of grass or low brush, I think of them as stepping stones and zig-zag from one to the other. Sometimes steep sand is best treated like snow and the easiest way up is a series of switchbacking traverses or a herringbone step in which the toes are turned outward.

Spring travel in the Sierra is often over old snow; sometimes I walk all day and scarcely touch dry ground. Hard and hummocky slopes of spring snow can be extremely tiring, and nothing short of wading tests the waterproofing of boots so severely. It is virtually impossible to keep feet dry. All one can do is carry several pairs of dry socks for a single day's travel. Since wet boots are extremely slow to dry, the Indians of northern Canada carry four pairs of sturdy moccasins or mukluks instead. By the time the fourth pair is soaked through the first pair has dried. My own solution, if I am rushing the season, is to content myself with day hikes and keep dry boots waiting at the trailhead.

In the spring there is the constant danger of falling through a thin crust of snow with painful, even serious, results. There is hardly an easier way to bark shins, twist ankles and even break legs. Whenever I cross a rock-studded spring snowfield I am reminded of a trip I made with my father when I was twelve. I was walking a little ahead and we were talking. When he failed to answer a question I turned around, and he was gone. There was nothing but a vast snowfield broken only by an occasional rock. As I followed his footprints back toward one of these, I heard what sounded like muffled shouting. Close beside the rock, which turned out to be a boulder, I came to a hole ten feet deep. In the bottom stood my father, uninjured, calling for help. It took half an hour to get him out. The cavern had been hollowed by heat from the sun transmitted through the boulder despite the fact that only a few square feet of rock actually rose above the snowfield.

The margins of spring snowfields should always be treated with suspicion. So should snow-covered logs and snow from which issues the muffled sound of gurgling water. The best strategy I know for testing suspect snow is to kick it without actually committing any weight to it. If it withstands the kicking it can probably support my weight. Sometimes a big step or jump will avoid the necessity of stepping on what looks like rotten or undermined snow.

In the spring it can be dangerous to ford creeks and streams, never mind rivers. If you can't find a log or a series of stepping stones, you'll have to wade. The first decision is whether to protect your feet but soak your boots, or take a chance on injuring your feet (and increasing the liklihood of falling) by going barefoot. If you choose the latter, be sure your socks and boots are tied securely to your pack or around your neck as you wade, so that they can't possibly be lost if you fall or go under—unless you're prepared to walk barefoot to the car! When wearing a pack on a dangerous crossing, always release the hipbelt and loosen the shoulder straps so you can jettison it instantly to protect yourself from drowning.

If conditions warrant, send the strongest man in the party across first with a rope but no pack. A fixed rope tied tightly between trees will provide a great deal of security and peace of mind. So will poles to probe for holes and brace like a third leg against the current. Choose a wide shallow ford over a short but swift or deep one. The job will be easier if you start on the upstream side of a good fording site and plan to angle downstream, because that's where you'll end up. If you can help it, don't cross immediately above a falls, cataract or other substantial hazard. Organize your party for the safest possible crossing. And remember that risks are enormously magnified when you're traveling alone. It's better to change your plans or make any detour than it is to take a chance when there's no one to help if you get in trouble.

Nothing consumes energy in such big gulps as maneuvers that require extra effort, like taking a giant step up onto a rock or log. If I cannot easily make my way around such obstacles, I transfer most of the extra effort to my shoulders and arms by placing both hands on top of the knee that is making the step and pushing down hard as I step upward.

On exceptionally steep rocky slopes, it sometimes becomes neces-

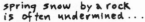

spring snow by a rock
is often undermined . . . .   so step over such areas.

sary to step forward onto the toe of the foot instead of the heel. Toe
stepping adds power and balance on steep grades, but soon tires calf
muscles. I find it helps to alternate heel and toe steps to prevent the
cramping the latter produce. By following ten toe steps with twenty
heel steps, I spread the work over two sets of muscles. The necessity
of counting helps distract me from the rigours of the climb. If this
arrangement continues to produce excessive fatigue, I sheer off from
the fall-line and climb in longer but easier switchbacking traverses.

When climbing cross-country it is sometimes necessary to remind
oneself that the easiest route up may not be the easiest way down.
Going up, I generally go out of my way to avoid sand, snow and scree;
coming down I go out of my way to make use of them. Nothing is so
pleasant after a hard climb up a mountain as glissading down a slanting
snowfield or gliding with giant, sliding steps down slopes of sand or
gravel.

Scrambling—climbing that requires the use of hands, but not
ropes—demands agility, good balance, endurance and desire. Success may depend on the scrambler's ability to discover a feasible route
by studying the slope during the approach and by consulting a large
scale topographic map. The basic rules for beginning climbers include: never climb alone; never go up a pitch you cannot get down;
never climb on your knees; lean out from, not in toward the slope
when exposure is great; and never take chances or attempt maneuvers
that are beyond your skill.

Despite the need for caution, climbing can be enjoyed by most
walkers, including women and children. Both my wife and daughter
have climbed a number of peaks with me; my daughter made her first
ascent when she was six. It is unfortunate that so many people think
climbing means inching up sheer cliffs by means of ropes, pitons and
limitless willpower. There is immense satisfaction to be gained in
scrambling up peaks that demand little more than determination and
offer no disconcerting exposure.

Climbing can be as safe as the climber cares to make it. As I come down a mountain late in the day, I remind myself that the majority of mountaineering accidents occur after three in the afternoon, and that twice as many falls happen on the way down as on the way up. The most expert climbers force themselves to descend with caution, thinking out difficult steps in advance to keep down the chance of injury.

Rock-hopping—crossing a boulder field by stepping or jumping from rock to rock—is probably the most demanding and dangerous way to travel in the mountains, but it is often unavoidable. I mentally try to keep a step ahead of my feet so when I run out of rocks I will be able to stop. I also treat every boulder, no matter how large, as though the addition of my weight will cause it to move. To slow myself down on a dangerous slope, I sometimes think back to a cross-country backpacking descent on which a companion, when forced to leap from a rolling boulder, opened six inches of his leg to the bone. Whenever I am forced to make a sudden or awkward jump, I try to land simultaneously on both feet with knees bent, to cushion the shock and minimize the danger of injury.

With more and more people heading for the wilds, the complaints grow louder and more frequent: "You can't get away from people anymore." . . . "There's nowhere decent left to go."

Nevertheless, I manage, with very little effort, to find plenty of places to camp, day hike routes, peaks to climb, even trout water to fish, where the country is handsome and wild and I see more wildlife than people. Others who find their wilderness getting crowded may be interested in some of the stratagems I use to get away from the mob and get closer to the country.

A majorty of hikers, or so it seems to me, are slaves to the trails. Many newcomers to walking are perhaps not aware that trails are the means, not the ends. The trail, however faint, is merely an extension of civilization. Wilderness does not begin until the trail is left behind. Trip planners, without thinking, plot their routes exclusively from existing trail systems. And many squander a whole vacation on wilderness travel that never leaves the beaten path. But the solitude—the true wilderness experience—does not materialize until the traveler is finding his own way through wild country, rather than following a route marked by others.

By far the easiest way to escape the trail is to day hike, carrying only sweater, lunch and first aid kit. More country can be covered in a day without pack than on a weekend under load. Hikers who want to spend a maximum amount of time in truly wild country may find it more fruitful to car camp close to the trailhead and spend the time dayhiking. I sometimes begin a wilderness weekend by backpacking cross-country for less than a mile to some unsuspected campsite by a spring or small creek; I then spend the bulk of my time dayhiking unencumbered.

The most heavily populated wilderness areas are those where fish are (theoretically) to be caught. It is my experience that most trail

the arms can help on a long step up.

networks link fish-bearing waters. A great many people who have little or no interest in fishing regularly camp in noisy over-used areas beside lakes, simply because that is where the trails take them. In heavily used country, the trails and the campsites along them are generally the poorest and certainly the least wild places. By planning routes that avoid well-known trout waters, I escape the mobs, find beautiful virgin camping areas with ample water, and occasionally I find exceptional fishing.

A good many trips have been ruined in the planning by the seemingly harmless assumption: "We ought to be able to make ten miles a day." On some days fifty feet would be too far. People have a habit of committing themselves to rigid goals: making 11.2 miles, fishing Lockjaw Lake, climbing Indian Peak. Somehow these achievements become substituted for the original or underlying reason for going—to enjoy roaming wild country. When people become so achievement oriented that they measure the success of a trip in terms of miles tramped, elevation gained or speed records, they often find themselves losing interest in wilderness travel. Working toward ambitious goals becomes too much like the rat-race at home.

I do not reject all goals when planning a trip, but I try to plan routes with maximum flexibility and minimum strain, thinking in terms of options and possibilities rather than achievement. I try to arrange for the possibility that I will find a place so perfect that I lose all ambition to travel farther.

One of the greatest sources of joy I know is climbing to some attractive summit. It has been a long time since I called myself a mountain climber, but I enjoy getting to the top as much as ever. And I get just as much pleasure from walking up a little granite dome after dinner to watch the sun go down as I do spending all day working my way up a mountain. The important thing to remember is that anyone can (and should) make his or her way to the top of an appropriate hill, ridge or peak. I know of no better way to savor the wilderness.

When I was a boy I had the good fortune to belong to a small group led by the well-known author-naturalist, Vinson Brown. Vince used to take us into wild places he knew in the hills and station us, out of sight of one another, perhaps a hundred feet apart, on conveniently located rocks and logs. After wiggling into comfortable positions, we would be instructed to sit absolutely still for five minutes, not moving anything but our eyes.

If we were quiet enough, Vince told us, the birds and insects and small animals in the area would come gradually to accept us as part of the environment, just as they accepted the rocks or logs on which we were sitting. It was truly remarkable how well it worked. I don't know a better way to get close to the country, and often when I am walking alone in wild country I will seat myself in some fruitful looking place and let myself once again become part of the country.

In most parts of the country summer style backpacking and wilderness travel have to be modified for mid-winter climates. Many people don't bother. The majority of those who like to hike in the summer give it up with a sigh when the weather turns cold and begin the long wait for the following summer.

But one needs contact with the earth just as much in the winter as during the summer. Maybe more. In the winter we spend most of our time confined to the cities and the insides of buildings. A majority of people, in the depth of winter, go to work in the dark and come home in the dark, seeing the sun dimly through the window or only on weekends. We lose contact with the real world, the natural order of things. And our retreat indoors from the cold and the dark contributes, I am convinced, to sagging spirits, and a liability to illness. Over the

"Getting to the top" can be a joy.

years I have discovered that I am happier, healthier, more vitally alive if I get outside often to work up a sweat and immerse myself in the natural landscape.

With more and more people walking in the wilds, trail manners have become more important. In most states discharging firearms, even during hunting season, is illegal across or in the vicinity of a trail. Equally objectionable is the boom of gunfire which invades privacy and solitude, and shatters the wilderness experience of other travelers for miles around. Guns are not needed as protection against wildlife and they have no place in today's crowded wildlands.

Horses and pack stock, once necessary to reach remote country, are now less common. But since stock can be unpredictable and difficult to control, it retains the right-of-way on trails. Walkers should move several yards off the trail, preferably downslope, and stand quietly while animals pass. Since walkers inevitably travel at different speeds, slower-moving parties should be considerate enough of faster walkers to let them move by. And fast hikers ought to politely ask permission to pass when the trail is narrow.

Over-riding the backpacker's concern for his comfort should be a sense of responsibility toward the country through which he passes. Increased travel in diminishing wild areas makes it necessary for all of us, consciously, to protect the environment and keep it clean. On the trail this means throwing away nothing, not even a cigarette butt, broken shoelace or match. In camp it means burning, then bagging, but never burying, garbage. Leftover edibles, not including egg shells and orange peels, can be scattered for the birds and animals. Everything else should go in heavy plastic garbage bags to be packed out. The thoughtful walker takes pride in leaving no trace of his passing.

11 CAMPING

For a majority of backpackers, a genuinely pleasant camp is essential to the enjoyment of any trip. Unfortunately, the more comfortable the camp the greater the quantity of gear that must be carried—and the harder the walk required to reach it.

The backpacker with no mattress, stove or tent travels comfortably light. He can go faster and farther than heavily laden hikers, and he is free to leave the trails and travel cross-country. But when the sun goes down he becomes increasingly vulnerable and must find comparatively ideal conditions in order to make a comfortable camp. The party carrying a floored tent equipped with mosquito netting and rainfly, stove, mattresses and all the trimmings is practically invulnerable to camping conditions, but its range and speed and traveling comfort are more limited, and it is more dependent upon trails.

The dilemma can never be completely resolved, but as a backpacker's experience, technique, and equipment improve, the cost (in pounds) of camping comfort can be considerably reduced.

The question of what to take must be reconsidered afresh for every trip. The likely weather, season and type of trip will influence the decisions regarding tents, tarps, ponchos and storm gear—so will the route, the type of outing, length of stay and familiarity with the country. There is no convenient way to avoid decisions, though some hikers persist in carrying the same gear on every trip. On a two mile trail haul to a family base camp I might seriously consider carrying the kitchen sink. On a thirty mile cross-country ridgewalk I pare my equipment to Spartan proportions.

No amount of mountaineering equipment, of course, can insure camping comfort in a steep, waterless, windy rockpile. There is simply no substitute for a wise choice of campsite. No skill is of greater value to the comfort-oriented backpacker than the ability to select the best possible spot to camp, and then to develop it for optimum comfort.

A persistent wind, damp ground, sloping bedsites, a lack of fuel or shelter, noisy neighbors, clouds of mosquitos, lack of water, etc., will rob the best equipped party of a pleasant night. There are times, of course, when bad weather, poor planning, inhospitable country or just plain bad luck make a terrible location unavoidable. The veteran backpacker will choose the least terrible site and devise the most ingenious development in order to make it yield minimal comfort.

First priority in site selection must go to bedsites since nothing is more important than a good nights' sleep. Damp and sloping ground should be avoided—so should roots and rocks that cannot be removed. Spare clothing and equipment should not be forgotten in the struggle to make a poor bedsite passable. Shelter from wind, unwelcome sun, evening downdrafts or intense cold may be essential to restful sleep.

As many a beginning camper has learned the hard way, there's more to a good bed than sleeping bag, mattress and ground cloth. A well-chosen, well-prepared bedsite may be even more important. Practiced backpackers will recognize a good place. Beginners will need to consider various criteria. The chief enemies of a good night's sleep are cold, dampness, wind, insects, running water, flying sparks, falling widowmakers, avalanche and the snoring of one's companion.

The most common mistake is to select a depression, dry ravine, streambank or dried up snowpool because it is sheltered from the afternoon wind. But winds have a habit of disappearing around dusk, turning an unfriendly promontory into an admirable camp. As the evening advances, a gentle but persistent night wind commonly rises to pour cold heavy air down the streambeds and ravines and into those inviting depressions, leaving them as much as ten degrees colder than higher ground only a few feet away.

Dry ravines and snow pools, besides collecting cold air at night, also collect running water quickly in a cloudburst. Meadows tend to be damp and attract heavy dew. Dew results when moist air cools, causing a fallout of condensation. Dew will be heavier near a lake, stream or meadow, and just after a storm. Heavy dew is capable of severly wetting an unprotected sleeping bag in just a few hours. Woe to the weary backpacker who, late on a night of heavy dew, has to climb inside a drenched bag left open or inside out.

There are enough advantages to sleeping beneath a tree to more than compensate for the filtered view of the stars. Trees serve as an umbrella to shield the sleeper from heavy dew and light rain. On a bitterly cold, clear night sheltering branches serve as insulation from solar radiation. The air temperture beneath a tree may be ten degrees warmer than a bedsite exposed to the chill night sky. Since I rarely want to be awakened at dawn, I regularly position my bed to the west of a good sized tree so that it can shade me from the early morning sun. The shade allows me to sleep an hour or so past sunrise without being cooked in my mummy bag. Trees frequently serve as windbreaks, clothes hangers, pack supports, tarp tie-downs, and a source of cushioning pine-needle mattresses. (The cutting of living boughs for a mattress can no longer be justified.)

It is generally important to know the direction of the prevailing wind in camp and to use this information in locating a bedsite, especially if the weather is unsettled or threatening. Even on a still night it is a bad idea to sleep directly downwind of the campfire. A wind in the night can fan the coals and bombard the bed with glowing sparks, each of which will burn a neat round hole in the nylon fabric. If the fire is utterly dead the sleeper will instead receive a shower of ashes.

Badly placed beds are rarely forgotten. One sultry night, making camp after dark, I placed my bed on the crumbled and cushiony remains of a thoroughly decayed log—usually an excellent location. I awoke after an hour, in the rain, crawling with big black ants whose home I had disturbed. Another time I was awakened by cold feet sloshing in a wet bag; a light rain had come up and though I was covered by a tarp a stream had materialized in the shallow gully containing my feet, soaking the bottom of my bag. The wakeful nights that followed both incidents were so grimly memorable that I now scrutinize prospective bedsights for disguised watercourses and concealed inhabitants.

Unusually good beds can be memorable, too. At a windy timberline camp on a rocky exposed mountain, I found a cleft in the rock beneath a prostrate whitebark pine that was just the right size and deeply filled with needles. All night the wind howled a few inches above my head while I lay snug and warm under the fragrant pine. On another windy high country night, I lay on a deep bed of needles in front of the fire in the mouth of a shelter made by roofing the space between two big fallen trees. Though the night outside was freezing, I was snug and warm in my little cabin.

Bedsites need to be very nearly level. If there must be a slope, it should run downhill from head to feet. Sleeping on a sidehill is nothing short of torture. One is generally better off with an inferior level site than a sloping bed that is otherwise perfect. It is not uncommon for the sleeper who made his bed on a slope to wake up in the morning ten feet away with the distinct impression of not having slept at all. I believe strongly that a bedsite's most important characteristic is its susceptibility to alteration, and I have yet to encounter one I could not improve.

As I view potential sites, bare earth is fine, deep pine-needles or duff are perfect, decayed tree trunks are excellent—when not inhabited—sand and gravel are satisfactory, provided I am carrying a cushioning foam mattress. Grass is poor because it cannot be contoured without removing the roots and permanently scarring the ground.

When I have selected the best available bedsite in all respects and decided where my head is to be, I dig a rectangular hip and shoulder hole. It measures about 18 inches wide, 28 inches long and 2½ inches deep with sloping sides and a slightly concave bottom. All of the excavated earth or sand is heaped into a pillow about three inches thick. From the bottom of the hip hole to the bottom of the foot area, I smooth the ground, removing sticks, rocks, pine-cones and twigs. If

the ground is sloping, I often use the earth excavated from the hip hole to build up the area that supports the legs, finding some other way to make a pillow. For maximum comfort, the feet should be a little higher than the hips and I find it well worth the trouble to make sure that they are. In seriously sloping or less than level ground it is sometimes easier to dig the hip hole deeper rather than pad the leg area. Like the highway builder, I try to balance my cut and fill.

Once the preliminary shaping is complete, I lie down on the bedsite on my back to test the contours. If the shoulder section needs widening and the hip hole deepening, I scratch some kind of a pattern with a twig, then get up to make alterations. When I lie down a second time, if everything feels comfortable (nothing pressing or cramped) I roll over on my side. This will generally feel less comfortable and additional excavating will be needed at the point of the hip and thigh. But I dig with restraint, knowing that no hole can fit perfectly both ways. The results must be a compromise which favors the postion in which one usually sleeps.

In an attempt to make a perfectly contoured hip hole, the novice will often build up an area to support the small of the back. This is a grave mistake and is guaranteed to produce an aching back before dawn. Women, because of their broader hips, usually are less comfortable on the ground than men; they will want a deeper hiphole that tapers to a shallower shoulder hole.

My contouring operation may seem a waste of time to some, but I can think of no better investment of time than the five minutes it takes me to transform a small strip of earth into a comfortable bed that will insure me eight hours of restful sleep.

If the wind is blowing and cannot be avoided I take pains to point my feet to windward, and if the night promises to be cold I build a small earth and rock windbreak at my feet. Even on a warm night a persistent wind can chill exposed limbs; the noise, the twitching of the bag and the breeze in one's face will rob even—perhaps especially— the most exhausted camper of hours of sleep. On an evening when the wind promises to blow, an extra fifteen minutes spent hunting for or constructing shelter from the wind will be time well spent.

The old prospector with whom I often camp in the desert considers me too finicky about my bed. After throwing his fifty pound bedroll (including mattress) from the truck, he is guided by just one consideration: his bed must be lined up north-south—with the head in the north—to assure a refreshing sleep. He believes that the magnetic lines of force must pass through him properly (head to toe) in order to recharge him with energy for the following day.

With a comfortable rest carefully prepared for, I sort through my pack and dig out everything I am liable to need in the night: personal kit, watch cap, bandana, flashlight, down sweater and socks for the following day. All of these are tucked in appropriate spots beside my sleeping bag inside the bivouac cover; a rock on top of my pillow assures that nothing will be dampened by the dew that will fall before I finally go to bed. The only exception is the small Mallory flashlight, which for the time being goes in my pocket. In the process of digging through my pack, I collect everything needed for preparing dinner: packets of soup and stew, herbs, condiments, pots, cups, stove, etc.

Since even a small breeze disturbs the flame and reduces the efficiency of most stoves, it's advisable to locate the kitchen in the most sheltered, protected part of camp. The alternative, especially if preparation requires a low flame, is to build a wind screen of some sort.

One morning I awoke with my family in a heavy breeze. My wife needed a cup of tea before facing the world, but the bleuet would not light in the most sheltered spot available. I pulled the six-foot foam pad from my bed, bent it into a circle around the stove and got my daughter to hold it in place while I made Sherpa tea and hot cinnamon oatmeal.

Once the stove is set up, water drawn from the lake, and the soup packet emptied in the pot, I know I am no more than fifteen minutes away from enjoying the first course of dinner. If hunger and approaching darkness do not urge me to start cooking, I usually see what can be done about preparing a campfire to cheer up the evening. A good many people like to get up early in the mountains and consequently they are ready for bed soon after dinner. I carry my city habits into the wilds, rising at a comfortable hour and sitting up rather late. Without a campfire, I can't indulge myself so easily.

If my campsite has been used before, I use or rebuild the existing firepit, taking care to turn the blackened sides of the rocks inward so I do not add to their discoloring. If I am on virgin ground, I try to dig a shallow pit in sand or mineralized earth (never duff, meadow, decayed wood or vegetation) so that I can safely build a fire without blackening anything.

If firewood isn't plentiful, I make my small campfire using rotten wood which another winter will render unburnable, chunks of bark, smashed pine cones and other junk wood. Since chunks of charcoal are unsightly in the wilderness, I try to burn all that I find in a

relaxing after breakfast

campsite, as well as all the fuel I use, down to an ash which will blow away and convert quickly to soil.

At sunset or thereabouts, I light the stove beneath my soup, put on warm clothes for the evening, zip extra food securely into my pack, take in the wash and stow it also in the pack, stir the soup to make sure it is not sticking, adding whatever butter, milk or bacon bar I can spare. If it's going to be dark before dinner is ready, I light and nurse my campfire past the critical stage. The best single rule I know for successful firebuilding is for the fire builder to be supplied with twice the tinder, matches, twigs, paper, etc., that should be needed.

A great many fires die while the builder is out looking frantically for more of something that burns well. Other common mistakes are packing the paper too tightly and smothering it with tinder: any kind of fuel needs plenty of oxygen to burn properly. At the other extreme, spreading the fuel so loosely that it fails to concentrate its heat is a familiar cause of failure.

Before the soup is ready, I arrange all the components of dinner—opened packet of freeze-dried food, sumptuous supplements and condiments and water so that as soon as the last of the soup has been poured the main course can be started. In parties of three or more, this usually means that the stove need not be shut down in order to conserve fuel—extremely desirable in gasoline and kerosene stove cooking—and the pot neither cools down nor scorches. Simplicity of meal preparation, of course, is essential to such exquisite timing.

Before the main course is ready, I lay out the makings for tea, and the stewed fruit or pudding that will very likely be eaten in the dark. If my craving for sweets and liquids promises to be hard to satisfy, I may also select a packet of lemonade. Since I tend to spend a good deal of time beside the fire in the evening, it is often worthwhile to drag or roll a boulder or log before the fire to serve alternately as a seat or back rest—providing, of course, that the dislocation does not disfigure the immediate landscape.

It is generally advisable to schedule dinner so that the meal is over—except for dessert, snacks and drinks—well before dark. I like to go fishing or walking between dinner and dark. These excursions, I have discovered, often turn out to provide the most pleasant experiences of the trip. After a long day, of course, it is easy to lie in camp, feeling comfortably tired, and often I do exactly that.

But the wildness I have come to see does not really begin until camp and trail are left behind. Campsites and paths are simply extensions, however faint, of civilization. To experience wildness one must wander away from all travelers' routes to see what lies in the country beyond. It never seems hard, even if I know the immediate area quite well, to find someplace intriguing to go walking after dinner. Since my jaunts have a way of running longer than planned, I always carry matches, pocketknife, jacket and flashlight.

Unless I am leaving early in the morning, I give the soup-stew pot only a brisk, brief cleaning after dinner, planning to wait for better light to finish the job. But quick attention after dinner—even before the pan cools (and food congeals)—will save considerable work in the long run. I scrape the pot with a big spoon to loosen all excess food and empty the contents in thick brush, for the nourishment of small animals, well away from camp and water. (There is nothing quite so grim as stepping down to the shore of a pretty pool, only to see the remains of someone's spaghetti dinner strewn across the bottom.) Then I add a little water (hot if the tea kettle has been on the fire), scrub briefly with a Chore Girl or abrasive pad and empty the scourings in the brush again. The pot, filled with water, is easily cleaned later.

When the campfire is really burning and the coals are hot, I toss in not only the paper and plastic refuse, but foil packages and Tea Kettle aluminum as well. If the fire is hot enough these are largely consumed; at the very least they are cleaned and much reduced in volume for the trip home. I usually drink tea in the evening, keeping the teapot warm in the fire even though the water is usually heated on the stove. In the city, I take nothing in my tea, but camp tea often suffers from boiling, debris, weakness or bitterness and I find I prefer it in the English manner well laced with milk powder and honey.

Since on short trips in small parties I usually do not carry pails, jugs or buckets for carrying water, it is often necessary to refill my plastic bottle. The great advantage of the Mallory flashlight over those requiring conventional sized batteries is that by holding the light in one's mouth both hands are left free for cooking, washing dishes, gathering wood or drawing water. It is even possible, with practice, to carry on a conversation.

When the time approaches to go to bed, I customarily brush my teeth in my last cup of tea and stir up the fire to coax as complete combustion as possible; partially burned sticks make unrewarding scenery. If the night is cold I put on a Navy surplus wool watch cap to ward off the cold (body heat is rapidly lost from the head). If I am putting on pajamas or long johns or other clothes to sleep in I warm them first over the fire and change quickly. I tend the fire until it has burned down to a safe bed of ash and coals. If there is a breeze or

dismantling a poorly-located fireplace.

danger of traveling sparks, I spread the ashes to reduce heat and cover with sand or water.

There are easier jobs than getting undressed in the cold and dark and wriggling into a dew-soaked mummy bag without getting cold or wet. I generally sit on my pillow, take off my shoes and turn them upside down; then I take off my socks and trousers and slip into bed in a sitting position in my shoulder hole. From this point it is comparatively easy to peel off the rest of my clothes and tuck them under the tarp or bivouac cover before sliding the rest of the way into bed. After pulling the drawstring that converts the top of my bag into a hood, and locking it, I zip up the bag, leaving my flashlight by the top of the zipper.

In the morning the first thing I do—after rising and getting on my clothes—is to dismantle my bed and set it to dry. Even if the dew seems already to have dried, there is liable to be ground dampness and condensation from my body. Weather has a way of changing fast in the wilderness, and it is nice to have one's bed bone dry and securely packed; the same goes for tents and tarps; anyone who has had to pack and carry a wet tent will go to some lengths to avoid repeating the experience. I spread my foam pad, bivouac cover and sleeping bag out flat on sunny rocks or breezy bushes until they are warm and absolutely dry, then I turn them over. When the outsides are nicely toasted, I turn them inside out and repeat the process. In the dry air of a high Sierra the whole process rarely takes more than half an hour, even after a heavy dew or drizzle.

Since I am more likely to wake up feeling sticky than hungry I usually wash, or possibly swim, before thinking of food. On most summer days my breakfast consists of cold cereal and fruit, along with Sherpa tea, so I am not obliged to clean the stew pot before eating. But if the morning is cold and blustery, and cold breakfast is unappealing, I clean the pot sufficiently (often by merely wiping it out carefully with a paper towel) to avoid unduly flavoring the hot spicy applesauce and instant oatmeal I customarily make; if the morning is really foul, I empty in my Birchermuesli too.

After a bad night, a very hard yesterday, or just for fun if there is no great hurry—I like to lie down and take a rest after breakfast on my foam pad. I sometimes read, make notes, study the map and make plans for the day, while lying confortably on my back. Often I just examine the treetops, and sometimes I accidentally fall asleep.

When it comes time to relieve myself I play a kind of game; I pretend to be a trapper who is traveling in the country of the sharp-eyed, sharp-nosed Sioux, and I hunt for a concealed spot unlikely to be visited by scouting parties—under a deadfall, in a thicket of brush, behind a boulder. I roll away a rock or kick a hole in loose soil, and slip the rubber band from the toilet paper roll around my wrist. When I have made my contribution, I burn the paper, cover the hole and jump on it once or twice to pack down the soil; then I roll back the rock, kick back a covering of leaves, duff or pine needles and branches, artfully landscaping the site until an Indian scout would never give it a second look.

I am careful to avoid any place that might serve as a campsite or trail. Running water, dry streambeds, empty snowmelt pools and any location within a hundred feet of a camp are also shunned. There is nothing more discouraging than finding that the second best campsite in an area has been used as a latrine by the people from the number one camp—unless it is streamers of used toilet paper fluttering in the trees.

In recent years I have increasingly become interested in cleaning up the country. Restoring a quality of wildness to the wilds by erasing the blighting marks of man has become one of my chief pleasures in the areas I travel. It seems the least I can do to repay the joy that wilderness has given me—and the one thing I can do to help make it last a little while longer.

Like many backpackers, I used to try to leave a camp as clean as I found it; it did not occur to me to try to leave it any cleaner, much less to go looking for other people's trash. I shook my head sadly at badly littered camps and passed them by in hopes of finding something cleaner. Then some years ago I spent several days on a cleanup party into Desolation Wilderness behind my cabin on Echo Lake. Carrying burlap sacks, we systematically scoured the trails, circled the lakes and worked our way through commonly visited areas, picking up litter, tearing down fireplaces, filling latrines, restoring battered campsites hiding blackened rocks, scattering firewood, and so forth. By the end of the trip I found myself hooked on cleaning up the country.

When I say cleaning up other peoples' trash can become addictive, I expect to raise a few eyebrows. How can picking old toilet paper out of the trees or broken glass from the ashes in a ruined fireplace possibly be fun? My answer is that the pleasure comes from the sense of accomplishment, from the restoration of an ugly site to its previous condition of natural beauty. For instance, a handsome little alpine lake may be marred by a sheet of glittering aluminum foil lying on the bottom. The act of fishing out the foil, crumpling it up and packing it

into a corner of the knapsack restores the beauty and naturalness of the setting. Simple acts of this sort, surprisingly enough, can provide immense satisfaction.

Sometimes I carry a burlap sack or plastic garbage can liner with me on these excursions. If I gather more than I can carry, I leave the partially filled bag on the edge of a prominent trailside campsite, then on my return I mention its location to the ranger. When I am backpacking, it is no longer possible to bend over and pick litter from the trail while wearing a full pack. And there is a limit, of course, to what I am willing to add to my load. My scavenging activities are necessarily limited to forays from wherever I am camped.

If the area is near a pack stock trail, I consolidate the trash, bag it if I can, and notify the authorities of its specific location, estimating the number of sacks and pack animals that will be needed. If the area is remote and cannot be reached by stock, and if carrying everything out is simply beyond feasibility, I set about trying to hide my collection so well that the likelihood of its being found again is exceptionally small. In an area of boulders and talus, for instance, quite large objects can often be stuffed out of sight into cracks and then covered again by a minor avalanche of loose rock, hopefully never to be seen again by anything larger than a Cony.

Both the weight and the volume of trash I collect must be greatly reduced for optimum carrying purposes. Raw garbage or spoiled food left in a campsite can often be scattered well back in the brush where animals, ants and decay can dispose of it. Egg shells and other indigestibles must be treated like foil, unless they will burn. Orange peels, plastic and discarded clothing can usually be burned, along with waste paper, if the fire is sufficiently hot. I save the more difficult items for the evening campfire, and I am careful not to breathe the often poisonous fumes of burning plastics.

I shake or rinse the dirt from ancient rusty tin cans before crushing them flat beneath the heel of my boot. Foil and new tin cans can be cleaned and partially consumed in a hot fire, before being crushed. Bottles can be shattered for reduction in bulk, but only if a suitable (heavy) container is available for safe breaking. Broken glass is best collected in an uncrushed tin can which should then be packed upright in its own plastic bag.

Often enough I have circled a small remote lake, visiting all the campsites, cleaning up several messes, collecting an empty six pack of beer, hiding blackened rocks after carefully dismantling inferior camps—all in less than an hour. And I have left, with less than two pounds of junk in my pack, well satisfied at having largely restored the area to a natural and inviting condition. Of course when I find such large or heavy items as skillets, life rafts or sleeping bags, disposal becomes something of a problem.

A friend of mine carries cleaning up one step farther. He carries with him a spray can of powerful oven cleaner with which to remove the names and comments of that strange breed of traveler who goes hiking with a spray can of paint. Oven cleaner also removes the soot from unfortunately blackened prominent slabs and boulders. By getting rid of the black and rearranging the rocks it is possible to discourage future use of an inappropriate spot.

The fact that 'trash begets trash' is as true in the wilds as it is in the city. Let litter accumulate and travelers will feel free to help swell the accumulation. But when a public place has been freshly cleaned people become reluctant to scatter their trash. And if containers are provided most people will use them. After the cleanup trips in Desolation Wilderness it was found that extra burlap sacks left behind in popular campsites were generally filled by the parties that followed.

Enthusiasm for cleaning up the country is not peculiar to me; it is shared by nearly all of my friends who have tried it. I have found that people who endlessly procrastinate about cleaning out their cellars will conscientiously clean up other people's campsites. And children whose rooms at home stand knee deep in litter will patiently pick the broken glass from someone else's fireplace. The annual cleanup trips in Desolation Wilderness have become so popular they simply cannot accommodate all the people who want to go; veterans take care to make their reservations early. The companionship, sense of accomplishment and the beautiful country combine to make these trips highly memorable.

Every hiking club, summer community or group of backpacking friends owes it to itself—and to the country it enjoys—to try a cleanup trip. The Forest Service stands ready to encourage serious groups by providing empty sacks and hauling collected debris.

Before leaving camp on short excursions—cleanup, fishing, an after dinner stroll—I always take a look around to make sure it is secure against the incursions of small animals, near neighbors, sudden weather change and fire. Brazen chipmunks, mice, bluejays and squirrels have more than once escaped with significant portions of my larder without even waiting for me to walk away from camp. Enticing food should always be stowed in a pack, preferably in a zippered compartment which can be tightly closed, before leaving camp, and

... *now he's ruining his boots!*

the pack shoud be hung from a tree or rope—depending on the type and voracity of predators.

One spring, I followed the snowplow into the mountains and made camp with a friend in an alpine meadow—after a long and heavy winter. Either the wildlife in the region was starving, or our food had unusual appeal. The first night, despite a fire that burned continuously, we spent half the night yelling and throwing pine cones at a bear who refused to leave us alone. We moved our camp the next day and that night we built a bigger fire, but the snuffling and stomping of the pacing animals that circled us all night gave us little rest. In the morning we found a ring of bear, coyote and deer tracks just beyond the firelight. After two sleepless nights fending off the wildlife, we gave up and returned home.

There was a time when one could leave money lying around camp in perfect safety—provided one was beyond the range of day hikers. Nowadays, it is a good idea not to leave anything valuable in camp. A camp that will be seen by a large number of hikers is far too vulnerable to leave. More than one group of hikers in recent summers has come back from a hike to find their camp entirely vanished. And backpackers in roadhead camps have awakened to find that everything but the bags they were sleeping in was gone. Packs, boots, down bags, parkas and the like have significant resale value and are easily sold, so it pays to protect expensive gear—and to camp well away from the boulevards whenever possible.

It should be a matter of common sense never to leave camp for even a few minutes if a fire is burning. A gust of wind can carry flaming embers into the woodpile, dry pine needles or a two hundred dollar sleeping bag and cause substantial damage in a matter of moments. The fire should be absolutely stone-cold dead whenever camp is left untended. Every summer I pass empty camps in which a fire still burns or smolders. The incidence of man-made fires is climbing every year.

Long excursions from camp require more precautions because weather must also be taken into account. Consider my recent experience. We had left our high Sierra camp close under a mountain on a clear summer day, without any thought of a possible storm. Our mistake was in forgetting that we really had no idea of weather conditions on the other side of the mountain.

By the time we reached the ridge the storm that had been hidden was almost upon us. By the time we returned to camp, late that afternoon, it had been raining steadily for several hours. Fortunately, our clothes and food were safe in our waterproof packs and our sleeping bags, though damp in places, were under tarps. The Bleuet stove was soaked and would not light, but we managed to build a big fire and stood before it in the wind and rain for another long hour before the sun came out a few minutes before sunset. There was just barely time to halfway dry out our beds and get them back under tarps before a drenching dew began to fall. Even without seeing the sky behind the mountain that morning, I should have been suspicious because the breeze, though faint, was blowing from the south. Wind blowing from the south, east or northeast is liable to bring a storm. Wind from the north, northwest or southwest generally heralds fair weather; the major exceptions are mountain thunderstorms which often come from the west.

Clouds offer the backpacker another aid to weather forecasting. Big fluffy cumulus clouds are harbingers of fair weather—so long as they do not join together and begin to billow upward. When they cease to exist as individual clouds and the bottoms darken and the tops form columns and flattened anvil heads—a thunder storm is on the way. High, thin cirrus clouds are generally filled with ice particles; when they whiten the sky or their mare's tails reach upward, a storm can generally be expected within twenty-four hours.

Stratus clouds, as the name implies, come in waves or layers or bands; when they are smooth and regular and rolling the weather should be fair, but probably cool; when stratus clouds are mottled or fragmented into a buttermilk sky, it will usually storm.

The astute wilderness traveler learns to recognize a number of signs of impending weather change. Sun dogs or halos around the sun forecast rain or snow; so does a ring around the moon. A red sky at dawn or an early morning rainbow, or the absence of dew on the grass—all of these should warn the traveler that bad weather is brewing. So should yellow sunsets and still, ominously quiet moist air.

Sensitivity to the signs should influence the backpacker's choice of camps and trip itinerary. If the signs are bad, he should erect the tent, lay in a good supply of firewood beneath a tarp and schedule close-to-home amusement rather than exposed activities like climbing. On the other hand, a careful reading of the weather may enable him to set out on a climb, confident of good weather, even before the rain has stopped. For instance, clearing can be expected despite heavy clouds,

lightning strikes prominent exposed places.

providing ''there's enough blue to make a Dutchman a pair of pants.''

The best aid I've seen to amateur forecasting is called ''Pocket Weather Trends,'' sold by Weather Things, Ltd. for $3. It's a 4 x 9 inch folder on which you match pictures of cloud conditions on a kind of slide rule with the direction of the wind to obtain a forecast as good as what your local weatherman can offer, and probably more current. It should easily be superior to old or broad area forecasts—providing you can accurately determine wind conditions in the sky (as opposed to capricious and often irrelevant ground currents).

Thunderstorms, those exciting, dramatic, generally shortlived phenomena, are nevertheless frightening to a good many people. I have seen tall trees virtually explode when struck by a bolt of lightning, sending huge limbs flying in every direction. But the danger is negligible for anyone willing to take the necessary precaution—leaving vulnerable locations before the storm begins. The places to avoid are high, open exposed slopes, hills, ridges and peaks, isolated or unusually tall trees, lakes, meadows, or open flats. The safest places are in caves, canyon bottoms and a part of the forest where the trees are comparatively short.

The hiker or climber anxious about lightning usually has considerable warning. When cumulus clouds have darkened and fused and still air has been replaced by sudden erratic winds, the storm is about to break and backpackers should already be snugly sheltered. Lightning usually appears to be striking closer than it is, especially at night. The distance can be accurately gauged by counting the seconds between flash and boom. Every five seconds in time means a mile in distance. Thirteen seconds between flash and boom means the lightning is striking two and a half miles away. No matter how fierce the storm may seem, summer afternoon thunderstorms characteristically are short, and the chances are good that the sun will be out before sunset. If my camp is battened down and I can watch in some comfort, I enjoy the noisy melodrama of an afternoon storm.

When the time comes to pack up and move camp, I like to see how wild I can make my campsite look. If I have camped on virgin ground, I take pains to restore it to its natural conditions so that a passerby would not guess it had ever been used. There are far too many campsites already in existence; my aim is to decrease, not increase the number. After collecting all the unburned foil and metal from the ashes and packing it in a garbage bag, I bury charcoal, ashes and partially burned twigs or scatter them well back in thick brush.

The firepit is filled in, blackened rocks are hidden and turned black side down in the brush, and the hip and shoulder hole from my bed are filled in and smoothed over. Pine needles, sand, soil, duff, pine cones and branches are scattered naturally about and if the area still faintly resembles a camp I sometimes roll in a few rocks and large limbs or small logs to fill up the bare spots. After firewood is scattered, all that remains are a few footprints. Once rain has fallen it would be difficult to tell that the area ever had been disturbed.

The extra effort I would invest in disguising a virgin camp, I am likely to spend destroying surplus or inappropriate camps in the neighborhood. Campers who arrive late at night or on crowded holidays often camp in gullies, or boggy meadow and even in the middle of the trail. These camps, which are rarely used a second time, can often be entirely obliterated with a little work, greatly improving the wilderness character of the area.

Even a day hike no longer seems to me complete unless I have dismantled a few fireplaces, disguised a few old camps, and stuffed a little debris in my pack. The blackening on granite from a single evening's fire will withstand erasure by the elements for as long as fifty years. Though I cannot hasten the process I can at least enjoy hiding some of the evidence.

12 FIRST AID & SURVIVAL

"Keep it short and simple," warned the backpacking surgeon who counseled me on this chapter, "and hope that people will read it. People get confused by complicated procedures—and remember to tell them that the best medicine of all is prevention."

From a safety standpoint, the greatest danger in wild country is traveling alone. Trail hiking is bad enough, but cross-country travel is infinitely worse, and climbing alone is idiotic. Unfortunately, some of the joys of wilderness travel are only to be discovered by traveling alone. I mostly hike by myself but, recognizing the danger, I try to minimize it by taking all possible precautions.

Protection comes from a combination of what gets carried and what gets left behind. What should be left behind is a knowledge of one's plans. I tell someone responsible—usually another member of the party or my wife, where I am going, what route I plan to follow both directions, when I expect to be back and the latest time (the time to begin worrying) that I could possibly be back. If the trip will take several days, I usually draw the route on an old map and make an 'X' where I expect to spend the nights. Lastly, I indicate in a general way my preparation for emergencies (tent, first aid kit, extra food and clothes), so the urgency of my situation can be judged if I fail to return.

First aid kits on the market are getting better (e.g. those made by Alpine Aid), but I make my own from scratch. Since it is little more trouble to make two than one, I constructed one for picnics, day hikes and easy trips, and a second for climbing, cross-country, family and more extensive trips. My 'little' kit consists of a dozen Bandaids in two sizes, four individually wrapped gauze pads in two sizes (2 x 2 and 3 x 3 inches) a roll of three inch Johnson & Johnson 'Kling' gauze, a roll of one inch old-fashioned adhesive tape, a small bar of soap, a sheet of Molefoam or a lump of foam rubber, a small pair of scissors, a needle, a backed razor blade, a selection of pills, a clean washcloth and half a dozen matches. The kit fits snugly in a screw-topped plastic ice-box jar three inches deep and four inches in diameter, which is marked top and bottom with big red crosses to distinguish it from the butter jar.

Plastic tape is all right on Bandaids, but it does not have the necessary strength for use on large bandages. Unfortunately, the adhesive on old-fashioned tape deteriorates; it should therefore be checked every season and replaced when necessary. Carrying soap is a problem.

I solved it, finally, by carving a chunk of soap to fit snugly in a waterproof aluminum 35 mm film can (marked with an 'S'); it is just the right size when used only for first aid. In a second film can (marked 'P'), I carry the following pills: six 500 mg vitamin C tablets to ward off colds, four 12-hour antihistamine spansules for cold symptoms or hay fever, half a dozen milk of magnesia laxative tablets, half a dozen aspirins and several aspirin with codeine tablets for severe pain. All pills are replaced at the beginning of each summer. I often wedge in half a roll of anti-acid tablets and a yard of folded toilet paper, along with the small washcloth. The needle and razor-blade are taped to the inside of the lid. My 'little' kit weighs six ounces and resides almost permanently in my day pack.

My 'big' kit, which fits in a five inch deep, four inch diameter jar and weighs nine ounces, contains the same ingredients as the little kit, but the number of Bandaids and individual gauze pads is doubled, a good pair of tweezers for splinters is included, and so is a three inch Ace bandage for sprains. There are several extra needles and half a dozen safety pins. Sprain-prone hikers should carry an ankle brace.

My surgeon friend advises against first aid creams, antiseptics, inhalants and tourniquets. "Soap and plenty of water are better than antiseptics," he says: "First aid creams seal in more dirt and bacteria than does a dry, clean wound. Tourniquets are dangerous and rarely necessary since pressure and elevation will stop all but the most serious bleeding. Amateurs should not attempt to set broken bones, but splinting protection is part of first aid. Either the patient should be moved to a doctor, or a doctor be brought to the patient."

My big kit—and the little one, too—is modified or enlarged for different country. For instance, in rattlesnake country (the foothill and lower elevations in the west side Sierra) I carry a Cutters Snakebite Kit (1 ounce, $3.50) and in Poison Oak country I carry extra soap, washrag and towel. In the desert or where water loss or perspiration is likely to be great, I carry salt pills. Other preparations that might be considered are Tetracycline for fever-producing infections, Pryidium for bladder infections and Tridol for nausea.

In addition to my first aid kits, which are only opened to give first aid, I also carry a personal (toilet) kit which contains items I expect to use every day. Included are vaseline, athletes foot powder, sunburn ointment, glacier cream, dental floss, toothbrush, and any special medicines. If the water is mildly suspect, it would include Halazone water purification tablets. Since they aren't effective against amoebas, in foreign countries or where pollution is likely, I use 5-10 drops of 2% Tincture of Iodine per quart of water.

Speaking of foreign lands, on an extended trek far from home I

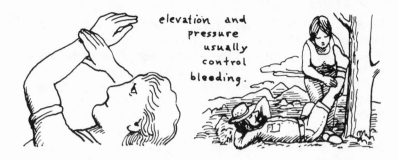

elevation and pressure usually control bleeding.

might take (or be sure someone takes) Tylenol for pain, Maalox or Gelusil for acid or upset stomach, Lomotil tabs for diarrhea (they've saved me more than once), Valium for high altitude sleeplessness and additional antibiotics and sun protection.

Thus armed, I am in position to give first aid treatment to myself or others for a variety of minor ailments and accidents. The ability to treat common injuries is one of the prerequisites of the experienced backpacker. Techniques are so simple (and potentially important) that no wilderness traveler can afford not to learn them. Take a Red Cross course next winter, and buy and read one of the good little booklets you ought to be carrying along with your kit.

Shock is a state produced by injury or fright. The victim feels cold and clammy and weak. The treatment is to lay the patient down on level ground and make him as comfortable as possible, usually by loosening constricting clothing and covering him if it is cold, until a feeling of well-being returns.

In case of a small or slightly bleeding wound, bleeding usually will soon stop if the wound is elevated so it lies higher than the heart; and pressure is applied with a gauze pad. (For a cut foot or leg, the patient lies down and props his leg against a tree; a cut hand should be held above the head.) A large or heavily bleeding wound may have to be closed by hand pressure. A puncture can be firmly blocked by the palm or a finger. On a slice or cut it may be necessary to draw the edges together with the fingers before applying pressure. Closing the wound to stop the bleeding is vital. Once bleeding has been controlled, the wound should be kept elevated to reduce the blood flow and aid clotting. One should never attempt to substitute a tourniquet for these procedures.

As soon as bleeding is under control, the wound should be washed with soap and water, or irrigated with water, to carry away bacteria and dirt. It may be necessary during the washing to keep the wound elevated to lessen bleeding. Once cleaned, it may be gently blotted dry with a clean cloth or towel (not to mention toilet paper or clean socks). The clean, dry wound can then be bandaged. On heavily bleeding wounds that do not respond sufficiently to elevation, it may be neces-sary to tape the edges of the wound together with a butterfly bandage in order to stop bleeding. In the majority of cases, however, a combination of pressure and elevation will be sufficient to control bleeding.

Minor cuts and scratches, especially on protected parts of the body, are better left un-bandaged. Protected but uncovered wounds are more easily kept clean and dry; healing is faster and the chances of infection are lower. Antiseptics (mercurichrome, iodine, merthiolate and the like) should not be applied; they tend to do more harm than good—inhibiting scab formation and trapping bacteria which cause infection. Small wounds need only bandaids. Larger ones will require a gauze pad held in place by narrow strips of adhesive tape. The largest may require wrapping the limb or body with roll gauze. Gauze and adhesive bandages should be applied directly on top of a wound held closed by a butterfly bandage.

The greatest enemy of wounds is dampness. A wet bandage inhibits healing by providing a favorable environment for the growth of bacteria. Once a bandage has become wet, whether from serum, perspiration or water, it is a menace to health and should be replaced. No bandage at all is far superior to a wet one. The drier the wound the less the chance of infection.

My backpacking doctor is a strong believer in foot care. "At the first hint of discomfort," he says, "stop, take off the boot and have a look. Wash and dry a place that is getting red, then tape a thin sheet of foam rubber over the spot." I had always relied on moleskin for covering blisters and inflamed places on my feet. Moleskin's disadvantage, the doctor points out, is that once it is stuck directly to the injured or tender area it cannot safely be removed (without removing the skin) until the end of the trip. In the meantime, of course, the moleskin is certain to get damp and dirty, encouraging bacteria growth. On his advice I have switched to either Molefoam or foam rubber and find both perfectly satisfactory. If I run out I can steal a fragment from a corner of my mattress. Scissors make the job neat and are worth their weight for foot care alone.

Often as important as bandaging an inflamed foot, is attacking the cause of the inflamation. On occasion I have had to hammer down a nail with a piece of granite or whittle away a protruding ridge of leather. More often the problem is solved by kneading new boots that pinch, removing a pebble, loosening laces, removing the wrinkle from a sock, adding an extra pair of socks, or changing to a dry pair. Of course prevention is the best answer. Wear only comfortable, broken-in boots that fit.

Dry socks are vital to happy feet. Wet, clean socks are far harder on feet than dirty, dry ones. Experienced hikers tend to do far more sock washing and sock changing than beginners, and they take off their boots and air (or wash) their feet at every opportunity. People unaccustomed to walking are likely to suffer from tender feet. Foot powders, Benzoin skin toughener and alcohol rubs may help, but are no substitute for adequate conditioning (see Chapter 9).

sprained ankles can be chilled in icy streams or with snow-filled plastic bags →

A good case can be made for carrying camp boots on the basis of sensible foot care. Many people like old tennis shoes, but feet tend to sweat in canvas and rubber shoes. I prefer Zoris (also known as thongs and go-aheads) because they are extremely light and air the feet although they offer scant protection. I have developed the habit, once the day's hiking is done, of immediately taking off my boots (before the sweat dries), washing and rubbing my feet, washing my socks and hanging them in a tree, then slipping on Zoris—if temperature and terrain permit.

Nothing is more common among backpackers accustomed to doing their walking on sidewalks than turned or sprained ankles. Severity varies greatly. Some sprains amount to nothing more than a momentary twinge. Others require the victim to be immobilized immediately. Often the wisest course for the person who has suffered a bad sprain (the ankle immediately turning black and blue) is to apply a tape cast and head for the car before the ankle can swell and stiffen.

Moderate sprains should immediately be treated with cold to constrict blood flow and prevent swelling. Putting the foot in an icy rill or applying cold compresses made by filling plastic bags with snow or ice water are fast and effective. Elevating the ankle also helps greatly to reduce the swelling. If sources of cold are not handy or it is inconvenient to stop, an elasticized ankle brace or three inch Ace bandage may be applied.

Braces are likely to be carried only by people with weak ankles who have come to rely on them. Ace bandages have the advantage of being usable on other parts of the body. In either case, it may be necessary to remove all (or at least the outer) socks to make room for the bandage in the boots. And people (like myself) who have sensitive Achilles tendons may find it impossible to wear an elastic bandage very long. Bandages need only be worn while walking. They should be removed at night and at any other time that the ankle can be elevated.

All of the swelling that is going to take place will happen on the day of the sprain or the day that follows. On the third day, with the swelling stopped, the treatment changes from the application of cold to the application of heat. The intent now is to stimulate blood flow through the injured area in order to reduce swelling. Hot compresses made from bandanas, towels, diapers, or washrags dipped in heated water are excellent, or the ankle can be baked before an open fire. Hot water bottles can sometimes be fashioned from large plastic bags, but care must be taken not to burn the patient. The exception to heat treatment is the ankle which is immediately encased in a cast of tape. Such casts should be left undisturbed for two or three days and heat applied only after removal.

While rattlesnake bites are uncommon, a snakebite kit ought to be carried in snake country. First prerequisites in prevention are caution and the ability to recognize poisonous snakes and the sort of terrain they like. I have spent a good deal of time in heavily infested areas and have encountered a great many rattlers. But by never extending any part of my body into a concealed place that could contain a snake, I have avoided being bitten. Although the Cutters kit offers more elaborate and valuable instruction, the treatment can be summarized in three words "Cut, Suck, Tie" (the order is important). Avoid the tendency to cut too deep (¼ inch is sufficient) and tie too tight (let the tourniquet just dent the skin). Since suction cups are useless on any but flat, fleshy, hairless skin, mouth suction will often be required. Once first aid is given, the patient should be made to rest to restrict blood circulation. He should also be taken to a hospital.

Salt pills (5 grain) are not required by most people unless the perspiration is literally pouring off the body. The usual dosage in such cases is one pill every 4-8 hours, but only while drinking a quart of water per 1-2 pills. Overdosing on salt is dangerous. Poison oak, like rattlesnakes, is a hazard that can usually be avoided by caution and the ability to recognize the danger. Poison oak in the west (and poison ivy in the east) have oily-looking distinctive three-lobed leaves that are easily remembered once they have been identified. Tolerance to the oil, which remains potent for some time on clothes and on the fur of pets, varies widely. Persons exposed have a second chance to avoid the itching, easily-spread rash, by scrubbing exposed skin vigorously with soap and hot water on the same day. Skin irritation generally begins four to five hours after exposure. In the west, poison oak rarely grows above 6000 feet.

Sunburn is a constant threat, especially at higher altitudes, to city dwellers who are not deeply tanned. At 6000 feet the skin burns twice as fast as at sea level, and the liability continues to increase with altitude. Sunburn often ruins a trip when a pale backpacker tries for a fast tan. Precautions should be taken to cover—or at least shade—all parts of the body for most of the day. Few people ever acquire a deep enough tan to expose themselves all day at high altitude without burning.

Glacier Cream is an excellent sunburn preventive: the red tube stops both burning and tanning, while the green tube allows some tanning. Sea & Ski greatly reduces burning up to 10,000 feet, while its companion, Block Out, prevents burning but allows some tanning. The lips are extremely liable to sunburn and should be frequently

coated with A-Fil Sun Stick or Chapstick. The best treatment for sunburned skin, says the doctor, is to keep it clean and dry, but I prefer, after washing gently in the evening, to lightly rub in petroleum jelly, wiping off the excess. For the inevitable burns from fire or stove, I also rely on petroleum jelly rather than carry a burn ointment.

As altitude increases the oxygen content of the air decreases. In order to adjust, the body strives to process more air by means of faster and deeper breaths, to better extract and utilize oxygen from the air. Adjustment begins at only slight elevation, but shortness of breath and dizziness do not usually appear until about 7000 feet. Individual tolerance to altitude varies widely. The more gradual the change in altitude, the easier the acclimitization (physiological adjustment). The well-rested, vigorous, healthy individual usually acclimitizes easily. Smoking, drinking and heavy eating before or during a climb make acclimitization difficult.

Failure of the body to adjust to reduced oxygen intake results in "altitude" or mountain sickness. Mild symptoms include headache, lassitude, shortness of breath and a vague feeling of illness—all of which usually disappear after a day of rest. Acute mountain sickness is marked by severe headache, nausea, vomiting, insomnia, irritability and muddled thinking. The victim must descend to a lower elevation. Mountain sickness can usually be avoided by beginning a trip in good condition, spending a night at the trailhead before starting out and choosing modest goals for the first day's walk. Most acclimitization occurs in the first two or three days.

People who acclimitize poorly, when they reach elevations in excess of 10,000 feet, are susceptible to high altitude pulmonary edema (HAPE) (fluid accumulation in the lungs). The first symptoms include a dry, persistent, irritating cough, anxiety, an ache beneath the breast bone and shortness of breath. If the victim is not evacuated promptly to lower elevation or given oxygen, breathing may become rapid, noisy and difficult, the skin often takes on a bluish tinge, and death may occur quickly.

Though HAPE is more common (in milder forms) than generally realized, the number one killer of outdoor travelers is Hypothermia, defined as 'rapid mental and physical collapse due to chilling of the body's core.'' When the body loses heat faster than it's being produced, you instinctively exercise to keep warm while the body cuts back blood supply to the extremities. Both drain your energy reserves. If chilling and exposure continue, cold will reach the brain, depriving you of judgement and reasoning power without your awareness. As chilling progresses, you lose control of your hands and body. When your body can no longer summon reserves to prevent the drop in core temperature, stupor, collapse and death await.

The first line of defense is awareness, awareness that most hypothermia cases occur during mild temperatures, 30-50° F. The greater hazards are wind and wet. Wind drives away the skin's cushion of warm air, and it refrigerates wet clothing. Remember that 50°F water is unbearably cold, and that the wet body can lose heat 200 times as fast as one protected by dry clothing! There is no better clothing for hypothermia protection than vapor barriers. If you can't stay dry and warm, do whatever is necessary to stop exposure. Turn back, give up, get out, make camp—before exhaustion can complicate your plight. Don't shrug off shivering. If you have to exercise continuously to prevent it, you're in danger. Get out of wet clothes, get dry and put on vapor barriers to stop heat loss, then take hot drinks, heap on the insulation, utilize whatever heat sources are available and stay awake.

SURVIVAL

Survival should not be a problem for the backpacker—unless he is hurt or lost. A first aid kit and the ability to use it should enable him to cope with all but the worst accidents and health failures. His equipment, experience and trip preparation should enable him to survive whatever bad weather or minor mishaps befall him with no more than extreme discomfort.

Getting lost—or thoroughly confused—is not uncommon in the wilds and rarely leads to tragedy if sensible procedures are followed. I have been unsure of my location a good many times without suffering unduly. The lost backpacker's ability to regain his sense of direction and rediscover his location (or make himself easy to find) depends largely on his ability to control panic and fear so that logic and reason can prevail.

The best insurance I know against getting lost in strange country is to study it as I move along. I consult the map and reorient myself with each new turning of the trail. I identify and study the configuration of new landmarks as they appear. I frequently look backward over the country just traversed to see how it looks going the other way. If I am traveling cross-country or on an unmapped trail, I stop several times each mile to draw the route on my map. And at critical points (stream crossings, trail branchings, confusing turns), I make appropriate entries in my notebook.

A compass is the easiest means of orientation, but the sun, the stars and the time can also be used to determine direction—and to act as a check on the compass. More than a few disasters result when lost travelers refuse to accept what their compasses tell them. Unaware that they are lost and convinced they have their bearings, they assume the compass is broken or being unnaturally influenced.

A roughly accurate watch will function as a compass on any day that the sun is out. If one turns the watch so that the hour hand points toward the sun, true south will lie halfway between the hour hand and the number twelve. An allowance must be made if the watch is set on Daylight Saving time, which is generally an hour earlier than standard (or sun) time.

If the time is known generally, even if only within two hours, a

rough but very useful idea of direction can be obtained simply by knowing that (in western America) the summer sun rises a little north of due east, stands due south at noon (standard time), and sets a little north of due west. In the winter the suns' path lies considerably to the south, rising south of east and setting south of west. Early and late in the day, one can easily determine directions with sufficient accuracy for most purposes.

Another useful strategy involves pushing a stick vertically in the ground, marking the end of its shadow, waiting about 15 minutes then marking the shadow again. A line between the two marks will run east-west (the first mark is the west end). A line drawn at right angles will run north-south.

If the night is reasonably clear (in the northern hemisphere), it is relatively easy to find the North Star (Polaris) which is never more than one degree from true north. Its location is determined from the Big Dipper (or Big Bear), a bright and easily identifiable constellation nearly always visible in the northern sky. A line drawn upward from the outermost stars at the bottom and lip of the cup will point to Polaris (see drawing). In the southern hemisphere, the long axis of the Southern Cross points toward a starless region that lies due south. The prominent constellation Orion lies in a nearly north-south plane, and the uppermost of the three stars in the belt rises due east and sets due west—from any point on the face of the earth.

There are so many variable in every situation that it is difficult to advise the backpacker who has managed to get lost. However a few general rules nearly always apply. The novice hiker has a tendency to plunge on through country that has gradually grown unfamiliar in hopes of reaching a familiar landmark. The veteran backpacker will resist this impulse, stop, admit to himself that he is at least temporarily lost, and sit down to review the situation. When he has overcome the anxiety that often accompanies such an admission, he will rationally review the situation, carefully considering all the information available.

After studying the map and thinking carefully, he may find a landmark he can identify that will reveal his approximate position. Or thinking back over the country he has traversed he may feel that by retracing his steps he can return to a known point in a comparatively

butter·
fly
bandage

day·pack
survival
kit

short time. After all the evidence has been sifted, the important decision is whether to try and return to a known point, whether to stay put and await rescue, or whether to head hopefully toward civilization. Only full consideration of the situation in a rational, panic-free manner will reveal the best course of action. The backpacker well equipped for recreational travel is generally well equipped for survival. Dayhikers are not so well provisioned and ought to carry, in addition to a good first aid kit, something that might be called a survival kit.

The one I carry in my creel or daypack whenever I go out (in addition to the small first aid kit) consists of an ancient tin cup, which can be used for cooking, a dozen kitchen matches, a yard and a half of toilet paper, about fifty feet of 550 lb. test nylon cord, a tiny one-bladed knife, two heavy-duty plastic bags, a quarter of a rum fudge bar broken into squares, three tea bags, three bouillon cubes, note paper and the stub of a pencil. All these items pack in the cup which in turn is packed in one of the plastic bags. Total weight is only six ounces.

There are many more items that might be worth carrying. A small waterproof match box with built-in compass and whistle might be worthwhile. So might the three ounce, 56" x 84" Rescue Blanket which is strong and a good reflector. In harsher seasons, when accidents can prove more dangerous, considerably more survival (and backpacking) gear can be justified. Fire starters, for instance, are part of my basic equipment when traveling in country that is cold, wet or other wise unfriendly.

In mild summer weather, if adversity fails to strike, I can always use my survival kit to brew a cup of tea beneath the shelter of a tree while I wait for an afternoon thunderstorm to pass.

13 FAMILY TRIPS

All parents who love the outdoors would doubtless like to instill the same feeling in their children. But many parents who badly want their children to enjoy the wilderness either cram it down their throats or fail to make sure those first trips are enjoyable. The world is full of people whose first experience in the wilds was unpleasant—and who therefore never went back.

So considerable effort should be invested in seeing that those first experiences are happy ones. This doesn't mean dragging children along on a short adult trip. It means carefully planning an easy trip into pretty, familiar country and tailoring all aspects to maximize the enjoyment of the children. The same principle applies to anyone who is a stranger to the mountains, whether girl friends, children, parents, brides, or even inexperienced friends.

In my view, there are a great many parents who are not ready to take children into the wilderness—and a great many children who are not ready to go. Every summer I see miserable families struggling up the trail or bickering in camp. The parents are bitterly disappointed because the children are spoiling their trip, and the children are tired of being hurried, picked on and yelled at. The parents vow never to take those "ungrateful brats" again, and the children are equally determined not to go.

Generally speaking, I feel parents should not take their children backpacking until: (1) they themselves can travel in the wilds with some degree of comfort and competence; (2) the children have been taken on several successful day hikes; (3) parents are willing to tailor an overnight trip to country they know, expressly for the pleasure of their children; (4) the children want (or are at least willing) to go; and (5) the parents genuinely want them along. Families able to meet these criteria have a fighting chance for a pleasant trip.

The most common cause of disastrous family trips, it seems to me, is the failure of parents to see the trip through their children's eyes. Any child will ask 'If it isn't fun, why do it?' He does not insist every minute be fun, but he will expect that, taken as a whole, the trip should be pleasant. After all, what good is a vacation if it isn't fun? The honest adult will find no satisfactory objection to this reasoning. If parents are not willing and able to make the trip fun—for themsleves as well as for the children—there is little point in going.

Parents with little experience in backpacking generally have difficulty enough without the added burden of children. People who cannot go into the woods with confidence are not likely to have the patience or the skill to provide children a happy time. There is rarely a good reason why children cannot be taken on a considerable number of day hikes before taking them overnight. I first took my daughter backpacking when she was eight. Because she had made many day trips with me, had walked up a few peaks and had slept overnight in the forest by our cabin—she took the trip in stride. Very little was strange to her and she required very little persuasion.

That first trip was simple and short. With another family, we walked no more than a mile and a half from our cabin. Though we traveled cross-country rather than on a trail, and climbed perhaps eight hundred feet, walking conditions were good and I knew every inch of the way. The campsite I had chosen offered a spring, a marvelous view, a cozy dell for sleeping, wildflowers and small caves. The children got to arrange their beds together, apart from the adults, before gathering wood and water for dinner. There were songs and marshmallows by the campfire before bed. Everything was planned with the children in mind. We were back at the cabin before lunchtime the following day.

Once it has been decided to take children backpacking, the trip should be planned with the tenderest, most timid member in mind. Backpacking parents might normally scorn camping at the first lake or stream on the trail, but if the children are young (under ten) that may be the wisest plan. Chances are that the country will be more than wild enough to excite them. Being relatively close to civilization (telephone, campground, motel, grocery) has its advantages. If the weather turns bad, the children get sick, the mosquitos are unbearable, or something else goes wrong—the car is a mercifully short dash away. And the shortness of the trail may seem a blessing to parents who find themselves carrying twice their normal loads.

I do not believe children should be taken backpacking for the first time to an area that has not been thoroughly reconnoitered by their parents. The campsite should be known in advance and selected on the basis of its appeal to a child. Adults often arrange their itinerary for the photography, fly fishing and rock climbing afforded, but a small child will be interested in none of these. Trips should be planned for the warmest weather and fewest bugs. In the Sierra, that means August. The fact that the traffic is heavy, the wildflowers past their prime and the fishing slow will not bother your children in the least. For a child's first trip, one or two nights will be long enough. If camp is to be moved it should be moved in the morning, with lunch and a leisurely afternoon planned in the new campsite.

Kids love tube tents

As on any backpacking trip, there is a limit to what can be carried. But parents should not expect children to be voluntarily Spartan—or even to be impressed with the size of dad's pack. Emphasizing sacrifice only makes it harder for them to understand where the fun comes in. Clothes must be carried to protect children from extremes of heat and cold. Sunburn must be guarded against with long-sleeved shirts, long trousers—and, if possible, hats. Extra quantities of sunburn cream should be provided so that children can carry individual tubes. The same goes for lip salve.

Extra aerosol cans of mosquito repellent (kept away from small children) are important for quick relief from a sudden invasion, and nylon netting and head nets may be required if the bugs are likely to be fierce. Too much protection is better than too little—even though it swells the pack. Rattlesnake country should be avoided if possible.

The first aid kit should be enlarged by the addition of extra bandaids and spare soap, and wash cloths and towels are certain to be needed. Petroleum jelly will be invaluable to ease chafing. Since children have an unfailing affinity for water, three pairs of extra socks will be needed, the heavier the better. Wool and synthetics are best because cotton tends to stretch and sag, producing first wrinkles then blisters.

In recent years, a great many cheap, small knapsacks and packs have appeared on the market, many of which are suitable for children. Flimsy plastic knapsacks that roll up into their own pockets cost as little as $5. Of course, canvas or nylon packs are preferable. For older children who can carry larger loads, a small aluminum pack frame (available from surplus stores, Jansport and Camp Trails) will be a better investment.

My daughter likes to carry a fanny pack (ski belt), which gives her greater freedom of movement than any shoulder pack. She often wears it with a knapsack which will just hold her sleeping bag. All but the youngest children should be encouraged to carry at least a token pack—of course, if the trail is too long or the load too large it may end up being carried by dad.

Extra sleeping bags tend to make dad's pack unwieldy, so children should carry their own bags, if possible. Since even an adult sleeping bag should not weigh more than five and a half pounds, most children old enough to backpack should be able to carry their own. If suitable bags cannot be bought, rented or borrowed, an adequate cocoon can usually be fashioned from cotton sheet blankets and old wool blankets or a quilted comforter fastened together with large safety pins.

For small children, a tube tent can be important, even if there seems no chance of rain. The small cozy space tends to be reassuring. Tents are extremely useful for afternoon napping and changing clothes out of the wind. And children fearful of the dark may insist on sleeping inside no matter what the weather. Children are usually intrigued by tents, and parents can often generate enthusiasm for camping by pitching one on the lawn at home before a trip, putting in sleeping bags and serving a picnic lunch.

A tarp tent, though more difficult to pitch, is also a good low-cost family shelter where insects and wind are not great problems. In addition to the tent, a sizeable extra tarp can serve as picnic blanket and dining table. When children are along, there is generally a need for something on which gear can be spread out.

Food that meets the adult backpacker's demands may or may not satisfy your children. Special emphasis should be put on snack foods and liquids. To maintain energy and prevent dehydration, children will need plenty of both. To encourage the between meal eating so necessary in the wilds, plenty of goodies are needed, especially gorp, cheese, salami, nuts and dried fruit. Children should be urged to drink small amounts of water often while traveling, and quantities of lemonade, Koolaid, Fizzies and reconstituted milk should be available in camp. Since kids will immediately notice that camp milk tastes 'funny,' powdered flavorings should be carried to transform it into chocolate milk, cocoa and milkshakes.

Young children will probably want to take along toys from home and since these will promote security and supply entertainment, parents ought to indulge at least one, so long as it is light and appropriate. Generous parents can sometimes be recognized on the trail by the teddybears and Raggedy Anns riding on top of their packs.

When the trailhead has been reached and the loads handed out, the real work begins. Getting children up the trail and into camp demands patience, a strong back and considerable psychology. Parents unwilling or unable to keep the children amused and moving—without losing their own sense of humor—will wish they had left them home. And so will the children. Without supervision, children tend to start out fast, which means they will soon want to rest. It is hard to curb the enthusiasm and effervescence that eats up their energy without curtailing the fun of the trip; it is also hard to keep them going when they feel tired and want to rest: and children fatigue quickly.

It is unfair to expect children to have the self-discipline necessary to conserve energy for the climb ahead. Instead, one has to supply

family camping means carrying a little more.

incentives, distractions, goals and just plain entertainment—with the minimum necessary discipline mixed in.

The rest of this chapter comes from notebooks carried on a number of trips with my daughter, other people's children and other families. Since, like kids, it seems to defy organization, I offer it more or less as collected.

Call the trip a 'walk,' 'walking' is fun but 'hiking' is work. Making the trip a lark for the kids means getting into the spirit of *their* adventure rather than fretting about the slowness of the pace. Keep children moving but don't try to make them hurry; it will only slow them down and rob them of their cheerfulness. Make sure they get away from the trail occasionally. Let them put down their packs and go investigate something they've discovered.

Take them off the trail to see mossy glens, snowbanks, waterfalls, a tree that looks like a witch. If they've been trudging along wearily for awhile, don't wait for them to ask for a rest or simply sit down. Stop voluntarily, give them something to eat and show them something interesting. If they're happy they'll recover from their fatigue with amazing swiftness. Keep in mind the fact that the long range goal is not just to get them to camp before lunch—it's to make the trip so much fun that they'll want to come again.

It's always a good idea to keep watch on childrens' feet. By putting a stop to chafing in the early stages you may avoid having to carry a child to the car! I have more than once discovered my daughter hiking happily along despite the fact that one sock had worked so far down her foot that it had disappeared entirely into her boot. Fortunately, children's feet take the abuse of rough country much better than their parents' and do not easily blister.

I find it important on the trail to talk to children a good part of the time. I give them progress reports ''We're more than halfway . . . It's only fifteen minutes until lunch . . . There's a spring where we can get a drink behind that big tree . . . It's all downhill to camp.'' Whenever I can, I praise their achievements. I try to distract them from the drudgery of the trail, and in doing so I find I have distracted myself.

When they grow weary of such temporal phenomena as birds' nests, rills and rock rabbits, I try to stir their imagination by pointing out a cloud formation that looks like a ship, a leaning tree that resembles a poised runner or patch of lichen that looks like a lion. Finding strange likenesses can be made into a contest in which children point out their own discoveries. The reward for the most imaginative can be a specially prized piece of candy.

I carry a considerable stock of snacks in wide variety, and I keep them concealed to add mystery and anticipation. It's less important that kids eat well at mealtime than it is to feed them snacks between meals to keep their energy and spirits up. I pass out food with the smallest provocation and often with none at all.

It's always important to keep the kids happy, but there's still the problem of getting them up the trail. A minimal amount of discipline, and self-discipline, is indispensable. So is a certain amount of desire on the child's part to please his parents and do his part. I explain at the outset that while we're going to stop and rest, play games, explore and generally have fun, we still have to make it to camp before lunch, so we'll have time to set up camp and spend the afternoon playing without our packs. And that means we have to keep moving. As we move along, I show kids easier ways to get around obstacles, help foot draggers, readjust packs, show how the Indians walk, and if the trail grows steep, I demonstrate the rest step, which I represent variously as the "polar bear shuffle," "kangaroo limp," "dromedary drag," etc.

If there are several children, I work most with the slowest ones. Sometimes the slowest becomes the fastest if you put them in the lead, explaining that they now have the responsibility for keeping the group on the trail, showing them how to recognize blazes and ducks and the footworn groove. It is usually best to bring up the rear when hiking with children, so you can help the ones who fall behind and so you'll

don't panic
at every danger

Kids are good at finding firewood . . .
. . . and mud!

know if a child quietly sits down on a rock or wanders off while the rest of the party marches by.

The hardest part of handling a group of kids is keeping them together and controlling the rest stops. Energetic older boys will want to keep going while younger girls will frequently want to rest. It's not difficult to spread your party all over the mountain. I urge the stoppers to keep going, and as a last resort I take their packs. If other kids get too far ahead, I may saddle them with the unwanted packs. When we stop for a rest I encourage the energetic ones to explore the immediate area while the tired ones sit and puff.

When the weariest seem to be somewhat restored, I simultaneously announce we must be off and pass out lemondrops all around. It is important after a rest not to let children dash up the trail with recharged enthusiasm or they'll burn themselves out after only a few yards and plead for another rest. If they fail to restrain themselves, after you've explained the reason for starting off slowly, there is nothing to do but nag. Chronic fast starters are best reminded at the end of the rest instead of after they take off.

Even with all these strategems, the trail can become monotonous, and when the group becomes dull or dispirited I call an early rest. Everyone takes off his pack and we make a little side trip to some interesting spot out of sight of the trail—usually a waterfall or a cool glade or a lookout point, and we have a drink of lemonade (powder and plastic bottle must be handy) or lie in the cool grass, or throw snowballs off the cliff. This side trip is likely to refresh the group and the time spent seems a worthwhile investment. Progress, in this fashion, will be anywhere from a quarter mile to on mile per hour.

When camp is reached (and by now it should be evident why it needs to be close and the trail well known) some kids will want to flop down and rest, others will want to explore. No one will want to unpack, lay out beds or gather wood. The best strategy is to let everyone squander at least half an hour before assigning chores.

Everyone should have something useful to do; if the tasks are thoughtfully assigned and described, previously exhausted children will go to work with surprising enthusiasm.

Limit the amount that thirsty children drink, but allow them—in fact invite them—to drink frequently from unpolluted streams and rills and your water bottle or canteen. Snowball fights and singing make good diversions. So do yodeling and echoing. Give kids the sense of helping you and finding the way. Don't communicate anxiety about reaching camp, snakes, storms, or mosquitos. You must be relaxed and at home in the woods if you want your children to feel the same way. Don't panic if they step near the edge of a cliff; their natural caution should protect them. Don't yell at them. Be alert for excessive fatigue, dizziness, blisters, chafing clothes, sunburn and chapped lips.

Explain in advance that you want to keep them comfortable and therefore they must let you know what's bothering them. They'll tell you all right! When you come to sand on smooth slab, wet slippery surfaces, loose gravel, mud, etc., calmly demonstrate how to cross safely. Celebrate all achievement; be liberal with praise and rewards. Teach your kids not to litter and get them to help you pick up gum wrappers and trash—if the going is not too difficult—to be deposited in one of your spare plastic bags.

Impress your kids that nothing must be left behind to mar the wilderness, especially used toilet paper! Children at all times should carry about three feet of TP folded up in a pocket. Teach them when traveling to choose a place that won't be found; supervise if necessary. Show them how to fold the used paper inward for easy handling and put it in a plastic bag for later burning. In camp, build a latrine and

Tarp tents keep the kids happy

furnish it with TP and a collection bag for used paper. Unless you provide instruction there are sure to be toilet paper streamers decorating the trees, and the responsibility will be yours.

It's a poor idea to plan to take children cross-country in rough terrain unless they are large, strong, proven hikers. Being closer to the ground, children see relatively small objects as real obstacles. A rock that's just a knee-high step to you will be a waist-high roadblock to a six-year-old; a good scramble for you may be a nightmare for them. Forget boulder-hopping altogether. Be wary of fussy eaters. Explain before the trip that the food—in order to give everyone more energy—will be a little different. Then serve them sample dishes or meals at home, making the change of diet an adventure.

In camp, find them rocks to climb, rills to dam, a snowpatch to slide on; define the bathroom area boundaries, explain camp rules regarding fire, food, muddy feet in the tent and the sanctity of the kitchen during meal preparation. Alert them to the continued need for wood and water. Explain that, like Indians, you plan to leave this camp so no one will know you've been there.

Taking children into the wilderness can be demanding, even maddening, but by allowing yourself to see the trip through their eyes you can share their wonder, joy and adventure. You can remember what it feels like to be a kid in the woods when everything is new and mysterious and exciting. And when the trip is over and you're homeward bound there is deep satisfaction in hearing your youngest ask "Daddy, when can we go again?"

14 TROUT FISHING

It has always seemed to me that many more people would enjoy catching and eating trout .... if only they knew how to go about it. Of course, catching trout is not the only measure of fishing success. The pursuit of trout, even when unsuccessful, is the best way I know to become intimately acquainted with a part of the wilderness. Whether following the rocky shore of a mountain tarn, watching trout feeding in a crystal pool or making my way cautiously along the bank of a brook, angling has shown me many more wonders than all the trails I ever traveled.

The hunt for solitude and challenging country often leads the backpacker past trout waters that would fill a fisherman with envy. More than once I have caught so many trout (and put them back unharmed) that the feathers were totally stripped from my fly. Of course, I also have been skunked on good trout water. I do not consider myself first of all a fisherman. I sometimes pass good trout water without setting up my rod. Sometimes I even fail to take a rod along. But I am fond of eating freshly-caught, wild trout. And I rely upon trout fishing and cross-country climbing to get me off the trails and into corners of the country that I otherwise never would see.

Some writers insist that it is enough for the backpacker to carry a few yards of line, a few feet of leader and a couple of hooks. The idea is to cut a willow rod, catch grasshoppers or grubs for bait and then go blithely forth to catch fish with this clumsy rig. An expert might catch unsophisticated trout on virgin waters, and a hard working angler might land starved fish, but this kind of outfit is utterly worthless for the beginner who would like the best possible chance of eating trout for supper.

Trout fishing gear, luckily, is neither expensive nor heavy. Basic outfits (rod, reel and line) for both fly casting and spinning are commonly offered for as little as $20. Neither pleasure nor fish-taking ability are much sacrificed in modestly priced gear. Of course, high quality backpacking outfits can easily cost $200. The fly fishing outfit I generally take backpacking weighs anywhere from 11 to 24 ounces. The cheapest equipment may weigh a little more, but the beginner should not have to carry more than a pound and a half for fly fishing or two pounds for spinning.

Trout fishing tackle is designed for maximum lightness, because the lighter the gear the more sensitive it will be to the antics of the trout. Fighting an eight inch rainbow on a three ounce fly rod is three times as exciting as playing the same fish on a five ounce rod.

Trout fishing gear sharply divides itself into two different types: fly casting and spin fishing. In traditional flycasting, it is the weight of the comparatively heavy line that carries the nearly weightless fly out across the water. The angler must lift the line into the air and keep it suspended there with alternate forward and backward casts until he is ready to place the fly on the water. Most people find fly casting harder to learn and more demanding then spinning.

In spin fishing, the comparatively heavy weight of the lure propels the almost weightless nylon line out over the water. There is no back cast to tangle and no necessity to keep the line suspended in the air. While the fly fisherman is largely restricted to flies the spin fisherman can cast spinners, plugs and bait, as well as flies.

Of course, the angler who has mastered both types of fishing and is prepared to use whichever seems most likely to be effective, will double his chances of catching trout. He need not carry two complete outfits since a fly-spin combination rod will suffice for both techniques. In recognition of the backpacking boom, tackle manufacturers are designing more and more gear for lightness, durability and easy carrying.

For years I carried a three-piece, split-bamboo, eight-foot fly rod weighing 5½ ounces and fastened together with metal furrules. And I held my breath every time the fragile tip caught on a branch. Today, I carry a virtually unbreakable, 2-piece Fenwick seven foot glass rod weighing 3 and ⅛ ounces, fastened together with hollow slip joints instead of furrules. Fenwick makes half a dozen rods that are admirably suited to backpacking. They range in length from seven to eight and a half feet tall; all weigh less than 4 ounces, and several break down into four pieces for easy carrying inside a pack. A seven foot combination spin-fly rod weighs 3 and ⅞ ounces, breaks down into four sections and offers remarkably good action for both types of fishing. Eagle Claw makes another good spin-fly rod and the cost is considerably less than the $70 required to buy a Fenwick. Lamiglass makes a marvelous 8-foot 5-piece backpacking rod that weighs 3½ oz. and costs about $70. Less expensive fly rods that should be perfectly satisfactory for the beginner can be purchased for as little as $20.

Single action fly reels of the simplest construction can be purchased for as little as $5, but the halfway serious angler will be better advised to spend $25 for a Martin MG7, or $30-35 for a Phlueger Medalist. Japanese copies of these and similar reels cutomarily cost $10-15 less. Automatic reels should be avoided. All good fly rods are rated for reels of a certain weight range and for lines of a specific weight.

Fly line is classified as either 'level' or 'tapered.' The tapering in the last few yards at the end (tippet) avoids an abrupt change in diameter between the line and the leader while retaining the line weight necessary for casting. Efficiency of casting and smoothness and naturalness of fly presentation are greatly increased by the use of a tapered line—especially for the novice.

Conventional tapered lines are tapered at both ends ('double tapers'), so when one tippet wears out the line can be taken off the reel and reversed to make use of the other taper. Double tapered lines (by Courtland, and Scientific Angler, for instance) cost about $18 for 25-35 yards, but cheaper makes are available in the $10 range. Level fly lines, though less than half the price of tapered, are not worthwhile investments for anglers interested in assembling competent fly casting outfits.

Depending on the water to be fished and the angler's experience, it may be necessary to back the tapered fly line with a length of level line. The junction of the two should be spliced and whip-finished, rather than simply knotted. The fly line tippet should have a whip-finished, spliced loop for easy knot-free attachment of the leader. A knot both catches the air to obstruct smooth casting and catches the water to disturb shy trout. A nail knot coated with Duco cement will substitute for a spliced loop.

trout
on
willow
stringer

Leaders are also either tapered or level, and the tapered leader is much to be preferred. The stiffer butt section helps transmit the thrust of the line while the delicate tippet allows the fly to settle lightly on the water after the leader has straightened out. The biggest benefit for the beginner—especially in brush—is that when the fly is caught on an obstruction the tapered leader always breaks at the weakest point—next to the fly, so the leader is rarely lost.

The rule of thumb for leader length is slightly less than the length of the rod, which avoids the necessity of drawing the leader-line junction through the guides. In murky water, spring fishing under cut banks, or lowering a fly through brush, as little as two feet of leader may suffice, while nine to twelve feet may be needed when casting in the fall over clear, glassy pools. Tapered leaders are rated according to tippet diameter (1X for heavy bass bugs down to 6X for the smallest flies on the clearest water) and also by breaking strength (from perhaps 5 pounds down to a pound and a half.) Creative Sports makes the strongest leaders.

Trout flies come in four basic types: dry, wet, nymph and streamer, but wet flies are scarce since they can only be fished wet, while dry flies can be fished either wet or dry. Dry flies are designed to resemble flying insects; streamer flies and bucktails imitate minnows and large bugs; nymphs are tied to look like grubs, aquatic stage insects, worms, caterpillers, larvae and other fish foods.

Most of the time, flies must closely resemble the insects on which trout are feeding in order to be effective. But a majority of fishermen

"natural" fishing rods mean frustration -not fish.

find that trout are more sensitive to size than shape or color. Rarely will they make any noticeable distinction between patterns, so the angler can choose the flies he likes best—as long as they are comparable in size to those on which trout are feeding. Even size is less important, some experts say, than the manner in which the fly is presented and fished. The most common mistake is to fish flies that are too large. For mountain trout, sizes 14 to 16 are more appropriate than the 10s and 12s that are most often available. It is a myth that "it takes big hooks to catch big trout."

A beginning fly fisherman on a three day trip should have at least a dozen flies, divided into three or four patterns. For variety I would choose a Royal Coachman because its white wings make it easy to follow, a grey hackle peacock with a thick body, and a mosquito, because these are among the commonest of summer insects. Flies cost anywhere from twenty-five cents to a dollar a piece. The cheapest flies, imported from Japan, often are not glued securely to the hook, have clogged eyes and tend to break easily, but I have used dozens of them and most were satisfactory. More than anything else, the price of a fly reflects the quality of its hook.

Another source of reasonable flies—in the long run—is fly tying, a common hobby among fly fishermen. Kits start at about $20. There is real satisfaction in devising and tying flies—and then taking trout on them. Since I pay nearly as much for fly tying hooks as I do for Japanese flies, dollar savings tend to be negligible.

Far and away the best fly box for backpacking is made by Perrine and sells for $4. This little marvel, the size of a package of cigarettes, easily holds a hundred flies in six spring loaded slips. Mine weighs only 2½ ounces, loaded. A variety of light, cheap plastic boxes are also available.

A creel is a considerable luxury for a backpacker, and the traditional woven willow basket is out of the question. On easy trips I sometimes carry a canvas creel if I plan to bring home fish to eat, but usually I rely on a V-shaped willow stringer or use a short length of nylon cord tied around a stick. Either can easily be threaded through the trout's gills and mouth for easy carrying.

Since it is necessary to be able to control the floating or sinking of the leader and fly, I often carry a small tin of Mucilin with Silicone and a plastic vial of Orvis Leader Sink. When it is vital to keep a fly floating on choppy water, Mucilin is invaluable. Of course, a fly can also be dried by vigorous false casting. A film of mud, mosquito repellant or sunburn cream rubbed on the leader will cause it to sink, but Leader Sink is more convenient. In the swiftest water, split shot clamped directly on the hook can be used to sink a fly—but casting becomes difficult.

A necessity in any angler's kit is a sharp knife, with a sharp point, but this the backpacker already has.

Spinning equipment is not quite so light as fly casting tackle, but it, too, has been developed during the past few years with the backpacker in mind. Fenwick makes two admirable spinning rods with hollow slip joints which sell for $60-70. The Shakespeare 4-piece, 7-foot Ugly Stik weighs 5 oz., costs $65 and will double as a fly rod. Complete spin outfits with telescoping rods often weigh as little as 14 oz., cost $20-30 and measure only 17 inches. REI offers a telescopic spin-fly rod of this sort called the Powerscopic for only $14 with plastic case.

spliced loop

Probably the best of the backpacking spinning rod packages comes from Daiwa, a rod that breaks down into 15 inch sections and, with tiny 6 oz. reel, weighs only 10 oz. and costs about $70. The best backpacking reels, besides the Daiwa at $47, are the Shakespeare Ultra-Lite ($50, 6 oz.) and President ($55-60, 9 oz.). The biggest recent advance in spinning reels is the highly recommended skirted spool. Unlike cheap fly reels, cheap spinning reels tend to be big, heavy, angular and lacking in durability—especially closed face plastic reels. Of course, since spinning outfits (rod, reel, line) are cheap, the beginner can afford to try spinning very reasonably before making a larger investment.

Backpacking spin fishermen commonly use either two or four pound test monofilament which serves as both line and leader. The lighter the line the lighter the lure it will cast. Backpackers need only 100-150 yards of line, which costs little more than a dollar per 100 yards if bought in bulk and wound on the spool at a sporting goods store. Several spare loaded spools should be carried.

ordinary knot

The principal use of spinning gear is to cast hardware: metal spinners, spoons and other lures. These commonly weigh from 1/16 to 3/8 ounces and cost 50¢ to $2 each. Most of the price of the more expensive lures pays for fine quality treble hooks. The Super Duper, Mepps and Panther Martin are the favorites. There is evidence that trout in heavily fished waters may actually grow wary of familiar looking lures, while accepting new ones with a different action. But

stalking grasshoppers gets harder once they're warm & awake.

most veteran anglers believe the lure or fly which the fisherman uses with the greatest persistence and confidence will catch him the most fish.

Beginners are advised to buy as great a variety of lures as possible—probably half a dozen to start—in the smallest sizes available. Considering the advice of the salesman is a good way to begin, provided he knows the type of water to be fished. Most accomplished spin fishermen use tiny swivels to reduce line twisting. Perrine makes a good aluminum lure box for about $3, but a number of much lighter plastic boxes are available for less than $1.

To make light lures cast farther and sink deeper, the spin fisherman should carry a small selection of various sized split shot or sinker putty, which can be clamped onto or next to the lure. Even more useful are plastic bubbles which can be filled with shot and fastened to the leader to make lures run deep. The same bubbles, partly filled with water, serve as floats and provide the necessary weight for spin-casting flies. Many bubbles accept water but not shot, so the angler must shop carefully to assure versatility. Bubbles are inexpensive and almost weightless, so three or four can easily be carried. Bubbles should be fastened two feet from the fly for beginners and three feet for more experienced casters.

The most popular bait for trout is the salmon egg. Small bottles of identical looking pink eggs may range in price from 50¢ to $3. The difference lies in the quality (firmness, toughness) of the egg and the appeal of the ingredients used to treat it. Trout rely principally on the smell of an egg rather than its appearance. Eggs are soaked in chemicals which toughen the skin and impart a flavor to the milk within. When the egg is punctured by the hook, the milk oozes out to flavor the surrounding water and attract the trout.

Pautzke's Balls O'Fire stay together, stay on the hook and do a good job of attracting trout. Despite their high price, they are the choice of regular egg fishermen. Salmon eggs are the most popular bait because they are neat, easy to use and do not wiggle. But they are generally

much less effective than such natural baits as worms, grubs, helgramites and grasshoppers; and heavily fished trout tend to ignore them.
Size No. 14 egg hooks, either snelled or unsnelled, are required to
completely hide the hook.

The most successful bait fishermen go prepared to catch whatever
wild creatures the trout are feeding on. They roll rocks to collect ants
and beetles. They dig in rotten logs for grubs. They catch grasshoppers with their hats in the early morning before insects become active.
And they prowl the margins of a stream or lakeshore for whatever
insect life is plentiful, digging in the mud beneath hovering dragon-
flies to capture their larvae and turning over rocks to uncover
helgramites.

Serious bait fishermen work in pairs, one holding a sheet of nylon
mosquito netting in the water while his partner turns over rocks just
upstream. The same netting will produce a variety of wildlife when
spread beneath violently shaken shrubbery. Worms, which should be
brought from home to save digging up the meadow, require worm
hooks which have two or three barbs on the back of the shank.

Trout, for the most part, are not very smart, i.e. they learn very little
from experience or association. But their instincts and senses are often
acute and serve to protect them. Trout see well underwater, but
distinguish only movement, not shapes, above the surface. And their
field of vision does not extend to the area behind their eyes—which is
why knowledgeable fishermen work their way upstream in order to
approach the fish from behind. (Trout generally face the current in
moving water.) Trout have demonstrated a preference for red, but
probably distinguish other colors as well.

Trout do not actually hear, but are extremely sensitive to vibrations.
They will often be frightened by the tread of a heavy-footed angler
they do not see. As demonstrated by the makers of various salmon egg
sauces, trout have a well developed sense of smell. This tends to
explain why natural live bait is successful while exact rubber imitations are not. Taste is closely related to smell and since trout are able to
discriminate between food and non-food, a good bait must satisfy both
the trout's taste and smell.

Trout feed most actively at dawn or dusk. Poor light early and late
conceals the angler and the artificiality of his offerings, and trout are
apt to venture farther from shelter to feed when protected by shadow.

Trout also have several spurts of appetite during the day, and if the
angler happens to hit one, the fishing is likely to be unusually good.
Another saying of some substance is that fishing will be better in the
dark of the moon. It is generally true that the brighter the moonlight
the better the fish can see to feed at night—and the less avidly it will
feed during the day. If I am making a trip primarily to fish, the phase of
the moon will be a factor in scheduling the trip.

More important than the time of day or the phase of the moon is the
angler's technique, and passable technique comes most readily from

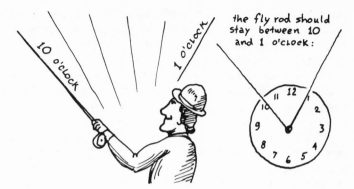

the fly rod should stay between 10 and 1 o'clock:

practice. The scarcity of fly fishermen stems from the fact that it takes a little time and patience to learn—and instructors are not easily found. An expert fisherman and tournament fly-caster friend suggests the following for beginners.

Using a seven to eight foot fly rod, matched reel, tapered line and leader and a fly from which the barb has been filed, the student should measure his fly line and wind it with different colored strips of tape at 25, 30 and 35 feet. On a stretch of lawn with plenty of back casting room, he should lay out a sheet of newspaper for a target. Fly casting demands a relatively stiff wrist and the student will benefit by fastening his wrist to the rod handle with a big rubber band to remind him to use his elbow instead. A book held in the armpit will discourage excess movement of the shoulder and promote good form.

Starting with about fifteen feet of line stretched out on the grass in front of him, the student, holding the rod in one hand and the line in the other, should lift the rod tip quickly from the 10 o'clock position—as viewed in profile against a giant imaginary clock—stopping at the 1 o'clock position. The motion's suddenness must lift the line into the air and into the backcast. The student must wait until the line is stretched out tight behind him before bringing the rod forward with enough force to carry the line out straight in front of him when the rod is returned to the 10 o'clock position.

False casting should be continued until the student can keep the line suspended in the air with a minimum of effort without exceeding the 10-1 o'clock range with the rod. To make the cast, it is only necessary to aim the forward cast to a point three feet above the newspaper and then drop the rod tip to 9 o'clock and allow the fly to quietly settle.

The student should become adept at dropping the fly accurately with 15-20 feet of line before trying longer casts. It will be helpful to use a highly visible white winged fly and to watch the path of fly, line and rod continuously at first to become acquainted with the paths they travel and to discover the necessary rhythm. When the fly can be placed gently on the newspaper every time at a distance of thirty feet the caster will be ready to catch fish.

Long casts are not essential to catching trout. The uncle who taught me to fly cast regularly outfished me on a stream with casts no longer than twenty feet. The most important factor in his success, it seems to me, was his knowledge of where trout lie. Nearly as important was his ability to present the fly in a natural manner without frightening the fish. Trout will choose protected feeding places during the day and will not venture more than a few inches away from that protection to take fly, lure or bait. Random casts into open water will only serve to scare them.

Placing the fly so that it floats on the current without drag past the likely lie, or casting quickly to a rise in a lake comes with experience. But approaching carefully so as not to spook the fish is largely a matter of patience and self discipline. The difference between scared trout and a full creel is often the angler's willingness to crawl slowly to the protection of a tree and then carefully cast from behind it. Concealment is far more important to the fly caster than to the spin fisherman because he is operating at closer range with trout on or near the surface, and will often be within the trout's field of view or vibrations.

Two other essentials for fly casting success are keeping a tight line and setting the hook. Only a small percentage of trout will hook themselves, and nearly all trout, given the chance, will reject artificial flies and try to spit them out. It is up to the angler to strike back when a trout takes the fly, before it can throw the hook. The angler's strike—lifting the rod tip with a snap—must be an instantaneous reaction. With a slack line, obviously, it will be virtually impossible to strike back in time. So the angler must balance the need to let the fly float naturally without drag, against the need to keep the line tight enough for setting the hook with a single jerk.

Since excessive casting tends to spook the fish, the fly caster must exercise restraint and emphasize accuracy. Whether in a lake or stream the closest lies should be explored first before working out toward the casting limit. Various retrieves can be tried to intrigue trout: leaving the fly motionless, twitching it, skittering it, or dunking it—until a strike is forthcoming. If fishing it dry fails, it should be allowed to sink below the surface. For wet fly fishing, only a single backcast should be used. If rising fish ignore the fly, either: (1) it is too large, (2) it is being presented unconvincingly, or (3) the fish are too small.

It is nearly always worthwhile to immediately examine the food in the mouth, throat and stomach of the first fish caught for a hint in the choice or modification of flies. For instance, finding a stomach full of small beetles, I might trim the hackles very short to make my fly more beetle-like—or go catch the real thing.

Once a stretch of water has been well prospected, even if unsuccessfully, it is a good idea to move on. If I get a good strike, but miss the fish, and several further casts bring no response, I immediately move away to rest the water, making a mental note to return later. When the water is still and well lighted it is next to impossible to catch trout on

stealth & concealment are
important in fly fishing

flies and casting will only frighten the fish. But the turbulence of
current, the shadows of trees or clouds, the swirl of rising fish, or a
wind ruffled surface will hide the angler, disguise his offering and give
the trout an illusion of protection, which will allow him to feed
uninhibited.

Fly rod fishing, though more limited in variety than spinning, offers
several variations. When the trout are numerous and receptive, but not
overly large, and casting room is ample, I often attach a dropper fly to
the middle of my leader by means of an eight inch length of monofilament. It more than doubles the chance of a strike and provides wild
action when two fish are hooked. Early in the year, I sometimes crimp
a split shot to the curve of the hook and, fishing off a ledge, jig for
bottom-feeding trout. And in desperation, I have even stripped the fly
off my hook to impale an ant or ladybug or grub when there seemed no
other way to catch my dinner.

Spin fishing is a good deal easier to learn for the beginning angler.
Spinning covers more water, offers less risk of frightening fish and
permits a greater variety of lures and baits, especially in lakes. The
elements of spin casting can be learned in fifteen minutes. All that is
required is the synchronization of the release of the line with the
forward thrust of the rod. Backcasting room is not required; neither is
false casting, nor the stealthful approach. The greater the weight of the
lure or lead or water-filled bubble, the greater the range of the caster.
The beginner is not limited to short casts; in fact he will easily cast
farther than the experienced fly caster. Of course spinning's advantage
lies in fishing big water: lakes and big rivers. In small or brushy
creeks, spinning is virtually impossible.

Spin fishing divides neatly into three categories: lures, bait and
flies. Lure casting, being easier, is naturally the most popular. It also
produces the most fish. The beginner should purchase spinners with
both wide and thin blades, wobbling spoons that are thick, thin, heavy
and light. Several sizes of split shot will also be needed. The angler's
imagination will suggest various combinations of lures and lead,
fished with various kinds of retrieves at varying depths. There is no
end to the possibilities. I have taken trout by skittering an unweighted

spinner-fly rapidly across the surface—and by bouncing a weighted spoon along a gravel bottom. Most fish, of course, are caught somewhere in between. The angler needs to be conscious of the depth at which a trout strikes in order to determine where fish are feeding.

The great advantage of spinning is the increased water that can be covered by longer casts which can be retrieved at any depth, but the advantage demands that the spin fisherman keep moving and experimenting in order to show his wares to a maximum number of fish. When trout follow a lure peacefully at a respectful distance they are only mildly curious, or well fed, and a change in lures is indicated. If trout follow closely or dart around the lure in an agitated manner they can sometimes be induced to strike by changing the action, or the depth, or the size of the lure, or perhaps by baiting the hook to add appeal. Lures should be connected to the monofilament by a swivel to prevent excessive twisting. Lure casting in streams or shallow water or weedy areas can be a very expensive sport!

Bait fishing looks deceptively simple. Unfortunately, it requires considerable art to make bait impaled on a hook attached to a line behave in a convincingly natural manner. There are two types of bait fishing: still fishing for the lazy and casting for the ambitious. The still fisherman hopes he has a likely spot, hopes the fish are feeding on the bottom and hopes the fish will hook himself. The bait caster at a lake generally attempts slow deep retrieves, tumbling his bait along the bottom, but also experiments with different depths. In some cases he is a still fisherman who occasionally moves.

In streams and rivers, the bait fisherman who can drift a bait along the bottom through likely lies with a tight enough line to feel a strike, but without tell-tale drag is an artist who will never lack for fish. The beginner who wishes to use bait will do better using a bubble for a bobber, attaching it at a point that will allow the lightly weighted bait to bob a few inches above the bottom.

Spin fishing with flies is much the same. A partially water-filled bubble is fastened two and a half or three feet from the fly and cast. Flies can be fished either wet or dry. Despite the splash of the bubble and its wake during the retrieve, the fish are not much bothered by relatively long casts on a wind ruffled lake.

a double fly can mean wild action

bait makes a spinner more
effective

There are certain techniques applicable to both spinning and fly casting. The most important is to keep moving. Ninety percent of the water contains no fish. The angler's objective is to eliminate much of it on the basis of experience, knowledge and inspection and to prospect the rest with diligence and imagination. The greater the area effectively fished the greater the chances of filling the creel. Beginners are apt to cast endlessly to water that has yielded a fish or a strike or a rise. The veteran angler will generally move after playing a fish, knowing the water is too disturbed to produce.

Trout lie facing upstream in running water and will generally hold in the same positions all day unless badly frightened. Under cover of dusk or darkness, however, they will move out into shallow or still or unprotected water to feed on morsels they would not have dared to pursue during the bright part of the day. The water that can be safely eliminated without a second glance during the day often yields the most fish in the evening. (Trout fishing is commonly permitted for an hour after sunset.)

Though difficult to reach and maddening to fish, the most productive water—even in heavily fished areas—will often be in brushy, swampy, heavily wooded country. Fishermen endowed with great patience—and some skill—often seek out just such hard-to-fish spots when they are determined to catch fish. The backpacker should not scorn accessible water because it is regularly fished, any more than he should depend on remote water to produce sensational results.

Trout are a roaming species in lakes and they tend to follow the shores near the bottom, patrolling the area they know. The best place to find them is where a stream feeds the lake. The second best place is off a point of land jutting into the lake. Coves are often good, especially if there is drainage into the lake. The foot of a dry watercourse is often attractive to trout, as are undercut banks and willow and alder thickets that overhang the water. Boulders, ledges, blankets of moss and submerged brush and logs all are favored by feeding trout.

Once the trout is hooked, two things become vital: to keep a tight line, and to keep him from reaching underwater obstructions. Slack in the line helps the fish throw the hook and invites knots and snags. Brook and brown trout instinctively bore for the bottom when hooked

and must be turned before they can rub the hook free or cut the leader. Rainbow and golden usually jump in hopes of throwing the hook and relatively little pressure is required to keep the line tight.

Beginning anglers tend to drag in their fish in great haste, often jerking them so violently from the water that the fish sails over the fisherman's head. This technique not only risks breaking the leader and pulling out the hook, it eliminates the pleasure of playing the fish.

For the backpacker—who cannot afford the weight of a landing net—playing the trout to exhaustion is more than just sport. Exhaustion greatly reduces the chance of escape. The trout should be maneuvered to the terrain most closely resembling a beach. The critical moment comes when the leader is grasped a few inches from the no-longer-flopping trout and it is gently beached, deposited several yards inland, and pounced upon before it can flop back into the water. Careless landing technique may cost the beginner one trout in two. The seasoned angler rarely loses a fish.

Of course, small trout or fish not needed for food should not be landed at all. The exhausted fish should be grasped gently but firmly underwater with one hand while the barb is backed out with the other. If the maneuver cannot be managed underwater, the hand grasping the fish should first be wetted to prevent it injuring the skin or ripping off the scales. Injured trout of any size should never be released. Nearly all trout taken on flies may be released unharmed, while nearly all fish taken on bait are injured by removal of the hook.

Once a trout has been landed, it should promptly be killed. Putting my index finger in the mouth, I quickly bend the head all the way back until it touches the back, breaking the neck and killing the fish instantly. After rinsing off the dirt, I usually lie the trout on a rock in the shade to let the breeze dry first one side then the other before putting it in my creel or on my stringer.

A creel should be well filled with grass or leaves to assure ventilation. Trout that are allowed to grow warm or stay wet or go uncleaned will lose texture and flavor in a matter of hours and will begin to spoil soon after. But by proper care and handling, I have often kept trout without refrigeration for three and four days in camp with no loss of freshness or flavor. By getting the trout dry to the touch almost immediately, and not allowing the sun to warm it, I can carry it in my creel for three or four hours before cleaning without risk.

Cleaning trout is simple enough. I insert a sharp pointed knife blade in the vent and with a short, rapid sawing strokes slit open the body cavity all the way to the base of the jaw. After cutting across from one gill opening to the other, I break the colon loose from the vent, and pull the viscera and gills loose. Then, running my thumbnail down the inside of the backbone, I remove the last blackness of the kidney and the job is done. After thoroughly rinsing the fish inside and out, and promptly drying all surfaces, it is ready for cooking, refrigeration or several days storage in a dry, cool place.

There are innumerable recipes for preparing trout, but fresh trout fried in butter is hard to beat. For years I have carried a plastic bag containing varying portions of corn meal, corn starch, salt, pepper, garlic and onion salt and other spices. After dampening the fish and putting it in the bag for a quick shaking, it is ready for the buttered skillet. Crumbling a little left over bacon bar over the frying fish enhances the flavor—so does a squirt of lemon juice. I am fond of smoked trout, but the process is not suited to most backpacking trips. Trout wrapped in aluminum foil and baked in ashes, on the other hand, is easy and saves the weight of a skillet. So does trout toasted on a stick.

When it comes to catching trout, there is no substitute for persistence. Almost anyone, equipped with reasonably efficient tackle and situated on reasonably stocked trout water, should eventually catch trout if the necessary effort is put forth. As one of my old fishing partners used to remind me: "You can't catch fish unless your line's in the water." He fished with great determination—and considerable imagination—and always caught fish.

The innocent angler should beware of guidebooks that promise marvelous fishing. Wild trout simply cannot be promised. The excellence of the fishing varies with the skill of the angler, recent fishing pressure, feeding activity, phase of the moon, available food, time of day, weather, season—and, of course, that great imponderable, luck.

Trout fishing has many allures. The chance of a big fish lends excitement to every cast. So does the yank of a striking trout. But what keeps me fishing is the pleasure of exploring the dependably fine country that trout call home.

15 a sample TRIP

In an effort to tie together the material on gear and technique, I provide here in some detail a composite narrative of a trip I take almost every spring, this time with my long-time traveling companion, Jorgy. The trip begins at my cabin on Upper Echo Lake on the edge of Desolation Wilderness on the crest of the California Sierra at 7,400 feet. Three little lakes offering three species of trout provide us with a destination. While none of them are reached by trail, access is not difficult, partly because we use a canoe. Probably most important is that the lakes are nestled in a small watershed with western exposure, so the swimming is good at a time when many of the lakes in Desolation are still frozen. So this is often my first trip of the year into the area.

I knew the three lakes would be thawed by early May, that insect activity would start the trout feeding on flies by mid-June, and that the nearby Boy Scout Camp did not open until immediately after the fourth of July weekend. To avoid the holiday campers, yet find the water warm enough for swimming, it seemed clear that the last week in June was the time to go. It would be the dark of the moon, which meant poor nighttime visibility, but probably better fishing. The only possible drawback was that mosquitos were likely to be active; since the country was open and well-drained, and since we meant to be prepared for insects, this was a negligible factor. (There are places, of course, where the mosquito menace is the *most* important factor in determining when to go.)

We decided to allow ourselves three days and two nights. Trip length was determined after considering several alternatives. The hike would be comparatively short, the country we wanted to see quite small; and there was a limit to what we could do to amuse ourselves. On the other hand, there would be several hours of driving each way and possibly an hour of canoeing. Alloting only two days and one night would mean going in one day and coming out the next; that would be too rushed. Four days and three nights was likely to lead to boredom. So we settled on three days—the average length of trip for recreational backpackers—sometime during the last week of June.

234

Normally, the next step is to work out a menu, buy the food and assemble the necessary clothing and equipment. But, since food, clothes and gear were already at the cabin in preparation for this and other trips, we postponed deciding what to take and turned to the decision of when precisely to go. The problem was weather. Few backpackers can afford to wait for perfect weather, but far too many see their trips spoiled for lack of knowledge about likely storms.

On the twenty-sixth of June at Echo, the sky was threatening all day, the wind was from the southeast and the barometer was low and steady. The forecast on the portable radio was for 'thunderstorms afternoon and evening' over the central Sierra. It rained a little in the afternoon and that night it snowed. The outlook was distinctly unfavorable.

On the twenty-seventh, the forecasts were for 'fair and warmer,' and the temperature climbed a little at Echo. The morning of the twenty-eighth the barometer was beginning to rise, and although scattered thunderstorms were still forecast afternoon and evening, these represented only the tattered remnants of the passing storm and would probably be weak and brief. Since the fourth of July weekend was almost upon us, we decided to leave the next day.

Most of my equipment is packed in cartons under a built-in bunk in my cabin. The first step in preparing for a trip is to prop open the bunk lid and fish out the notebook containing my latest checklist. It may be possible to remember everything needed on short notice without such a list, but before I made lists I nearly always left something vital home.

I like to postpone final choices and making up my pack until the last possible minute at the trailhead, so I begin by finding two empty cartons: one for food and community gear and the other for my own personal gear. Items on my list in general use, and therefore not stored beneath the bunks I usually skip over the first time around.

Because in years past the weather has ranged from sweltering to below freezing at this time of year, I decide to take my Cosy Quip foam bag to be assured of comfort (and no sweaty feet) whatever the temperature. Since the trip will be easy and short, the extra weight and bulk can be afforded. For added cushioning and protection from ground cold and moisture I add a 72-inch EVA pad. Both bag and pad are unrolled, inspected and aired. Since I prefer to sleep out I decide to take along a Marmot Burrow (bivy sack) for protection against rain, wind, bugs, dirt, etc., and leave the tent at home.

Cooking gear is the next consideration and I decide on the Coleman Peak One stove because of its easy simmering, wide burner, stability and capacity. A full tank will see us through the trip so extra fuel can be forgotten. I fire up the stove to make sure it's not clogged, fill the tank and put it in the gear box. In my own box goes a large, single-bladed jacknife (the blade is sufficiently pointed to clean trout, yet broad enough to spread butter) and my folding aluminum spoon-fork. With it goes my large plastic cup marked with lines at every quarter cup. Since weight is not vital, I add an almost weightless aluminum measuring cup as well.

Although our menu is still to be determined, I know we will want a big pot for soups and stews. A teakettle will function as a second pot. The single burner of the stove limits the possibilities (thereby simplifying menu planning). I put in the gear box a two and a quarter quart Sigg kettle, the lid of which has been fitted with a small knob so that it can be lifted with aluminum hot pot tongs, and my squat one quart teakettle.

For carrying water to camp and making fruit drinks, I choose a wide-mouthed polyethylene quart bottle. For this weekend-sized trip my half empty shaker containing a mix of various salts and pepper does not require refilling. One quart of milk will be more than ample so I open a quart packet of powdered Milkman and empty the contents into my plastic milk squirter bottle (originally a mustard dispenser). After tightly plugging the spout from within with a matchstick, this, too, goes in the gear box. I know my partner Jorgy prefers coffee to tea and will bring along his own, so I throw eight tea bags in the box (powdered tea may be simpler in the city, but bags are still best in the woods).

From my container box comes a plastic squeeze tube that was boiled clean after the last trip. I make sure the cap is screwed on tight, and fill it approximately half full of apricot-pineapple preserves through the open bottom. After cleaning the opening with a wet cloth I fold it over, leaving plenty of room in the bottom, and force on the plastic clip. I give the tube a hard squeeze to make sure it will not leak under pressure in my pack (it never has), then I wipe off the remaining stickiness and toss the tube in the food box.

It cannot be denied that margarine keeps better than butter, but I much prefer butter, and with minimal precautions it will always stay fresh for the three to five days I am usually out. Butter and margarine are heavy and many think of them as luxuries, but they are high in food energy and probably the most palatable source of badly needed fat. I find it possible to consume an almost unlimited quantity: in soups, stews, on crackers and frying trout, and even, like the Himalayan Sherpas, in my tea. So I select a large, wide-mouthed plastic jar and take two quarter-pound cubes of fresh butter out of the refrigerator and set them on the kitchen table to warm to a workable consistency.

A slightly smaller jar is chosen for cheese, and into it I fit wedge-shaped chunks of the four varieties I find in the refrigerator. Hard orange cheeses like cheddar are more melt-resistant than, say, Monterey Jack. After screwing the lid down tight, I put the can of cheese back in the refrigerator.

In my supply boxes beneath the bunks, I keep a variety of heavy duty plastic bags—containers that have become indispensable to backpacking. I choose six large ones (two of which are for bringing home trout) and two smaller ones, and stuff them all into the bottom of

deciding what to take

my pack. A Chore Girl, dish cloth, and a half-empty one ounce tube of Paket biodegradable hand and dish soap go into a small plastic bag which is closed with a twisty. I find half a roll of toilet paper secured with a rubber band, and since that looks like plenty I throw it in the box. Paper towels are more easily used in the wind, and they also serve as dish towels and hot pads, but I could not find a partial roll and a full roll is much too bulky for three days.

Next comes my small (six ounce) first aid kit packed in a screw-top plastic icebox jar. It contains a dozen assorted plastic Bandaids, a pair each of 2 x 2 and 3 x 3 inch gauze pads, a one-inch roll of adhesive (not plastic) tape, a roll of three inch Kling gauze and a clean washcloth. There are a few lumps of foam, a sheet of Molefoam and a pair of nail scissors to cut them. Taped to the lid is a needle and a backed razor blade. Scattered about are matches.

One aluminum film can contains a dozen aspirin, half a dozen 500 mg vitamin C tablets for fighting colds, a sprinkling of anti-acid and milk of magnesia tablets, and several long-lasting anti-histamine spansules. A second can contains a lump of soap. I test the backing on the adhesive tape (which deteriorates after a year) and replace the short-lived vitamin C and crumbling milk of magnesia tablets.

The next item is my personal kit, packed in a plastic zippered pouch. There was a time when I painstakingly gathered the contents for every trip, but it soon became evident that it would be easier to keep a kit permanently assembled. Mine contains a toothbrush, a tiny flat plastic container of dental floss, a spare tube of chapstick, one ounce tubes of Sea & Ski suntan lotion and Desenex athlete's foot ointment, half a roll of anti-acid tablets, a stub of pencil and the remains of a tube of glacier cream. The little packet weighs three ounces, and I put it directly into an outside pocket of the pack.

I decide to take the ancient Trailwise frame with the coated fabric bag an old girl friend made for it before any were available commercially. I choose it for the comfort of its padded harness and full mesh backband and because I don't need anything bigger or heavier. After trying it on to make sure it's intact and complete, I set it out, along with the Antelope frame I'm loaning Jorgy. Mosquitos in the area are liable to be active so I toss in my box a half empty 2 oz. bottle of Jungle

Juice. With it goes a 3 oz. Mallory flashlight—after I test the batteries and tape the switch closed so it can't turn on in my pack. A spare bulb travels in the first aid kit.

The best existing map of the area we are visiting is the seven and a half minute USGS topographical map. I have an old, but still service-able copy that shows not only the area we will visit but also the surrounding territory, so we can identify the peaks we will use as landmarks. To orient the map, we will need to know directions, so I dig out a liquid-filled plastic-cased compass that weighs only half an ounce and put it in the gear box.

With it goes a four by six inch Spiral notebook with a section of pencil pushed snugly through the spiral binding. Pencil and paper also make it possible to leave notes for other party members in camp or on the trail. And my notebook pages have served as emergency toilet paper, started fires in rainstorms and supplied mountaintop registers. My notebook and pencil weigh two ounces.

Except for food, that takes care of the equipment kept under the bunks. To make sure nothing has been overlooked, I quickly sort through the remaining boxes of gear. My search turns up a film can containing a tiny G.I. can opener and I toss it in the box in case we take along a can of apricots or peaches. It is difficult to open a can of fruit packed in heavy syrup on a mountaintop with nothing but a sharp rock!

Next, I turn to the selection of clothes. First comes a long-sleeved Hickory shirt because there are going to be bugs. Over the shirt in the evening (or in the wind) goes an unlined pullover nylon shell parka with a drawstring on the hood, elastic at the wrists, a drawstring at the bottom (over the hips) and a front zippered pouch into which both hands can be stuffed. The parka weighs only 7½ ounces and is rarely left home.

Beneath the cotton shirt goes a short-sleeved string shirt which is superior to a t-shirt or undershirt in almost every way; it is cooler and dryer in hot weather, warmer and dryer in cold weather, lighter and more easily washed and dried enroute. I also prefer it as a pajama top. To protect against the possibility of really cold weather, I also put in the box my 4 oz. Stephenson VB shirt, which of course also can serve as windshell, raingear, pajama top and emergency garment.

Since I plan to hike in shorts and also spend a good deal of time sunning and swimming (possibly in public) I select an old canvas boxer-style bathing suit with pocket in which I have probably logged 200 miles. In the evening I'll need protection from bugs and cold so I add to the pile the trousers with the wrap-around zipper and velcro waist that were modified for me by Synergy Works. While the trousers are before me I fold a yard-long strip of toilet paper and button it into a back pocket. Into a front pocket goes a clean bandana, which may also function as a wash rag, pot holder, towel, neckerchief, etc. A pair of boxer shorts will be worn with the trousers.

This takes care of all but the extremities. I have tried a good many

GORP
is good
any ol'
time.

powdered
milk in a
plugged
mustard
dispenser

mallory
flashlight
with
switch
taped
shut.

different hats and sun shades. In the warm and friendly summer Sierra I am concerned with sun protection and maximum ventilation, not rain protection. Summer days are long and the high altitude sun beats down relentlessly, so that a hat brim that partially shades the nose and neck and ears can make the difference between developing a protective layer of tan or a painful sunburn. For the country we will visit I choose an old, shapeless, once-white cotton tennis hat that weighs two ounces. The underside of the two and a quarter inch brim is dark green for reduced glare, and fully a third of the crown is nylon netting that provides good ventilation. Since I rarely wear dark glasses, I always take a hat when I go out overnight.

The hiking won't be strenuous or the load heavy, so my 2¼ lb. DMC PTF 1000 Goretex boots will be more than adequate, even if we decide to do a little cross-country scrambling. Since they require no waterproofing (or break-in) I merely tug on the laces to make sure they're strong before tossing them in my box, along with two pairs of stretch rag wool socks. For backup protection against unexpected cold, I stuff a couple extra Baggies in a side pocket of my pack to serve as VB socks. My footwear is completed with a pair of featherweight foam rubber sandals (Zoris) to protect bare feet in camp.

Many walkers will take a change of shorts and an extra T-shirt on a three day trip, but I expect to be able to wash and dry both my trunks and my string shirt without inconvenience. Having selected clothing to cover all contingencies, I make a pile of what I plan to wear the next morning—which is everything except the boots, spare socks, nylon shell and VB shirt—and put the pile on my bed, where it cannot be missed.

The fly rod I plan to take is a 2-piece, 7-foot, two ounce Fenwick of furruleless fiberglass. The attached Phlueger Medalist reel is loaded with fifty feet of level backing, a tapered fly line, and a seven and a half foot leader tapered to a one and a half pound tippet. I reel the No. 12 mosquito dry fly to the tip of the rod, disjoint the two sections and fasten them side by side—the tip protected by the butt—with stout rubber bands at each end.

Though reduced to 3½ feet the rod will still stick a foot above my pack, but I am accustomed to making the necessary allowances, and this arrangement leaves me ready to cast within thirty seconds of stopping. Because the rod does not fit well in a box, and because leaned against the wall it is easily forgotten, I set it inside the open pack.

In a pocket of my pack goes a Perrine fly box the size of a cigarette package which comfortably holds 50 flies. Fastened to it with a stout rubber band are three extra cellophane-enclosed rolled, tapered leaders. The top one contains my fishing license. I also toss in a small tin of Muselin for dressing my line and fly.

My Konica 35 mm camera weighs 13 ounces loaded with a 36 exposure roll of Kodachrome-X (without case, which is the way I carry it). I find the camera empty and have no spare film, so I write myself a note to buy a roll on the way to the trailhead. The camera goes in my box while the note stays on the kitchen table. As protection against adversity I fill a small plastic bottle with about four ounces of brandy and put it in an outside pocket of the pack.

Late in the afternoon Jorgy arrives to help decide what we'll take to eat. I carry several boxes of backpacking food out to the back porch, and while Jorgy picks through the collection to see what looks good, I retrieve the notebook and pencil. We will need provisions for three lunches, two dinners and two breakfasts.

We discuss our preferences (within the limits of our food supply) and decide on the following: for breakfast both mornings there will be the Birchermuesli Familia with milk and freeze-dried strawberries and Sherpa tea. Since Familia will constitute the bulk of the meal we will need four ounce servings. A fresh 13 ounce package and a third of another are emptied into a doubled plastic bag, which is then knotted at the top. For Jorgy's coffee, cereal, etc. I add a small bottle of sugar; for myself there's a squeeze bottle of honey.

For dinner we decide on Mountain House Beef Almondine for one night and beef stew, which I have offered to concoct that evening, for the other. Both meals will start with soup and we select foil packets of Maggi ham and pea, and mushroom, each of which will yield four full cups. I empty about six servings of bulk freeze-dried apples into a plastic bag and add a heaping teaspoon of cinnamon and half a teaspoon of nutmeg before knotting the top. Dessert one night will be Richmoor Banana Cream Pudding; the other night we will splurge, since weight is not crucial, and take a can of Del Monte sliced peaches in heavy syrup.

Lunch always seems the most complicated meal to plan for. To the cheese, butter and jam already packed we add half a package (four

making the stew from scratch

ounces) of salted wheat crackers, two Wilson's Bacon bars, an 8 oz. package of Westphalian pumpernickle slices, a half pound mixture of raisins, chocolate drops and salted almonds (gorp), half a dozen sticks of jerky, dried pineapple, and small bags of date bits and banana flakes, left over from a previous trip.

Provisions are completed by adding five packages of Wyler's Lemonade—one for each lunch and dinner—and a three ounce plastic bag of 'trout dip,' a mixture of corn starch, corn meal, salt, pepper, onion and garlic salt and probably other now forgotten ingredients. Having suffered in the past from taking too little or leaving home something vital, I spread all the food on the table grouped by meals, and we give it a hard look. The lunch, which must supply three meals, and snacks as well, looks a little skimpy, so I get half a salami from the kitchen while Jorgy adds a handful of dried apricots to the fruit mix and puts in the other half box of crackers. Satisfied now, we dump everything in the food box and turn on the portable radio for the hourly weather report.

Scattered afternoon and evening thunderstorms are still forecast locally, with fair weather both to the east and west. The late afternoon sky, though more than half filled with billowing, black-hearted thunderheads, is not particularly threatening, and the barometer has continued to rise. We plan to meet at 9 a.m. the next morning at my pier.

After Jorgy leaves I inspect the EVA pad, bivy sack and sleeping bag that have been airing in the sun. Both bag and bivy have several pitch spots and these I wipe off with gasoline, taking care to immediately wash away the gasoline with soap and water. When both are thoroughly dry, I stuff them into the small, waterproof stuff sacks and put them into the pack.

Back in the kitchen, I find the butter has softened and after removing the wrapping I have little difficulty pressing both cubes into the plastic jar. After screwing the lid down tight I put the jar in the refrigerator, along with the cheese. Then before I forget, I write boldly on a large sheet of paper "Butter and cheese in icebox" and put this reminder on top of everything else in the food box.

That evening, I spread out on the kitchen table the various ingredients for my stew. In order to make some record of my creation, I decide to make two identical dinners, combining ingredients in a double plastic bag for the one we take, and keeping them separate in individual small bags for the one I leave behind. That way, if the stew is successful or needs obvious modifications, I am in a position to measure portions and make adjustments.

The ingredients I choose are: dehydrated potato cubes and mixed carrots and peas, a beef bouillon cube, half a package of instant gravy, dehydrated mushrooms, half a quart package of Milkman dehydrated milk, three ounces of freeze-dried ground beef, salt, beef flavored TVP, pepper, and onion and garlic salt. It is my intention to cook this in the uncleaned soup pot for added flavor, and to add half a cube of butter—if we can spare it—and any bacon bar left over from lunch. I knot the top of the doubled bag and toss it in the food box. Everything, now, is ready to go.

The following morning dawns cloudy and threatening and the weather forecast is unchanged, but the barometer has continued to rise. When Jorgy arrives, my pack, fishing rod, and the two boxes— including the butter and cheese from the refrigerator—are stowed in the outboard motor boat at my dock. We have decided, both to add variety to the trip and to save three and a half miles of hiking, to canoe the mile and a half width of the lake from the end of the road. So we tow the canoe from my dock down lower Echo Lake to the resort, where I buy a roll of film. With the canoe lashed on top of the station wagon, we load up and start off.

Our principal concern is still the weather, which remains murky as we drive west and then north along the western slope of the range, listening for a change in the forecast. At the end of the gravel road on the shore of a large mountain lake, we unload the car under an overcast sky, launch the canoe, and spread the food, cooking equipment and all other community gear on a shelf of granite. I ask Jorgy if he wants to divide the gear; he says no, but he would prefer weight to bulk since his pack is small. By now it is nearly noon and we decide to eat lunch here rather than pack it away and start out hungry.

We sit on a glacially polished slab, looking out across the lake to the mountains in the east as we make all kinds of sandwich combinations from the bacon bar, four kinds of cheese, jam and salami and buttered crackers. After eating our fill of fruit and nuts and finishing a quart of lemonade, we close the plastic bags and pack all the lunch food in a large heavy-duty plastic garbage bag. Hefting an item of community gear (or food) in each hand, I quickly divide everything into two piles of roughly equal weight, taking the bulkier pile for myself.

By this time, we are happy to note, a band of blue sky has appeared in the west, and is steadily growing larger as the gloomy cloud mass moves slowly to the east.

I attach my sleeping bag to the bottom of my pack, then make a layer of the heaviest items (food, pots, stove, etc) against the back of

canoeing across the lake saves many miles of walking.

the packsack (closest to my back). Since the day is warming steadily, I take off my trousers and switch to shorts before closing up my pack and checking all zippers and lashings. At the top of my pack are my trousers and shell parka in easy reach in case of insect attack, or a sudden change in the weather.

I rub a little Sea and Ski on my face and the back of my neck, put on my boots, and carry my pack, mattress and fishing rod down to the canoe. Jorgy loads the canoe while I return to lock up the car. After pocketing a couple of dimes because I know there are pay phones at nearby trailheads, I lock my wallet in the car, then hide my keys under a nearby rock, thus saving pocket room, a few ounces and the possibility of losing either valuable. As I climb into the canoe tell Jorgy where the keys are to protect against emergency, then I settle myself in the stern, and as we paddle slowly out into the lake the last of the preparations can finally be forgotten. The trip, itself, has begun.

The small, heavily-laden canoe moves slowly through the light chop, but the wind is with us and we cross the lake in less than an hour—an estimate, since Jorgy shares my unwillingness to wear a watch in the woods. We drag the canoe some distance up the bank and hide it, well separated from its paddles, in some brush to discourage borrowers. I lash my fly rod to the pack by means of two nylon cords attached to the right side, and lash my full length foam mattress to the top of the pack by two more loops of cord.

We put on our packs and move up through the brush for a hundred yards before finding the well-marked trail which follows the lakeshore. By now the western half of the sky is blue and clear and I know it will be hot in the bright sunlight, so I take off my shirt and stuff it in the top of my pack. For awhile the trail climbs gently away from the lake, but when it turns to the east toward a pass and grows steeper, I tell Jorgy to go ahead. From past experience I know his comfortable pace uphill is faster than mine, and there is no need for either of us to travel at an uncomfortable speed. I know he will be waiting at the pass when I arrive.

As he takes off, I stop to adjust my shoulder straps to make the pack ride more comfortably and to prevent my shoulders from growing sore. A hundred yards farther I stop again, and this time I get it right. As the pitch steepens, I automatically shorten my stride and cut my speed to maintain an unchanged energy output. After a little while my hips begin to ache, reminding me to loosen my hipbelt and tighten my shoulder straps to put a larger potion of the weight on my shoulders. On the steepest stretch my knees start to hurt, but after three limp steps the discomfort goes away.

When I reach the pass, Jorgy is waiting in the shade, sitting on a rock, looking out over the lake-dotted granite basin to the east. I take off my pack and join him. Both of us are better acquainted with the basin as viewed from the opposite direction, so we try to identify all the visible lakes and peaks before bringing out the map and compass. I need to be sure I am properly oriented because the route from this point to the lake is mostly cross-country. After a snack of dried pineapple we put on our packs and start off.

When we reach the turnoff area, I hunt until I find the small, unobtrusive duck that I built beside a tree the previous year. The cross-country trip is pretty and easy, passing up a broad grassy draw and dropping over a little rise to the small, sparkling lake. Tucked in a shallow depression in the rolling granite woodland, the lake is flanked by a thicket of willow on one shore and a small, glacially polished dome on the other. We take off our packs in a choice campsite on a little peninsula between two bays. Apparently, we are the first visitors of the year, and there are only a few mosquitos—both excellent signs. The little peninsula has no fringe of marsh to harbor insects, and the parklike stand of pines upon it serves to break the wind, but let through enough air for good ventilation.

I show Jorgy a tilting slab that forms a beach on the more sheltered bay and, after testing the temperature of the water, we immediately take off our boots and dive in, wearing our shorts and shirts. After an exhilarating swim we peel off our wet clothes, rinse them, wring them out, and stretch them to dry on a flat topped boulder. We lie on the hot slab, talking and dozing and watching the clouds for perhaps an hour before putting on our dry shorts and returning to set up camp.

I unload the main cavity of my pack onto a convenient ledge, and unroll my foam bag and mattress to give the cells a few hours to refill with air. We gather all the food which might be of interest to birds or mice or squirrels and zip it into my pack. Jorgy folds down the legs of the little stove and selects a little bench to serve as a kitchen while I take the butter and cheese cans and our quart water bottle down to the lake. The tins I partially submerge and secure with rocks; the bottle I rinse and fill with water.

My feet are fully restored by a swim and an hour going barefoot in the sun, so I put on my spare pair of heavy socks and my sandals. Next, I set about making my bed. I want a level spot well-shaded in the east from the morning sun, where the ground is soft enough to be shaped to the necessary contours.

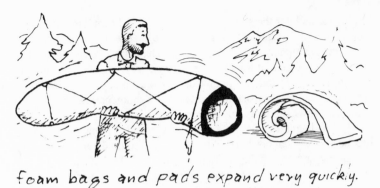

foam bags and pads expand very quickly.

I find an ideal patch of granite sand in the lee of a boulder and go to work scooping a shallow depression about two and a half feet long and a foot and a half wide with tapered sides and a relatively flat bottom, placing the excavated material in a mound on the end I propose for my head. To test the result, I lie down on my back, make mental notes for repairs, then roll over on one side to check the fit again.

After a little more scratching, I test it again and find it satifactory. I know that if the bare earth feels comfortable I am sure to rest well with the addition of 1½ inches of foam plus my bivy sack. I now assemble my bed by sliding the mattress inside the cover and positioning it over the hip and shoulder hole. After lying on it once more to make sure it is aligned, I lay my sleeping bag inside the cover on top of the mattress. From the pockets of my pack I take my string shirt and personal kit and tuck them inside the bivy, making sure everything is covered from what will likely be a heavy fall of dew. Now I can forget my bed until time to crawl inside.

My experience the previous year was that the fly fishing was good after the sun went down, but not before. Since the lake surface is still, with no sign of feeding fish, we decide to eat early and fish until dusk. While Jorgy drags in some old logs and rearranges already blackened rocks into a campfire circle, I tear open the foil package of ham and pea soup, empty it in the large Sigg pot, along with the quart of water from the bottle, and set the covered pot on the stove. I light the stove, taking care to hold the lighted match to the burner *before* turning on the gas, then turn down the flame.

I take the teapot and the water bottle down to the lake and fill them, coming back with the butter can. While the soup is cooking, I get the salt and pepper shaker, sugar, pot tongs, forks and spoons, applesauce and Beef Almondine and spread them on the ledge near the stove. Then I empty the dried applesauce (with sugar, cinnamon and nutmeg previously added) in the teakettle and add enough water so that, after stirring, all the apple bits are wet and rehydrating. I put the lid on, leaving it to soak, then lift the lid of the big pot with the tongs to give the soup a vigorous stir, using the opportunity to add about a third of a cube of butter.

Moments later the soup comes to a boil and I turn down the flame until the boiling subsides to a slow bubble. The recipe calls for five minutes of simmering, but at a mile and a half above sea level I let it go more than twice that long before calling Jorgy. Using the aluminum pot tongs as a handle, I pour it in our plastic cups. By now it has cooked to a thick consistency that makes a spoon helpful, but we still get nearly two delicious cups apiece.

The moment the last cup is poured I scrape the remains of the soup loose so they cannot burn, add the water required for the Beef Almondine and empty the package into the pot. This is contrary to the directions, but provides better hydration of the meat at this altitude (6,800 feet). While we are waiting for the stew to cook, we go to work on the succulent applesauce. When the Beef Almondine begins to bubble I turn down the flame to a low simmer, stirring from time to time to prevent scorching. Since the flavor seems a trifle bland, and to add caloric power, I add crumbled bacon bar, Fines Herbes seasoning, my salt and pepper mix and a gob of butter. Then I rinse the applesauce from the teapot and refill it with lake water.

When taste tells me that dinner is ready, I call Jorgy, who has been rigging his fly rod, take the stew off the stove and put on the teakettle.

We eat and eat, and by the time we are full and the teapot is boiling, there is still a little stew left for later in the evening. I turn off the stove now and drop a tea bag in the teapot. While the tea is steeping, Jorgy takes the three cups to the lake, fills them with water, loosens the clinging food with a spoon and tosses the resulting garbage into the bushes well back from the lake. In the meantime, I am similarly cleaning our stew pot, after saving the leftover stew in a plastic bag.

Though I am too full of dinner to think of eating, I know something sweet will taste good after we come in from fishing, so I empty the Banana Creme Pudding mix into the still wet pot and add two cups of water. After stirring briskly for a minute or so, I cover the pot and put it aside to thicken. Unlike jellos which need an icy rill or a snowbank to help them set, puddings need only a little time. I put a good sized rock on the lid as insurance against disturbance, and, after a cup of hot tea apiece, we are ready to go fishing.

Since fly casting at dusk around the shore of a Sierra lake can present difficult footing, I change back into my boots, put on long trousers over my shorts, and my long sleeved shirt over the string t-shirt. And since my skin has an unusual attraction for insects of all kinds I rub repellent on my face, hands, neck and ankles. It takes me less than half a minute to assemble my rod since reel, line, leader and fly were never removed. Carrying my nylon shell and flashlight in addition to fly box, leaders, license and muselin, I make my first casts in the little bay where we draw our water. Jorgy begins in the bay where we swam, planning to fish in the opposite direction.

The sun has now set, but only just, and it is still light and warm. There are only a few clouds to be seen in the east and the breeze is

cleaning up the lakeshore can be satisfying.

hardly sufficient to ruffle the darkening water. There are only a few rises and these suggest small trout. I cast to several avidly feeding fish, but the rises merely move away from the fly, confirming my suspicion. The year before there were fair numbers of fat eleven inch brook trout. Could they have frozen out during the previous winter? Or have their tastes turned from flies to the fingerlings which evidently had been air planted since my last visit?

Out of the corner of my eye, I see the widening circle of a larger rise. I turn back into the woods and circle toward it, making my way to the water's edge behind a good-sized tree. On my third cast to the area of the rise there is a strong underwater strike and I set the hook. The fish runs for deep water, taking line off the reel, then surges toward the shore and I am alarmed to feel it rooting on the shallow rocky bottom, trying to tear the hook from its mouth. I lean out over the water and lift with all the weight I think the leader will safely stand. The fish comes to the surface, beginning to tire, and within another minute I have safely beached a deep bodied brook trout of over thirteen inches.

In less than an hour we hook and play nearly a dozen good trout between us, keeping four of the best and returning the rest unharmed. By now it is nearly dark, but Jorgy volunteers to clean the catch if I will hold the flashlight. The entrails he puts well out of the way in thick brush, where they probably will be enjoyed by a garter snake, and the washed trout are hung from a willow stringer threaded through gill and mouth, which in turn is hung from a limb on the west side of a small pine so the fish will not catch the morning sun.

The night air has grown chilly and our wet hands are cold, but Jorgy's campfire blossoms quickly and after a sip or two of brandy we are soon warm and relaxed by the fire. Jorgy finishes off the stew in front of the fire, and since both of us are thirsty, I make up a quart of Wyler's lemonade which is promptly consumed. Hiking in the dry air of the summer Sierra often results in a daily water loss through perspiration of several quarts. By evening, even after frequent drinks during the day, the hiker craves liquids and sweets. We therefore plan on drinking a quart or two apiece every evening to maintain body fluids. Menus, of course, must be planned accordingly.

It is my habit—and Jorgy's too—to sit up late beside the campfire until I am so drowsy that I go to sleep promptly and stay asleep until the morning sun has warmed the air. We polish off the pudding and a fresh quart of water before our fire burns low. When we find our way to our beds they are as wet from condensation as though it had rained. A corner of Jorgy's sleeping bag, not covered by his tarp, is soaked. I wriggle carefully into my foam bag, roll my trousers in my shirt and stuff them into my sleeping bag stuff bag to enlarge my pillow (which goes under the mattress to smooth out the lumps), and fall asleep almost at once.

In the two days that follow, we spend our time swimming in the little bay, dozing in the sun on the slab beside the water, and hiking cross-country to fish and swim in two nearby lakes. The storm has vanished entirely and the humidity quickly drops so there is far less dew on the second evening. In the other lakes we have good luck, finding a few large brook trout in one and a dense population of smaller cutthroat, brook and rainbow in the other. Between the lakes, we climb a high dome that yields an excellent view of the surrounding country.

For dinner the second night we try my stew, which Jorgy kindly rates as equal to the Beef Almondine. At least it is easier to prepare: we simply add water and boil, then simmer. After dinner, tired of fishing, we scale a second dome and find an abandoned trail on the far side, marked by ducks which we idly follow until darkness forces us back to camp.

On the third day, the eve of the fourth of July weekend, we pack up, and before leaving camp try to obliterate all sign of our passing, except for a little charcoal inside a ring of already blackened rocks. Carrying a dozen good trout in the cool interiors of our packs, we return to the trail and make good time back to the canoe on the shore of the big lake. Then we paddle upwind for an hour against a brisk chop to the opposite shore and the car. Driving home through the mountains to the cabin, my reluctance at leaving the wilderness is nicely balanced by my anticipation of a hot shower and a trout dinner with my waiting family.

GOING BACK

When I get back
to the high bright world
of the windblown sun
and the meadowed rock
things will be all right.

When I return
to the mountain wild
on a turning trail
through a summer rain
my rhythm will return.

When I can escape
to a land left wild
on a still starred night
drowned deep in peace
my life will turn around.

When I get back
to the wilds again
and the easy peace
of a dreaming fire
I'll be content again.

LIST OF SUPPLIERS

Alpenlite
39 West Main St.
Ventura, CA 93001

Antelope Camping Equipment
21740 Granada
Cupertino, CA 95014

Arcata Transit Authority
650-A 10th St.
Arcata, CA 95521

Banana Equipment
Box 1076
Longmont, CO 80501

Black Ice
120-P Woodland Ave.
Reno, Nev. 89523

Bugaboo Mountaineering
170 Central Ave.
Pacific Grove, CA 93950

Camp Trails
4111 West Clarendon Ave.
Phoenix, Ariz. 85019

Camp 7
802 So. Sherman
Longmont, CO 80501

Cannondale
35 Pulaski St.
Stamford, CT 06902

Caribou Mountaineering
P. O. Box 3696
Chico, CA 95927

Coleman
250 No. St. Francis Ave.
Wichita, KS 67201

CosyQuip
P. O. Box 1631
Santa Fe, NM 87501

Dolt
10455 West Jefferson Blvd.
Culver City, CA 90230

Donner Mountain Corp. (DMC)
2110 Fifth St.
Berkeley, CA 94710

Down Home
P. O. Box PP
Arcata, CA 95521

Early Winters
110 Prefontaine Place So.
Seattle, WA 98104

Eureka Tent
Box 966-E
Binghamton, N.Y. 13902

Eastern Mountain Sports (EMS)
Vose Farm Rd.
Peterborough, NH 03458

Feathered Friends
1314 Northeast 43rd St.
Seattle, WA 98105

Forrest Mountaineering
1517 Platte St.
Denver, CO 80202

Frostline
Frostline Circle
Denver, CO 80241

Gregory Mountain Products
4620 Alvarado Canyon Rd.
San Diego, CA 92120

Great Pacific Iron Works (Chouinard)
P. O. Box 150
Ventura, CA 93001

Hine-Snowbridge
P. O. Box 4059
Boulder, CO 80306

Holubar
Box 7
Boulder, CO 80302

Jansport
Paine Field Industrial Park
Everett, WA 98204

Kelty
10909 Tuxford St.
Sun Valley, CA 91352

Kletterworks
P. O. Box 1676
Bozeman, Mont. 59715

Lowe-Alpine
P. O. Box 189
Lafayette, CO 80026

L.L. Bean
Freeport, Maine 04032

Mark Pack Works
P.O.Box 6332
Albany, CA 94706

Marmot Mountain Works
331 South 13th St.
Grand Junction, CO 81501

Mojo Camera Protective Systems
P.O.Box 99
Bozeman, Mont. 59715

Moonstone Mountaineering
P.O.Box 4206
Arcata, CA 95521

Moss Tent Works
Mt. Battie St.
Camden, Maine 04843

Mountain Safety Research (MSR)
631 South 96th St.
Seattle, WA 98108

The North Face
1234 Fifth St.
Berkeley, CA 94710

Outdoor Gal
116 East Chestnut St.
Burlington, WI 53105

Robbins Paraphernalia
Box 4536
Modesto, CA 95352

Shasta Llama
Rt. 1, Box 183-A
Mt. Shasta, CA 96067

Sierra Designs
247 Fourth St.
Oakland, CA 94607

Snow Lion
1485 Park Ave.
Emeryville, Ca 94608

Stephenson's (Warmlite)
RFD #4
Gilford, NH 03246

Trailwise
2407 Fourth St.
Berkeley, CA 94710

Recreational Equipment (REI)
P.O.Box C88125
Seattle, WA 98188

Vapraflect
P.O.Box 588
Kenmore, WA 98028

INDEX

ABOUT THE AUTHOR

Long a tinkerer with backpacking equipment and a searcher after comfort in the wilds, Robert S. Wood has been walking and climbing for twenty-five years in the Sierra Nevada, the Cascades, Mexico, Europe, South America, New Zealand and Australia. He has written and edited for a number of magazines, including *Time, Life, Sports Illustrated, Sierra Club Bulletin, Wilderness Camping* and *Outside.*

A forestry graduate from the University of California, he is the author of the trail guide *Desolation Wilderness* and other books. Although a native and resident of Berkeley, he lives with his wife and daughter during the summer at a cabin on Upper Echo Lake near the edge of Desolation Wilderness at 7400 feet in the California Sierra.